DATE			

Follow the Wild Dolphins

Also by Horace Dobbs

Camera Underwater

FOLLOW
THE WILD
DOLPHINS

by Horace Dobbs

ST. MARTIN'S PRESS · NEW YORK

To my own family of "dolphins,"
and to Kay, whose zest for life
and spirit of freedom took her on a
sailing voyage into the Pacific Ocean
from which she never returned

Design by Victoria Gomez

Library of Congress Cataloging in Publication Data
Dobbs, Horace E.
    Follow the wild dolphins.
    1. Bottlenosed dolphins. 2. Cetacea. I. Title.
QL737.C432D6   599.5'3   82-5712
ISBN 0-312-29752-1   AACR2

First Edition
10 9 8 7 6 5 4 3 2 1

Contents

PART TWO

A section of photographs follows pages 96 and 192

Acknowledgments

This book is not just my story and the photographs were not all taken by me. It has been compiled from a mass of tales and pictures from a great variety of sources. I am pleased to acknowledge all of those who have so willingly provided me with material. It would be virtually impossible to detail all of you by name. I hope, therefore, that those of you who read this and are not listed below will be able to identify yourselves and will accept a very sincere thanks from me.

Of those with whom I have corresponded, I feel I must offer special thanks to John Denzler. *The Daily Mail* is also thanked for allowing me to quote extensively from John Edwards' report on the dolphin slaughter at Iki. The picture used to illustrate this tragic story was taken at considerable risk by Suzie and Dexter Cate of Greenpeace and reached me via Hardy Jones of the Living Ocean Society and Glenn Chase of The Fund for Animals in Washington.

I thank Gordon Ridley for telling me of his experiences in the Faroe Islands and for allowing me to choose from his excellent collection of photographs.

Chris McLoughlin kindly presented me with a selection of photographs of Sandy, the dolphin who became his special friend, and my thanks also go to Pat Selby who gave me a greater insight into the character of the elusive dolphin.

The photograph of Anne Rennie was provided by the *Eastern Province Herald,* Port Elizabeth.

Barry Wills, D. J. Nunn, Mrs. Skinner, John Pile and Norman Cole all kindly provided me with pictures of our mutual friend Donald, and numerous people have written to me telling me of their encounters with this mischievous dolphin. Doug

Godwin did the art work for the figure illustrating Donald's Odyssey and Doug's expertise in the darkroom is reflected in many of the black and white photographs in this book.

I have also to thank my correspondents in far away New Zealand for telling me of the exploits of my namesake, Horace, and for the considerable efforts they made to send me illustrations. They include Quentin Bennett, Frank Robson and Ros Rowe. I also thank Margaret Bingham for her touching poem.

I thank the indefatigable Estelle Myers, the Australian director of Project Interlock; and the founder of the Interlock project, Wade Doak, with whom I have developed a bond despite the fact that he lives halfway around the world from England. Wade's own story is told in his book called *Dolphin, Dolphin*.

My filming partner, Chris Goosen, a person of incredible drive and energy, never gave up hope in our hunt for the elusive dolphin in the Red Sea. Without his involvement I would never have met another friendly wild dolphin under the sea.

I also gratefully acknowledge the help I have had from my family—wife Wendy and children Melanie and Ashley—without whose unswerving support I would not have been able to champion the cause of the dolphins.

Finally, I thank Kerry Davis for transcribing my tapes and embarrassingly untidy scrawl into a typed manuscript.

H.E.D.

Foreword

Two things are required to achieve the conservation of endangered species; scientific facts about the life-cycle, habitat and the threats to its survival, and secondly, the will to introduce appropriate conservation measures. The former depends on objective study, the latter depends on propaganda and the stirring of human emotions. The author has used all his intricate knowledge of dolphins for the latter purpose and in so doing, I believe that he has made a most valuable contribution to the conservation of a particularly attractive species of wild animal.

H.R.H Prince Philip, The Duke of Edinburgh K.G., K.T.,
International President of the World Wildlife Fund

Buckingham Palace,
July 1981

Parting day
Dies like the dolphin, whom each pang imbues
With a new colour as it gasps away
The last still loveliest, till—'tis gone—and all is gray.

—Byron, *Childe Harold's Pilgrimage*

PART ONE

1 · A Frightening Experience

On March 26, 1972, Henry Crellin sat on the wall of his inflatable boat, put one hand on his facemask and rolled backwards into the water. He was an experienced diver laying a new mooring chain. He was deliberately over-weighted, and as he landed on the sandy seabed, clouds of silt stirred up by his arrival temporarily reduced the underwater visibility.

Henry Crellin was familiar with such conditions and set about the task of joining the chain that was lowered down to him to the ring in a block of concrete half-buried in the sand. As he pulled the chain across the seabed, more clouds of silt swirled into the water, giving it the eerie appearance of dense fog through which the weak spring sun glimmered as a deep orange disc. Crellin knelt down and once again heaved on the end of the chain to bring it closer to the eye in the concrete block. As he did so he noticed that the light intensity was suddenly reduced. He looked up.

In a fraction of a second he registered a huge gray shape with a large dorsal fin moving silently past him just a few feet away. The open jaws were lined with sharp triangular teeth. At that instant he felt a massive dose of adrenalin, his instinctive flight-response took control of his body and he hurtled to the surface as fast as his flailing fins could propel him. He came up alongside the inflatable and heaved himself, complete with aqualung and 45-pound weightbelt, over the side, slithering into the bottom of the boat like landed fish. His companions, Dave Wood and Colin Bowen, who had been busy sorting out more chain and getting their diving gear ready, looked at him in amazement. Never had they seen Henry make such a rapid, unexpected and acrobatic reentry into the boat.

Before Henry could compose himself he blurted out "There's a bloody great shark down there."

Dave and Colin were incredulous. A big shark in the sheltered waters of Port St. Mary was unheard of.

"How big was it?" asked Dave as Henry slowly regained his composure.

"Bloody enormous," replied Henry.

Both of his companions knew that Henry was a quiet man, not given to exaggeration, and certainly not easily frightened. What could he have seen that had upset him so?

As they peered over the side into the water, a few yards away a large dark gray domed head broke the surface. On the top of the head was a hole about an inch in diameter.

There was a loud puff of exhaled air that sent up a tiny cloud of spray. The short puff was followed by the lower noise of air being sucked in. The two noises followed so closely one upon the other that there was no detectable pause between them; in a fraction of a second the blowhole had closed and the head vanished. The entire sequence from the glistening dome breaking the surface to its disappearance took no more than three seconds.

As the head submerged the three divers caught a glimpse of a large black dorsal fin. It cut briefly and silently into the air before following the head back into the water. Although both head and the fin were large, they left barely a ripple.

But that brief appearance on the surface of the sea resolved the question of the frightening creature's identity.

"It's a bloody dolphin."

"Well it looked like a shark down there."

As if to confirm their identification, the dolphin surfaced again a few moments later, made its characteristic puff, and descended once more.

Once he realized that the dark dorsal fin he had seen belonged to a dolphin, Henry Crellin's heart rate slowed down. He even managed to smile when his partners burst into uncontrollable laughter. Well, it was an easy mistake to make in the underwater half-light. On the surface the dolphin looked large. Underwater it would appear even larger—as all underwater objects do to divers. He was the senior diver of the party and he decided to bring the merriment to an end.

"When you two have finished laughing you can get in the water and finish the job."

So after a half-serious debate on the prospects for their survival, Colin Bowen and Dave Wood accordingly pulled their aqualung cylinders on to their backs and tightened the harnesses. Sitting on opposite sides of the inflatable they rolled backwards simultaneously, in spite of their recent laughter a little apprehensive of what might happen in the next few seconds. The familiar swirl of bubbles hurried to the surface and the two divers hung in the green water looking at one another. They each turned to see what was behind them.

Their senses were alert and ready to register any strange happenings, and their nerves were geared to take considered defensive action—not uncontrolled flight. However, no such action was needed for there was no sign of the dolphin.

Colin and Dave exchanged the OK signal, then allowed themselves to drift slowly toward the seabed. The underwater visibility was good, about thirty feet, and the silt stirred up by Henry Crellin's earlier activities had settled. The two divers spotted the chain and the mooring block and, with their hearts still beating a little faster than normal, they peered into the limits of their horizons. They could not see anything unusual, so Dave picked up the end of the chain and started to pull it toward the block. Then he looked up and as he did so the dolphin appeared slowly out of the mists of the limit of visibility. Dave's heart rate increased.

The dolphin approached slowly and seemed to be taking a kindly interest in what was going on. Dave sensed no aggressive intent and watched as it slowly circled him. He could not help but admire the graceful, easy way the dolphin moved through the water. Very soon he relaxed completely and decided to get on with the job. He unscrewed the pin on the shackle and hooked it through the ring in the top of the concrete block. He pulled the length of new chain across the seabed and attached the last link to the shackle before inserting the pin and screwing it tightly home with a marlin spike. As he did so the dolphin approached even closer and stopped with its curious smiling beak just a few inches away. When the shackle was fastened, it swam off and was gone in a second, with two sharp upward beats of its tail fluke. Dave felt no turbulence from its flashing tail.

Dave continued with his job and pulled the chain over the bottom toward the next block. The dolphin seemed to become excited at this activity and appeared and disappeared several times. Colin helped Dave with the task and thoughts of danger slipped from their minds. They were both after all seafaring men, and to sailors through the ages the sight of dolphins around a ship has never been a threat, but, according to traditional belief, a sign of good fortune.

This belief indeed goes back at least as far as the ancient Greeks and Minoans, who seem not only to have held the dolphin in a benevolent relationship with man, but attributed to it a peculiarly sacred relationship with the Gods. Homer tells for instance how Apollo disguised himself as a dolphin and led a Minoan ship to found the Shrine at Delphi, to which it gave its name and which for a thousand years was one of the greatest religious and cultural centers in the world. And the history of the sea ever since has been rich in legends about the benevolence of these mysterious sea creatures.

Yet the incident off the Isle of Man was more extraordinary than perhaps even the three divers knew, for the traditional lore about dolphins almost always involves them accompanying ships to sea. A school of wild dolphins will not play around a stationary boat, and they keep well clear of submerged divers.

This the descendants of those ancient Greeks discovered, when in the early days of deep sea diving the sponge fishers in their copper helmets—"coppernobs" as they were known— and lead-soled boots began to work in deeper and deeper water along the coasts of Greece. Trailing their hoses behind them, at the mercy of the dreaded bends, equipment failure and the unpredictable sharks, theirs was a hard and hazardous living.

4

Dolphins often frolicked around the fishing boats when they were on their way to the sponge grounds, and their presence invariably had an uplifting effect on the crew. It was a good omen—for one thing, the sponge gatherers knew that sharks and dolphins are seldom seen together, and that when dolphins appear sharks disappear, so a sponge boat in the company of dolphins was a happy boat. The crews were able to see the dolphins at very close quarters, when they surfaced alongside to breathe, and often a school would stay close to a vessel for a long journey. However, once the boats stopped and the divers prepared themselves for their work, the dolphins moved away.

Thus the incident with Henry Crellin and his partners in Port St. Mary on the Isle of Man was something new, and special.

2 · The Dolphin Makes Friends

The Isle of Man has a comparatively small resident population, and news travels fast—particularly in the winter months when tourists, a major source of income to many of the islanders, are not present to distract the locals from their gossip. Immediately before his encounter with the dolphin, however, Henry Crellin had been away in England, so he had not had time to catch up on local affairs. If he had been at home he would already have heard about the arrival of the dolphin, which had made itself known just a few weeks earlier to Dr. Joanna Jones and Michael Bates, both divers who worked at the Marine Biological Station. The incident took place in the bay at Port Erin, the same fishing village where Henry Crellin had his diving business and shop.

Port Erin, whose name is derived from the Manx words *Purt Chiarn* meaning Lord's Harbor, has a natural charm that is unspoiled by the commercial amenities of a modern seaside resort. Bradda Head to the north, almost a sheer cliff, rises 350 feet above sea level and is capped by a tower built in 1872. It was erected to the memory of a famous safe maker, William

Milner, and the shape of the tower is said to resemble a safe key. Milner's Tower can be seen for miles from the sea and is a valuable reference point for boatmen when navigating around the southwest corner of the Isle of Man. In the summer Port Erin is noted for its clear water and smooth sheltered sandy beach, and that above all is what most holiday makers remember.

The local residents, however, know that Port Erin has another very different face. The mouth of the bay is open to the southwest and is subject to the full fury of the southwesterly gales that can lash the coast in the winter. In the middle of the ninetheenth century work started on the building of a breakwater to dampen the energy of the mountainous waves that were often funneled toward the shore. Huge concrete blocks, some weighing as much as seventeen tons, were spilled into the bay. But when work had reached an advanced stage in 1884, a mighty storm smashed the rampart with astonishing ease, and the project was abandoned. The jumbled underwater profusion of rocks now provides a sanctuary for fish and crustaceans.

Brilliantly colored wrasse will often swarm around a diver there, if he makes unhurried movements. The fish are expecting to be fed, for just above the ruined breakwater, on the southern side of the bay, is the Marine Biological Station and fish hatchery, run by Liverpool University and the British government, and staff from the station, when setting off from the shore on underwater research projects, often take titbits with them to feed the wrasse.

It was thus perhaps a happy accident that the dolphin first made its presence in the Isle of Man known to marine biologists, who would possibly have a greater understanding than laymen of its friendly character and benign behavior when in the presence of man. Mike Bates certainly showed no fear of the dolphin when he first encountered the surprise visitor to the doorstep of the Marine Biological Laboratories.

It happened at a time when the scientists of the station were interested in measuring underwater light intensities. For this purpose they used two light recording devices mounted on a metal frame. In January 1972 it was decided to move the apparatus. The research vessel *Cuma* was detailed to haul up the equipment from its site off the lifeboat station slipway, then to ferry it to a new station at the end of the ruined breakwater. It was a short run, and the *Cuma* was accompanied by a small rowing boat containing Joanna Jones, Michael Bates and a two-man crew. The rope slings had already been attached to the apparatus and the job of the divers was simply to attach these slings to the wire lowered from the winch aboard the *Cuma*.

The divers were in position over the submerged equipment when Mike Bates got his first sight of the dolphin—a seemingly gigantic tail disappearing into the water alongside the rowing boat. A few seconds later a grinning head appeared. The dolphin eyed the occupants of the boat for a few seconds, then submerged. On board, the two divers hastily fitted their masks. Quick checks were made, and they dived, with a great deal more splashing than the animal they were so eager to meet. Mike Bates gives an account of what happened next:

> While we were fixing the wire to the rope slings he stood on his head and surveyed us, first out of one eye and then the other. When I copied the action, pushing my mask to within an inch of his eye, he became very excited and rushed around us, performing somersaults and leaps. We would rush at one another, veering off at the last second so that we passed within inches of each other. It was a pity we did not really have time to get to know him better but there was a job to do and we could not very well spend the time with a dolphin, however playful he was.

That was the first of several meetings Michael Bates and Joanna Jones had with the dolphin. It would appear, often without warning, when they were working underwater, and became progressively more friendly.

The newcomer to Manx waters was given the name Donald the Dolphin, and he rapidly established himself among the diving community who began to look forward to his sudden arrivals which could turn any routine dive into a memorable event.

He was identified as a male bottlenose dolphin, or *Tursiops truncatus*—the common name being derived apparently from the shape of the head, which resembles the neck and shoulder of an early wine or brandy bottle. The bottlenose is one of the largest of the dolphin family (Delphinidae), and males reach a maximum length of about twelve feet. In America, bottlenose dolphins are sometimes referred to as common porpoises. This had led to some confusion because in Britain common porpoises are members of another family which taxonomists call the Phocoenidae. The common porpoise *Phocoena phocoena* is found all around the British coast, the males reaching a maximum length of only six feet. It lacks the narrow beak of *Tursiops truncatus* and has an evenly rounded snout. The teeth of the common porpoise are also comparatively small, being only about one tenth of an inch in diameter at the gum.

One person to take a particular interest in Donald was a very remarkable Manxwoman, then living in England, named Maura Mitchell. She was one of the people Henry Crellin had stayed with on his visit to England just before his encounter with the dolphin, and on the night after the incident he had written to Maura giving her a full account of it. He went into some detail because he knew that Maura was an enthusiastic diver and that she was about to move permanently to the Isle of Man.

He may also have known that she had a very special gift for handling animals, but he could hardly have foreseen that he was introducing Maura to one of the most important, and extraordinary, relationships of her life.

Just as the gift of the musical child has to be nurtured if it is to flower in later life, so the intuitive rapport which Maura had with animals was developed during her childhood in a farming area. One of Maura's earliest memories was of lying on her back for a long, long time in a hayloft watching a barn owl feeding its young.

She had an innate understanding of nature. She married her girlhood sweetheart, Peter, who had a passion for motorcycles, a quiet disposition and red hair. In the early 1960s Peter, who was running a motorcycle engineering business, built himself a twelve-foot speedboat, then a powerboat which was regularly trailed to Wales and the Isle of Man. Their boat gave the Mitchells access to the sea and it was natural for them to take up diving.

Maura took to diving like the proverbial duck to water. She enjoyed the spirit and the companionship of the diving club and became an unashamed sub-aqua enthusiast. Most of all she enjoyed her diving trips to the Isle of Man. And as their two boys grew out of babyhood, Maura and Pete began to question their life style. Rather than spend the next few years satisfying the ever-increasing demands of a growing business that would allow them to spend less and less time in the sea, they decided to sell and start a new life on the Isle of Man. They settled in the village of Ballasalla in the southwest corner of the island.

It was only a short while after Maura had settled into her new home that she had her first meeting with Donald, a meeting that was to prove the beginning of a long and extraordinary relationship. Unlike Henry, Maura first saw Donald from the shore one evening when she was sitting on the jetty off Fort Island. The dolphin appeared suddenly, as was his way, and began playing like a huge aquatic kitten. He raced between the moored boats, graceful and precisely controlled, turning like a slalom water skier to avoid them at the last possible moment, sending spray and waves crashing against their rocking hulls. He hurled himself into the air with explosions of energy that filled Maura with awe—she could well appreciate Henry Crellin's fright when a creature of such size and power had appeared unexpectedly underwater.

So it was not without some apprehension that Maura first went into the water when Donald appeared one day outside the fort at Derbyhaven. Maura eventually suggested to her male companions that they should abandon their planned aqualung dive and have a snorkel swim with Donald instead. The dolphin was not in a boisterous mood, and as the trio swam slowly out from the jetty Donald made his way toward them. First he inspected one male diver, then the other, before making his way toward Maura. The dolphin was swimming gently around them and then stopped. He looked at Maura head-on. Maura slowly stretched out her gloved hand; the dolphin backed imperceptibly away so that she could not reach him. Then he swam slowly around her legs and she again extended her hand and stroked the dolphin very gently under the chin. This time the dolphin did not swim away; he seemed to like it. Maura

9

talked gently to Donald, as she would to a horse, and the dolphin responded. The next time he swam by she held out her leg so that the rubber tip of her fin stroked the dolphin's abdomen. This he thoroughly enjoyed, and for the next thirty minutes he ignored the other two divers and stayed swimming gently with Maura. When all three snorkelers eventually swam back to the jetty, Maura's newfound friend swam alongside until she left the water.

The two men, who expressed themselves as much affronted at the attention Donald had devoted to their female companion, told the story at the club room. They decided that Donald must have a preference for female divers in wetsuits. Then, in a more serious vein, they remarked on the extraordinary rapport that Maura had so quickly established with the wild dolphin.

After the first encounter, Donald and Maura met frequently. Club dives took place every weekend, and if Donald was in the vicinity he would join the divers, inspecting them all but devoting most of his attention to Maura, who spoke to him and stroked him.

Indeed, to divers and non-divers alike Donald was making his presence on the Isle of Man a source of amusement and pleasure. And not all of those who remember him from that time were human. One was a Jack Russell terrier by the name of Spratt. Spratt belonged to Bill Dawson, who owned a yacht with his father. The yacht was kept moored in Port St. Mary, and often when Bill rowed out to it Spratt, dressed in a red lifejacket complete with handle on top, would accompany him. Then, when Bill arrived at his yacht he would tie up to the stern and often leave the dog happily sitting in the dinghy. Donald, on his by then regular visits to Port St. Mary, took to swimming around the dinghy as Bill rowed. And this in itself would set Spratt barking. One evening, when very few people were about, Maura watched Donald take what had been an established game into his own hands. She saw Donald accompany Bill as he rowed out; then, when the owner was below in the cabin of his yacht, Donald apparently decided to have a closer look at the strange four-legged creature in the red lifejacket with the handle on top. The dolphin rose in the water alongside the rowing dinghy with his head well clear of the water and peered in. This set Spratt barking, and he stood with his paws on the gunwale yapping at the dolphin. Donald opened his mouth to reveal his handsome set of sharp triangular teeth, and moved forward, imitating the dog's yapping movement with his own jaws. This sent the dog into a frenzy—to Donald's immense delight.

Having elicited such a good initial response, the dolphin submerged and reappeared to look over the other side of the boat, which brought the terrier forward to defend his territory in a pose of fearlessness that Donald soon discovered was false; when Donald made another advance with his jaws opening and closing, the dog almost fell over backward. The two animals spent a long time playing their game of dare. Then Donald thought up a variation on the theme. He slipped quietly underwater, turned upside down and started swimming with his belly pressed against the keel. The dog burst into a new spasm of barking as soon as Donald appeared alongside to assess the effect of his latest tormenting trick. Having satisfied himself that he had extracted the maximum response from the poor dog, Donald performed a couple of spectacular leaps that sent spray raining down on the yacht and dinghy, then set off to find another source of amusement.

In his behavior with Spratt, Donald displayed the irrepressibly mischievous side of his character that was to become so familiar to all who knew him. He also revealed again the joyous exhibitionism that had already impressed Maura. He seemed to be aware that people were watching him and he would put on an extra special display if they were.

3 · Attempted Murder

On September 13, 1972 a story appeared in the *Daily Mirror*, under banner headlines:

GUNMAN'S VICTIM—DON, THE PET DOLPHIN
Angry animal lovers are hunting gunmen who pumped bullets into Donald, the friendly dolphin.

For some months Donald frolicked off the Isle of Man coast and became a holiday attraction.

But the twelve-foot dolphin was wounded by two bullets in his head and three shotgun wounds in his body.

Mr Harold Blundell, Chairman of the Manx SPCA, said yesterday, "this has outraged us all and we want to find out who is responsible."

He added, "There have been rumors of threats by fishermen because they thought the dolphin was causing poor catches."

The news of the shooting fell like a bombshell on Maura, her diving friends and the other folk who had come to love the dolphin. For some the shock quickly turned to anger of a most violent kind. They became so incensed that several of them swore severe retribution to the culprit.

Many stories about Donald's demise circulated. One was that he had been killed and eaten by French fishermen—who were intensely disliked by the Manx fishermen, partly for reasons of rivalry, and partly because of their habit of shooting seagulls and hanging the corpses from the halyards to deter other gulls.

The Manx Society for the Prevention of Cruelty to Animals offered a reward for information leading to the detection of the criminals. But although a number of suspicions were voiced, none could be corroborated with evidence. The most plausible story was that Donald had played around some fishermen who were illegally netting salmon. The fishermen disliked Donald for three reasons: first because he ate their salmon, second because he could damage their nets, and third because he attracted unwanted attention to their activities. If such was the case, and as yet there is no public evidence to support the story, the fishermen were wrong on the first two counts. There is no data to support the conclusion that Donald would take salmon in preference to the other fish that are bountiful around the Isle of Man. Dolphins are also extremely clever at avoiding being caught in nets, as those who have tried to net dolphins have discovered. No one could refute the third point however—for everywhere that Donald went he certainly attracted attention to himself.

One day a dolphin of about Donald's size was spotted near the coast, though it kept well clear of human contact. Was Donald alive after all? There were other sightings, and in time it became clear, to the relief of his Manx friends, that he was alive and swimming. Anger at the shooting subsided, but the hunt for the would-be murderers continued, and Donald kept his distance from humankind.

It so happened around this time that the European Spear Fishing Championships were held in the Isle of Man. As is usual at such functions, a medical officer was appointed and the man who took on the task was Dr. Raymond Goyne. Donald became interested in the activities of the spear fishermen, although he remained very wary of them. However, Dr. Goyne, who spent a lot of time snorkeling, gradually gained Donald's confidence and got close enough to take a photograph of him. The photograph showed a deep wound over Donald's right eye that was consistent with what might have been expected from a shotgun fired at close quarters. The dolphin was incredibly lucky that the shot had not damaged his blowhole. Without proper control of the very sensitive mechanism for keeping water out of his lungs, the dolphin could easily have drowned.

Gradually, Donald became his old friendly self again, seeking the company of the Manx fishermen, frequently getting in their way and even giving them an occasional helping hand at their work. One fisherman who received the dolphin's attentions was Norman Crellin, coxswain of the lifeboat. Norman Crellin had a small lobster boat, and Donald quickly learned that there were games to play when lobster pots were to be hauled in. He would follow the boat out from the harbor, and the dolphin always knew what was going to happen next: before Norman could grab hold of the buoy on the end of a string of pots, the dolphin would take the rope between his teeth and deliberately tow the buoy away. But Norman remembers one day when Donald helped instead of hindering: he actually tossed the buoy that Norman wanted right into the boat!

It might be argued that the dolphin's behavior in this case was accidental—he did not really understand what he was doing. However, most of the divers who got to know Donald well do not take this view. Many of them can quote incidents to indicate that the dolphin is rapidly able to assess what divers are doing in the water, and then to prove his understanding by his actions. One such person is Dave Wood, who was in the boat with Henry Crellin when he had his first encounter with Donald when laying the mooring lines in Port St. Mary harbor.

Donald often joined Dave on dives around the Calf of Man. Usually there would be no sign of the dolphin until about halfway through the dive, when Donald would appear out of the underwater mists. On one occasion Dave's diving partner, Colin Bowen, was collecting crayfish. Donald watched carefully, disappeared and came back. Colin watched the dolphin as he swam off a short distance, and then started to swim in a tight circle. Intrigued by this unusual behavior, Colin swam over to see what Donald was doing. When he arrived he saw that he was circling directly over a crayfish, which the fisherman promptly added to the collection in his sack, thanking the dolphin warmly for his help.

A story perhaps even more convincing is told about a snorkel diver who was out one day catching plaice for his supper. The main mode of defense of plaice is camouflage. They lie flat on the bottom, often half covered in sand, and their backs change color to merge with their surroundings. An experienced diver watches for a break in the contours of the seabed, then swims quietly down to the fish and impales it with a knife or prodder of the type used by park attendants for picking up paper litter. On this occasion Donald followed the diver, and with his usual curiosity watched him impale a fish. The dolphin then swam ahead a little, and suddenly took a nose dive at the seabed. When the diver swam over to investigate at close quarters he found that Donald had pinned a plaice to the ground but was making no attempt to eat it.

Despite these signs of returning friendliness, however, it took some time for Donald to allow himself to be approached as closely as he had before the shooting. Indeed, it might be said that the relationship between man and dolphin was not really set right again until the drama that is recounted in the next chapter. But what is remarkable is not Donald's wariness of human contact—it is his readiness to entrust himself to it once more.

One of the essential elements in the observed behavior of dolphins recorded down the ages is in fact a complete absence of aggression toward man. Dr. David Taylor, a veterinary surgeon who has specialized in the care of dolphins, is among the many contemporary scientists who have confirmed this ancient observation. He has remarked that many large animals become difficult to handle when they know they are to be injected, but that dolphins show no such resentment, regardless of how painful the procedures they are subjected to. My own experiences in veterinary medicine bear this out.

In his book entitled *The Dolphin Cousin to Man*, Robert Stenuit reviewed the classical and modern literature on dolphins, and made the following unequivocal statement:

> A dolphin could kill a man with a blow of its snout. It could dismember him with a blow of its jaws, because it possesses a double row of strong conical teeth, eighty in all, which sink in with precision. But never, absolutely never, has a dolphin or a porpoise attacked a man, even in legitimate defence, with a harpoon in its side, or when, with electrodes in its skull, it has been massacred in the name of science. On the contrary . . . .

Many people are killed or maimed by animals, including pets such as horses and dogs, every year. Man himself, if struck suddenly, reacts immediately, most likely by retaliating in a physically violent manner. Such an immediate response is instinctive, and involves the lower centers of the brain—those that govern the behavior of the lower animal orders to which, for example, belong the sharks. A deliberate and carefully considered response will involve the higher centers of the brain which are most developed in the higher primates, including man, and the Cetaceans. Thus in man's immediate response to aggression it is the lower centers which tend to take precedence over the higher.

Yet it would appear from a dolphin's behavior after a sudden and unprovoked attack by man that it is the *higher* centers of the brain that take precedence over the lower. Does this suggest that the dolphins may have made an evolutionary step not only beyond any other animal, but beyond man?

4 · Stranded

The tide was slowly ebbing from Derbyhaven. As it did so, the vessels that had been bobbing on the water with the regular rhythm of the gentle waves became still as the keel of one after another settled on the seabed. When the tide had receded the boats were left resting on the exposed sandy flats, waiting for the next incoming tide to lift them off again.

It happens twice a day as regularly as the sun rises, and it was a scene as familiar to John Moore as it is to all those who live on the coast in a tidal area. It was part of the rhythm of the sea that he never tired of watching. On a day in March 1973, however, the tidal rhythm held an extra significance for both John Moore and a relative newcomer to the Isle of Man—Donald the Dolphin.

John Moore was supervising new building development overlooking Derbyhaven. It was time for the midafternoon tea break when his companion, Willie Kneale, commented that there was a seal in the haven. Willie had just seen it moving by one of the yachts. John peered in the direction indicated by Willie and could see a dark gray mass beside the white hull of the *Nemesis*. Then he saw something move. It looked more like the tail of a huge fish than any part of a seal.

"Are you sure that's a seal?" John said to Willie, puzzled by the unusual shape he had seen rise and then drop again.

"It is certainly not a seal," he commented when he had observed more closely the heavy dark mass struggling on the sand, and a tail again waving briefly in the air.

The two men left their mugs of tea. John tucked his trousers into the tops of his socks and they paddled across the muddy sands toward the *Nemesis*. As they got closer they realized that the object they had seen was not a seal but a dolphin.

As the dolphin struggled he sank more into the mud. He raised his tail fluke uselessly into the air and splashed it down. They inspected the huge animal and from the scar on its body they realized with mounting excitement that it was Donald. Now the poor animal, recently so nearly killed by a shotgun, lay helplessly stranded. They tried to move him manually, but as they slithered on the mud they knew that they stood no chance of pushing his heavy body back into the sea.

The two men knew that the first thing they should do was to keep Donald alive. Already there were signs of cracking on his delicate skin. Willie Kneale ran back to the building site, collected a bucket and then ran out to the receding sea to fill it with water.

John Moore was working out a rescue operation as he hurried back to the building site. The group of workmen abandoned their tea break and a couple went to help Willie Kneale with the dousing of the stranded dolphin. John Moore then headed for the skip-loader on the site and discussed the problem with the driver, Nigel Warren. Nigel agreed to attempt a rescue, provided the wheels of his Massey-Ferguson digger did not sink too deep into the newly-exposed mud.

The water-carrying team, who had been walking back and forth to the ever more distant surf, was pleased to hear the noisy staccato chug of a powerful diesel engine as Nigel Warren's Massey-Ferguson came bumping across the sands. Nigel maneuvered the excavator so that the leading edge of the scoop bucket eased gently under the dolphin. But in this position the men could not get close enough to manhandle the animal into the scoop without damaging both the *Nemesis* and Donald. So they decided the boat would have to be moved. In a few minutes a line was attached, the powerful engine spurted black exhaust into the air as it took the strain, and the boat slid smoothly over the sand leaving the dolphin fully exposed, with plenty of room all around him.

Again the scoop moved in. The steel talons along its leading edge bit into the sand, then stopped. The gang of men heaved on the fluke of the dolphin to pull him into the steel bucket. Others pushed the dolphin's head. Slowly they managed to maneuver Donald into a suitable position, the powerful engine throbbed again, and the steel shovel moved forward, tilted and lifted its unusual cargo.

Like children alongside a float in a carnival procession, the team of rescuers delightedly followed the excavator as it headed toward the sea.

When the water reached a depth of two feet the bucket was slowly lowered. The life-giving sea flushed over the passive body of Donald.

But the problems were not over. Nigel Warren could not risk taking his digger any further into the water. So some of the men took off their shoes and socks and waded into the water. The bucket tipped and they eased Donald free. The dolphin was only half submerged and remained pressed to the seabed by the unsupported weight of his body out of the water. Each time a gentle wave came in the men pushed Donald forward.

At last, with the added push from Donald's own swimming efforts, the dolphin was free of the bottom, and it was only a matter of seconds before he was in water deep enough for him to swim. But he did not swim away immediately. Instead he swam around in circles offshore. Then as if in a final gesture of thanks and farewell he turned in a tight circle, jumped high into the air and swam away out to sea.

The following day he was spotted beside his favorite boat in Port St. Mary, apparently none the worse for his excursion ashore. The efforts of John Moore and his colleagues did not go unacknowledged. They were later given awards by the Manx Society for the Prevention of Cruelty to Animals.

It is interesting to speculate on just what effects the incident would have had on Donald. For his entire life Donald's considerable body had been supported by the sea. In the sea he was weightless. So as the water became shallower and shallower the stress on his body would have been increased as the surface became increasingly exposed. The weight settling on his belly would have made it difficult for him to expand his lungs to breathe. Fortunately his respiratory system had evolved to be very economical in its use of air. Other factors however would have added to his discomfort. In the sea he was continuously bathed in cooling fluid and his metabolic rate was adjusted to keep his core temperature at the normal mammalian level of about 98.4°F. But he had no sweat glands and could not pant to keep his temperature down when his skin began to dry. Although he could control the amount of heat dissipated through the blood vessels going to the surface of his body, the thick insulating layer of blubber so essential for his survival in water could outside the water have become instrumental in his death. Finally, his very thin skin, uniquely adapted to help him slide through the water with the minimum of resistance, had started to shrink and crack upon exposure to the air.

Just why many whales and dolphins become stranded and die is a question that has puzzled scientists and non-scientists alike for many years. One reason that has been advanced is that stranding is a voluntary method for animals to bring their lives to an end, akin to the legendary graveyards to which elephants are reputed to make their way to die. But I have been told by hunters in Africa that such places exist only in the minds of those who write scenarios for Tarzan movies. And although many of the dolphins that are found stranded are old, relatively young specimens have also been reported. So I am inclined to discount the "graveyard theory." In Donald's case, he certainly showed a will to live after the shooting incident. And after all, if he wished to die he had only to sink below the waves and inhale.

Another even more fanciful theory suggests that built into the genetic make-up of all the whale family is an urge to get back to the land. It stems, the proponents of the argument say, from the days way back in the dolphins' evolutionary past when their predecessors made the transition from being purely land animals to amphibians.

Such speculation takes science beyond the extent of our present knowledge. We know, for instance, that the genes within all living cells contain the master plans that govern the structure of all forms of animal life. Basic behavioral patterns such as migrating instincts are probably also laid down in the genetic code, but in a less precisely defined way, for behavior is influenced by a host of external factors, such as the environment and the availability of food. It is possible therefore that

19

strandings are the result of two or more influences—a deep instinctive force coupled with some unique external circumstances.

My own theory is that in this case Donald's curiosity got the better of him. He probably discovered something new, to which he devoted his attention, causing him to forget that the tide was receding from a flat area with a very gradual slope. The sea was calm, so there were no wave surges that he could ride piggyback into the sea until he got into water deep enough to swim free. His fins and his tail fluke touched bottom and he could not move forward. A small depression was scoured out alongside the vessel as the tide receded and he was trapped.

That incident, though perhaps the most dramatic, was only one indication of how thoroughly, within a year of his arrival off the coast, Donald had won the affection of the Manx people. Already, his peculiar emotional impact on human beings was changing individual lives. One of the first people—apart from Maura, to whom Donald was already a friend—to be deeply influenced by the wild dolphin was a fisherman by the name of Michael Kneale. Those who understand Manx fishermen will know that they are an extremely conservative and superstitious community. Many of them cannot swim. So it is all the more remarkable that one of their number should actually have learned to dive in order to get closer to the dolphin that came alongside his fishing boat when it was making its way to and from the fishing grounds.

Once he learned to dive, Michael Kneale also caught the bug that grips many of those who swim underwater—photography. On his birthday Michael Kneale received an underwater camera, and he delighted in the challenge of trying to get pictures of Donald.

Intense though Donald's human relationships tended to be, however, they were not all friendly. At the same time that the MSPCA were considering the presentation of an award to John Moore for his rescue, another incident occurred that enraged the dolphin-lovers on the Isle of Man. It concerned a wealthy new resident on the islands, owner of a thirty-foot twin-engined cabin cruiser which he kept moored off Port St. Mary. And it followed as the direct result of one of the mischievous

20

tricks that Donald played when the opportunity presented itself. When residents were rowing out to their moored cabin cruisers, Donald would bump against the bottoms of the small rowboats and give them a hefty shove.

When Donald tried out this latest trick on the new resident as he rowed out to his cabin cruiser, he was not at all amused. He wrote to the Board of Agriculture and Fisheries complaining about the dolphin, The exact wording of his letter has not been made public but it was rumored at the time that he had reported that the dolphin was a menace and should be destroyed. An uproar shook the normally placid inhabitants of the quiet fishing village of Port St. Mary when news of the contents of his letter leaked out. It was not unnatural for the local populace to resent rich newcomers who used their island home as a tax haven. And when one of these "comeovers," as they are called, suggested that the dolphin they had taken to their hearts should be got rid of they vented their feelings without inhibition. Many of them openly expressed the view that it was the wealthy newcomer, not the dolphin, who should be despatched.

A local newspaper investigated the accusations and reported the story. The Examiner quoted Mr. Bill Martin, Chairman of the Port's Commissioners, as saying: "It has come to my notice that a certain gentleman has made an application to have the dolphin destroyed." He said the Harbor Board had confirmed that an application for Donald's destruction had been lodged with them.

A spokeman for the Harbor Board said "We sought the advice of the Attorney General's Department and we were told that the dolphin is a protected fish, which is accorded something of the royal privilege extended to the sturgeon."

Although the Attorney General's Department showed a certain lack of knowledge of the dolphin — which is certainly not a fish — the Harbor Board's stand was made quite clear in the statement reported in The Examiner as follows: "Therefore, if anyone does anything to harm this particular dolphin, they will find themselves in very embarrassing circumstances. There would be no hesitation to take action . . . He is very welcome in Manx waters."

21

The storm of indignation subsided when the residents of Port St. Mary were thus assured of the safety of their dolphin. However, they did not forget. Although the "comeover" died a short time after the incident, feelings against him still ran high when residents were questioned by Maura Mitchell on the subject over two years later.

5 · My First Encounter

Some people plot the course of their lives and direct their efforts and energies single-mindedly toward long-term goals, but I have discovered that in my life the most exciting things have happened when I have let the wind of chance blow me where it will.

It was just such a turn of circumstances, indeed it was literally a wind of change, that first brought me into contact with Donald the Dolphin through Maura Mitchell.

Underwater photography is the most popular activity taken up by underwater swimmers once they have mastered the techniques of aqualung diving. In my case, it was the films of Hans and Lotte Hass taken in various remote and exotic parts of the world that triggered my interest in diving in 1957. I had recently graduated from London University, and taken a job with the Atomic Energy Authority at Harwell. For the first time in years I found myself with a few hours to spare, so I joined the Oxford branch of the British Sub-Aqua Club. From the moment I first put on a facemask and dived in the sea, I realized that I had made a big discovery, and that I would be able to combine this new-found interest with my other passion—photography.

Within a few weeks of joining the diving club I appeared at the poolside with my cameras encased in waterproof and not-so-waterproof housings. There was very little literature available on underwater photography, and I had to work out for myself solutions to the innumerable problems that were stopping me from getting good pictures. (I was fortunate in having a scientific background with which to approach some of these puzzles, and in 1962 the first edition of my book *Camera Underwater* was published. It has since become a standard text on the subject.)

At the same time I gathered around me a group of divers who were keen to engage in serious underwater projects in their spare time, and with them I formed the Oxford Underwater Research Group. One day Kay, the secretary of the group, and the wife of a law professor, showed me a picture taken on a family diving holiday in the Aegean Sea. It was not an underwater photograph but an ancient painting illustrating an underwater scene. It was a frieze of dolphins that had decorated the bathroom of a queen in the Minoan palace at Knossos. Those stylized common dolphins (*Delphinus delphis*) seemed to capture the marvelous feeling of joy and freedom that I experienced when I was released from gravity and drifted down into clear blue water; they emanated a spirit that bridged the sea of time that separated me from the artist who painted them in 1600 BC. So I incorporated one of the dolphins in the logogram of the Oxford Underwater Research Group, and painted the same dolphin symbol on my aqualungs. Thus it was that in a manner of speaking I took a happy dolphin with me on nearly all my dives after 1962. I had always had a keen interest in whales—the big cousins of the dolphins—but it was with my identification with the beautiful dolphins in that classical picture that my love affair with dolphins really began.

The members of the Oxford Underwater Research Group made the first full-length underwater television documentary in which all of the sequences were filmed in British waters. The film, called *Neptune's Needle*, was highly acclaimed and won a gold medal at the International Underwater Film Festival in Brighton in 1966. A year later I changed my job and moved to North Ferriby in Yorkshire, where I named my new house "Dolphin."

Although my passion for underwater exploration and photography remained unquenched, I found my new post as head of the radioisotope unit in a large pharmaceutical company both demanding and interesting. I was awarded the degree of Doc-

23

tor of Philosophy as an external student of London University for some of my work using radioactive tracers to study chemical reaction mechanisms, and started work on the mode of action of a series of drugs. I worked closely with veterinary surgeons and doctors and was elected a Fellow of the Royal Society of Medicine.

I presented papers on my research at conferences in different parts of the world. In Geneva, at such a conference, I met Dr. Luciano Manara. We discovered that we were both interested in underwater photography, a common interest that has caused our lives to intertwine ever since.

One outcome of this friendship was that Luciano agreed to join me and my family on a diving holiday at Dale Fort in Pembrokeshire in August 1974. All arrangements were made. Then a day before he was due to arrive I had a telephone call to say that the holiday was canceled as diving would be impossible because of the unprecedented force of the winds.

What could I do? One possibility was to find a new location where we would be less affected by bad weather. Even moderate onshore winds can make diving difficult close to the coast, but when the wind is blowing away from the land, the sea remains calm close inshore and diving is possible. I considered that I stood the greatest chance of finding a suitable venue for our holiday if I chose an island, for it is axiomatic that if there is an onshore wind on one side of the island there is an offshore wind on the other. Knowing from personal experience that excellent diving was to be had round the Isle of Man, I telephoned my diving contact there—Maura Mitchell.

She reported that the conditions were far from good. Then, as we exchanged our diving news, she happened quite by chance to mention that she had made friends with a wild dolphin. What were the chances of meeting the dolphin even if conditions were not too good? Maura was diffident. However, in an instant I made up my mind. If there was the remotest chance Luciano and I could dive with her friendly wild dolphin, then the one place I would consider taking my Italian friend was the Isle of Man. Somewhat overwhelmed at my enthusiasm, Maura agreed to see if she could make arrangements for us. With what I was to find out later was her usual organizational efficiency, she rang back having booked us all—

Luciano, my family and myself—into a hotel in Douglas, and had made arrangements for us to dive.

Luciano flew from Milan to London, and caught a plane to Yeadon, near Leeds, by a hair's breadth. As soon as he arrived we squeezed him into our four-seater car, which already had four people in it—me, my wife Wendy, our daughter Melanie, and Ashley, our son. We headed in the wind and driving rain for Liverpool and the Douglas Ferry.

As one of the last cars to go on board, we were parked high on a flying ramp on the stern of the *Mona's Queen*. It was a vantage point almost as good as the ship's bridge. From inside the car we could look down on the deck, the dock and the River Mersey. In the shelter of the quay, conditions for the eighty-five-mile crossing appeared reasonable. It was not until we were well clear of land that the full impact of the Force Eight gale hit us. The sea was a blue-gray mass topped with a meringue of whipped spray that was occasionally flung right over our car. The car was not secured to the deck and it rocked and shuddered in the buffeting wind. Fortunately the vessel was fitted with stabilizers which kept it on a reasonably even keel, but I must admit that there were moments when I questioned the advisability of staying in the car, especially when a number of the cars on the ramp leading to our elevated platform started to slither. Luciano said he had never encountered such conditions before as he struggled to open the door against the pressure of the fierce wind, and what his apprehensions were about diving in such seas I do not even know.

But we arrived safely on the Isle of Man, and all misgivings were forgotten. It was not long before I saw Maura and Donald together for the first time, and that first encounter is firmly inscribed on my memory. It was pure magic.

It was a clear bright blue morning. The sky was dotted with white cotton-wool clouds pushed along by a stiff breeze from the southwest. Outside the harbor at Port St. Mary the sea was summer blue and the waves were occasionally crested by whitecaps.

I parked my car on top of the harbor wall and surveyed the scene. It was one of peace and beauty. I felt inclined to regard it as typically English until I remembered that the Isle of Man enjoys an independence that is hotly upheld by its inhabitants. It has its own Parliament, and its own coinage and stamps. Placed between England, Ireland, Wales and Scotland, the harbor scene was a subtle blend of ingredients from all of its neighbors, with a character all its own.

Small runs of ripples occasionally skated across the surface of the sea, driven by eddies of wind that sneaked past the protective harbor wall. The sea inside the harbor was quiet and had a blue-green tinge. The boats rose and fell gently as the waves at the entrance to the harbor dissipated the last of their unreplenished energy.

This place, Maura told us, was where we were most likely to find the wild dolphin. On the jetty, a group of divers in black wetsuits were busily maneuvering a red speedboat toward the slipway. The speedboat trailer was parked amidst a group of dinghies whose halyards rattled against the alloy masts. We climbed out of our cars and I introduced myself and Maura to the divers. They had come over to the island from Blackpool for a few days' diving and were anxious to get off for their dive before the rising wind made conditions impossible, so I posed the question foremost in my mind.

"Have you seen the dolphin?"

"What dolphin?" came the reply.

I explained that a wild dolphin had been observed in the harbor on many mornings during the past few months and I was very anxious to find it and if possible dive with it.

"Sorry, we haven't seen it," said the short stockily built man who I had detained.

He hurried away to join the rest of his party on the slipway, as they pushed the trailer into the water and floated their boat free. We watched from out vantage point on the top of the harbor wall and I looked at my own diving bags and aqualung cylinder stowed in the back of Maura's small car. Even if we could not find Donald, what were the chances of getting a dive, I asked myself? Slim, I concluded, and looked enviously at the divers now pulling the starter rope on their heavy outboard engine. It fired into life and the boat turned and slid easily forward.

Fifty yards ahead of it a silver arch formed briefly on the water and disappeared in a shower of spray.

"There's Donald!" cried Maura.

A few seconds later he surfaced close by the speedboat, which had changed its course as the result of the sighting and was heading toward the spot where Donald had just surfaced. The speedboat changed course again and there was obvious excitement on board. As the pattern repeated itself those aboard quickly realized that attempting to chase the dolphin was a fruitless way of making contact with him, so they wisely tied up to one of the boats moored about a hundred and fifty yards offshore and the divers tumbled into the water.

The sighting of the dolphin had an immediate effect on all of us standing on the harbor wall. We rushed to Maura's car and hauled out the bags containing our wetsuits.

"If they go out to sea Donald could well fellow their boat out," said Maura.

Now Luciano is the most meticulous diver I know, but in the urgency and excitement of the moment he was pulling on his tightfitting wetsuit as if his life depended upon it.

At the same time I was getting into my own wetsuit, which was nylon-lined and therefore relatively easy to put on, I was instructing my thirteen-year-old son Ashley on the art of getting into his newly acquired wetsuit. His was not nylon-lined and required liberal lubrication with talcum powder before it would slide over his skin. Clouds of perfumed talc billowed into the air around him as he fervently dispensed the contents of the tin into the trunk and arms. When his head finally popped through the neck seal in a small cloud of dust his hair was snow-white and his excited face looked as if he was half made up as a clown.

Maura got into her wetsuit with a speed that would have been gratifying to a quick-change artist, and helped Ashley.

Luciano took his underwater camera and exposure meter out of the plastic box in which it was carefully stored and joined Ashley and Maura, who were already heading down the slipway carrying their fins, masks and snorkels. I had decided to use an aqualung to stay underwater if I needed to. By the time I had it on my back and had got my cameras ready, assisted by Wendy, the other three were already in the water and heading out across the surface toward the area of activity around the moored boats. Excited shouts were coming from the scene as the divers caught glimpses of Donald. Fins flashed and splashed on the surface as the divers made frantic attempts to swim down to him. Donald added to the confusion by darting from one place to another in what appeared to be a completely random manner.

At last I was ready and plodded down the slipway into the water. When it reached my waist I fell forward into a snorkeling position and finned toward the activity. I watched the gravel and sand pass beneath me as I progressed into deeper water. I looked up to make sure that I was still heading in the right direction. Ashley and Luciano, who were well ahead of me, had nearly reached the boat. Ashley raised his head. He shouted something I could not hear, treaded water, and pointed down.

A few seconds later a shape like a gray submarine passed beneath me. It looked huge. I saw the pale, white-gray snout followed by a domed, dark gray forehead which in turn widened into a massive shoulder section, also dark gray but scratched with numerous light gray scars. Behind that came a vertical dorsal fin that passed just eighteen inches beneath me. Beyond the dorsal fin the body tapered and then fanned out again into a fishtail-shaped fluke. As the tail moved up toward the surface in a powerful vertical stroke, the head dipped slightly.

When the tail swept downward again the head of the dolphin rose, giving the entire body a smooth undulating motion as it passed. In two such movements Donald had passed into the blue-green haze at the limit of my underwater vision and was gone.

True to form, he had come to investigate the latest happening—my arrival—in his self-appointed territory.

His introduction to me had been so swift that I had had no time to set my camera. The next time I saw him was when he surfaced briefly amid the excited divers near the red speedboat.

The aqualung on my back impeded me and I was annoyed at my slow progress, but eventually I reached the other divers. When I had regained my breath I put the mouthpiece into my mouth, inhaled and allowed myself to sink slowly. I watched as Donald approached one of the divers who was snorkeling on the surface. With a wild flailing of his fins the diver tried to submerge quickly and made a violent grab for the dolphin's dorsal fin. But with a single powerful upward thrust of his tail fluke Donald accelerated away, leaving the diver with nothing but water between his grabbing hands. Even to my untutored eye it was apparent that Donald took exception to such human behavior.

One thing that struck me immediately, as I watched the diver swimming back to the surface for air, was how smoothly the dolphin moved through the water in comparison to the man. After that I got only fleeting glimpses of Donald as he raced from one person to the next. There was no telling where he would appear. Then the divers decided that they had seen enough of Donald and they climbed aboard their boat and headed for the harbor entrance, leaving Maura, Luciano, Ashley and me grouped in the water.

That was the last I expected to see of Donald, but I had not reckoned on his special relationship with Maura. She called out to him under the water and started to talk to him gently. He was still very excited and would stay with her briefly and then rush away again. Gradually she calmed him down with a sympathetic understanding that I too could sense. Maura snorkled down beneath the surface and nodded her head gently. Donald opened his mouth, his expression extraordinarily similar to a human grin, and nodded his head in return before darting away.

I realized as I watched the two of them together that I was witnessing a complex relationship, something rare and curiously exciting that I could not analyze.

Donald came to inspect me a couple of times and stayed still long enough for me to take a few photographs. I noticed again the upturned line of his jaw that gives the bottlenose dolphins their famous "smile." Some people have said that the smile is simply a chance configuration, but in the fleeting moments I had with Donald on this first encounter I could not decide. I thought this might well be my one and only opportunity of photographing a wild dolphin in the sea, and I concentrated on getting pictures.

After another five minutes in the sea, in which there was no sign of Donald, I surfaced. None of the others, still snorkeling on the surface, had seen him either. Donald had gone.

29

That day was Luciano's birthday, and in the evening we all sat in The Crow's Nest Restaurant overlooking Douglas Harbor to celebrate. Luciano was as excited as the rest of us. In his first dive in British waters he had had an experience that does not befall many divers in a lifetime, and our talk throughout the evening was almost exclusively of dolphins.

After the meal Maura suggested that we meet some of the other divers on the Isle of Man who had dived with Donald, so we moved to a pub on the waterfront. The saloon bar of the Britisher was dimly lit with yellow light, and the air was thick with tobacco smoke, adding no doubt a further tinge to the ceiling which had mellowed to a dark cream from a hundred other such nights.

We eased out way past the holidaymakers to a group of locals in the corner, raised our voices above the noise and then listened to other tales of Donald. There was no doubt about it, every person who had dived with him had found the experience more memorable than almost any other in their very varied diving careers. These were not just divers' tales told to entertain and impress their friends in a bar. When they were all added together it was apparent to me that there was much more to diving with a wild dolphin than to encountering any of the many other creatures in the sea.

We made plans to dive with Donald again the next day.

But we had not taken into account the vagaries of the British climate. The next morning the weather made headlines, and newspapers showed pictures of the southern coast of England being pounded by gales, with columns of spray and spume rising high above cars on seaside roads. The bad weather had not confined itself to the south coast, but had blown up the Irish Sea.

We drove south out of Douglas up the coastal road that rose high along the top of the cliffs. Huge waves thundered against the rocks and whisked the water into white foam. Out from the rocks the wind whipped the surface of the sullen sea into a white mottled meringue. It was awesome to see the elements air and water locked in battle, and we huddled in out parkas to watch the spectacle.

What, we asked ourselves, does Donald do when the

weather is like this? Does he run for shelter in a harbor, or does he join the giants on the battlefield of the open sea?

We pondered the answers as we plucked wet wild blackberries to which the gale-blown spume had imparted a slightly salty tang. Such was the force of the storm that all prospects of diving had to be abandoned.

We never did see Donald again during our brief holiday, but I resolved, come what may, to come back to the Isle of Man and get to know Donald much better.

6 · Return to the Isle of Man

After that first brief encounter with Donald I resolved to go back to the Isle of Man as soon as I could, to see if I could get some photographs of Donald and Maura together. Just two days of my annual vacation entitlement remained, and I decided to use them. However there were two major obstacles to my success. The first was the weather, and the other was the technical difficulty of photographing in the relatively low visibility underwater.

The weather is always unpredictable, so the best I could do was to listen to the forecasts, get Maura's report on local conditions and then set off if the weather looked as if it might stay settled.

The underwater visibility—know as "the viz" in divers' jargon—is all-important, for it governs just what the diver is able to see. In Port St. Mary I could expect the underwater visibility to be in the region of fifteen feet, with a maximum of about twenty-five feet. Experience had taught me that to get clear pictures underwater it is essential for the cameraman to be separated from his subject by a distance not greater than one third of the visibility. In effect, then, I would have to stay so close to Maura and Donald that the standard camera lens would limit me to "head and shoulders" shots only. More distant shots would be so indistinct as to be virtually worthless.

The answer to the problem was to use a wide angle lens.

Nikon had recently introduced a very wide-angle lens with a focal length of 15 mm, for use with the Nikonos cameras I used underwater, but its price, which was approaching that of a new small car, was completely beyond my means. And I knew of no one who had one that I could borrow.

One of my friends, who was working for a large photographic company, had been experimenting in his spare time with a cheaper supplementary lens that could be attached to Nikonos cameras. He told me that he was ready to produce it commercially and had coined the name "Vizmaster" for it. I ordered one of his first production models, and a few days later it arrived, well protected in its box by a mass of polystyrene foam chips.

It was an impressive-looking attachment with a plastic domed front about three inches in diameter, protected by a red woolen hat knitted for the purpose by his wife. It clipped onto the standard Nikonos 35-mm lens underwater, thus enabling standard shots, as well as fish-eye shots, to be taken without the need to surface to change lenses. It came with a special viewfinder which slotted into the camera accessory shoe. The viewfinder was essential, for it indicated what the supplementary lens was taking, its field of view being greater than that normally visible to a diver unless he turned his head from side to side.

Once the lens arrived I was ready to go and decided to travel on October 3 unless the weather forecast was very bad. When the day arrived the forecast was for unsettled weather. But I decided to take the risk, on the ground that further delay would only lessen my chances of success.

I also decided that it was more important for my son Ashley to have some days in the company of a dolphin than to have a few more facts crammed into his head at school. So a note was sent to his headmaster and Ashley and I set off by car to Liverpool, and thence to the Isle of Man by ferry, where we were met by Maura.

The following morning we made our way to Port St. Mary and were delighted to see that one of the unmanned dinghies was behaving in a very unnatural manner. It was moving forward to the full extent allowed by its mooring rope, then sliding backward across the water apparently of its own accord.

We knew no freak of the wind was moving it, so we concluded that it was being propelled by an unseen animal swimming upside down with his belly pressed against the keel. Donald was at home.

The wind was blowing strongly from the northwest, whipping up small waves that scurried into the slipway where we planned to launch the small C-Craft inflatable. We tried to shelter from the wind as we changed into our wetsuits, but even so I was chilled by the time I was ready to help carry the inflatable to the water's edge. Ashley stood in the water holding the inflatable off the rocks, while Maura and I dashed back and forth to the car to collect and load our diving equipment and cameras.

At last we were ready. I heaved my air cylinder onto my back to be ready to dive immediately, and pushed the boat, with Ashley at the oars, out into the choppy water. As Ashley started to row, I climbed in over the stern. For the first minute, with Ashley rowing as hard as he could, the vessel made headway, but the surface area presented by our bodies and by the sides of the inflatable provided the gusting wind with plenty to push against, and as soon as Ashley tired, which he did after a few minutes, the inflatable was pushed broadside to wind and blown rapidly toward the rocks despite his strongest efforts. Maura, who was close to him, jumped into the rowing seat, took the oars and with some short sharp pulls had the vessel pointing back into the wind. I sat impotently in the stern firmly anchored by my aqualung and cluttered with cameras.

Maura was able to row the heavily laden boat out into the bay until we could tie up to one of the fishing boats. As soon as we were tied up I rolled backward into the sea and felt the cold water seeping into my wetsuit. Ashley handed me my camera and I slung it around my neck. I released my handhold on the side of the dinghy and allowed myself to sink, calling to Donald as I descended. I looked around waiting for the gray submarine shape to appear out of the gloom. There was no sign of him. I called again and again, but he either did not hear or chose to ignore my cries.

After five minutes I surfaced and reported to Maura that her friend was not being cooperative. I clung to the side of the dinghy, which was bobbing up and down vigorously in the choppy swell, and between us we decided that Maura would snorkel around on the surface and call him. She slid over the side and swam with powerful strokes of her fins across the surface of the sea, rising and falling with the waves like a flexible blue log. In a few moments Donald appeared and she enticed him back to the inflatable. I could hear her talking to him. Why he had accepted her invitation but not mine I did not know, but as soon as I saw him I was filled with pleasure.

When Donald and I had made our introductions, Maura joined me at the dinghy and agreed to put on her aqualung for the underwater pictures. She put her arms over the side of the inflatable and lifted herself inboard as easily as a seal hauling itself out of the sea. I hovered just off the boat, bobbing up and down while Ashley helped Maura on with her gear. A few minutes later she was back in the sea with Donald, who was swimming excitedly in and out of the gloom. We both sank together and I watched the plumes of bubbles rising from her aqualung. Everything was set. Donald followed her down. I reached down for the camera with its new wide-angle lens, that I had slung round my neck. But it was not there. I felt again. It was definitely no longer around my neck. For a moment my stomach felt as if it had been gripped and squeezed by a pair of strong hands.

I looked up and down, as my vision was limited by my face-mask, and felt all around me with my hands. I could neither see it, nor touch it. I signaled to Maura and we surfaced together.

"Have you seen my camera?"

"No. I thought you put it around your neck."

"I did."

"Well it's not there now. Does it float or sink?"

"The new lens floats and the camera sinks."

I could not remember whether the combination of the two sank or floated. And I had no idea when it had come adrift.

"My guess is that it just floats," I decided.

"In that case we had better look for it right away," replied Maura.

We looked across the water and searched intently for any sign of the plastic dome gleaming in the light. But the choppy water made it unlikely that we would see anything floating, unless it was very close by.

I groaned. "With this strong wind blowing it could have drifted a long way."

"Let's unhitch the inflatable and drift with the wind," she suggested.

"Good thinking, Mrs. M."

We unhitched our weightbelts and aqualungs in the water and Ashley stowed them in the boat before we climbed back inboard. I untied the mooring rope from the old car tire on the side of the fishing boat. With the three of us sitting on the inflated walls of the "Buc," scanning the water surface, we bumped gently up and down in the choppy water as the wind jostled us across the harbor.

After about five minutes, which seemed very much longer, we had drifted close to the line of the fishing boats moored to the harbor wall. We looked along their waterlines and in between them, but there was no sign of my camera. The camera was black and the new lens mount was dark gray. Apart from the clear plastic dome it would be difficult to see in the water.

"Are you sure it floats?" Maura asked.

"No, I'm not absolutely sure," I replied.

"Well, what shall we do then?"

"Let's row back to the fishing boat and look on the bottom. I'll row."

As I pulled at the oars with short, hard jabs I added: "You two keep on looking."

The "Buc" jumped over the waves and we eventually tied up to the fishing boat again without sighting the camera.

My training told me that finding lost objects on the seabed is difficult and I should have commenced with a systematic search pattern, but I was impatient and decided to start with a random search. I took no heed of the fact that I felt a little exhausted after my row. Ashley lifted my aqualung cylinder onto my back. As soon as I had buckled the quick release fastening I put the mouthpiece into my mouth and rolled into the water. I was so preoccupied with my loss that I did not feel the cold as I headed down into the green water.

I arrived at an outcrop of broad-leaved seaweed known as Laminaria that I recognized, and I scanned it carefully from above. It hardly stirred. That was a good sign, for it indicated that there was little current. I realized that if the camera had dropped into the kelp I would be very lucky to find it, for it would slip down beneath the brown blades that obscured the seabed like a blanket. I swam round the kelp patch and headed in the direction I thought I had taken when I first entered the water, but the seabed was devoid of any other specific features that were fixed in my memory. I glided over the muddy sand with odd outcrops of small boulders, some of which provided the necessary foothold for the holdfasts of Laminaria and other seaweeds. Donald zoomed in out of the blue-green haze and looked at me.

"Hello, Donald,"I spoke into my mouthpiece. "You've just cost me a lot of money."

He nodded at me. I continued to look at the seabed, not taking much notice of him. He swam in close to me and nodded again.

"No, I can't take your picture," I said, "I've lost my camera."

I put my hand out and stroked him gently along the top of his head, being careful not to touch his blowhole, which I knew to be a very sensitive area. He responded by shaking his head and swimming slowly forward. Without thinking I followed. He swam ahead. Then he nosed down to the seabed excitedly and, with his body vertical in the water, he flexed himself a couple of times. I looked down. There lying on the sand, just below his snout, was my camera.

I swam quickly down and picked it up.

"You clever fellow," I chortled into my mouthpiece, intensely relieved.

I discovered that one end of the neck strap, which should have been attached to the camera via a split ring, had come free. The ring was partially open because it had been put on and off the camera several times. Nonetheless, to remove it required a deliberate rotational movement of the ring. I concluded that, although the chances of this happening were very small, it must have happened when I was bobbing in the water alongside the dinghy. What was even more remarkable, however, was the fact that I had found the camera again with its new, unused, fish-eye lens still in position.

I hurried up to the surface and waved it at Maura.

"You've found the camera, Horace," she cried, as excited as I was.

"Yes, with Donald's help. He's here in the water just below me. Come on. In you come."

I decided to hold on to the camera after that, and held the viewfinder up to my eye. When I looked through it I found that my view of the underwater world was marvelously expanded. There was distortion around the edge of field where the image was curved, but the view through the viewfinder was brighter and much wider than I could see through the tunnel of my facemask. I was fascinated because I could see both the surface of the sea and the kelp on the bottom. I watched Maura's bubbles chasing overhead to the bright silver-blue surface, and contrasted that image with the dull brown sand on the bottom.

As I peered into the wide-screen circular picture in the viewfinder, I saw Donald's gray shape appear in the edge of the frame and rapidly become larger. Maura was visible in the distance and I swam toward her until she nearly filled the frame. My view of her seemed exceptionally clear. Donald was there too. Excitedly I clicked the shutter. Donald disappeared and I looked away from the camera, surprised to see that I was only about nine inches away from Maura.

I was overjoyed. If the pictures were anywhere near the clarity of the image I had seen through the viewfinder, they would be excellent. With my new dolphin-eye lens, I would have broken the "underwater visibility barrier"—something I had been trying to achieve for fifteen years.

With Donald in the water, and Maura posing for pictures with him, I was extremely happy. And those moments of joy were heightened by the small tragedy of a few minutes before, just as pleasure is always enhanced when it has been hard won.

Donald was intensely interested in the shiny plastic dome of my new lens. He came and put his snout in contact with it and then hovered a few inches away, looking at it intently. Such lenses give a very exaggerated perspective and when I held the camera up to my eye I could see Donald's head clearly and could see the length of his body, which appeared to become tapered and thin, as if it was a long way away. I could also see Maura swimming near his tail. She too looked small. The vision I had through the viewfinder was of a huge whale in clear water, with a diver in the far distance.

Having inspected my camera Donald next moved his attention to my leg. I could feel the gentle pressure against my thigh. I looked down and could see Donald with his jaws open wide and my leg between his teeth. I realized that with his immensely powerful jaws he could probably sever my leg. In a moment of complete irrationality I said to myself, "If it's going to come off, at least I will have the first picture of a dolphin biting a diver's leg." I pointed the camera toward my midriff and clicked the shutter. Donald started for a moment and then continued to feel the texture of my wetsuit with his teeth and jaws.

In a moment his curiosity was satisfied and he swam away skittishly to inspect Maura and Ashley.

As time passed I became cold. Donald made fewer and fewer appearances, so after nearly an hour in the water in all, we abandoned the dive and climbed back into the inflatable. The wind helped to push us back to the slipway and I shivered as I pulled off my sopping wetsuit, hanging it over an upturned boat to drain. Gray clouds scudded across a gray sky as we headed for Port Erin to get our cylinders recharged with air.

As we drove we discussed Donald. I had noticed that he had a new injury on the top of his head, where an approximately circular chunk of flesh about four inches in diameter had been completely cut out. The wound was deep and at its center was a patch of red-raw vascular tissue. This was encircled with a ring of gray-white blubber. It did not appear to be infected.

Maura explained that Donald had been playing with a power boat when it happened. He was riding the bow wave, which would drive him forward at the same speed as the boat with relatively little effort. The dolphin probably then got into a position where he no longer had the benefit of the forward-moving water, and before he could accelerate away the boat had passed over him. He was struck by the metal skeg which projects down below the propellor, with such force that the mountings of the outboard engine had been distorted and taken to Maura's husband Pete for repair.

It must have been a stunning blow, and if the skeg had hit his blowhole the dolphin would almost certainly have died from drowning. Donald seemed to lead a charmed life, I reflected.

In the height of the summer Port Erin is alive with vacationers who swarm over the sands, and along the streets, like ants. When the season closes they disappear, leaving the town to the locals and the seagulls.

On the cool October day Maura, Ashley and I were the only people to stroll along the foreshore. We entered an empty cafe—painted pale blue with white. Water in a chromium-plated urn behind the counter boiled continuously, waiting for the few customers who strayed in from the road. Steam condensed on the windows. Although it was not cold outside I was glad to get inside to the muggy warmth and have a hot cup of tea. The proprietor was pleased to see us and we told her of our adventures with Donald. She, on her part, remarked on the quiet at the end of the season, when Port Erin was preparing to decline into its hibernation until the tourists returned the following year. Maura, however, pointed out that it was only an apparent hibernation. Behind the surface quiet many activities went on. The divers on the island dived throughout the winter months—although less frequently than in the summer, with the influx of "comeovers."

It was mid-afternoon before we returned to Port St. Mary and I was glad to see Donald still surfacing regularly in the same area where we had seen him during our late morning dive. He still appeared to be enjoying himself and I wondered if he was ever unhappy. Maura and Ashley were pleased, as always, to see Donald but they were less enthusiastic about going in the water with him again that day.

"Come on, let's get suited up," I said, in a voice that I hoped sounded like a request. A fishing boat was making ready to leave the harbor and Donald was happily diving around it.

Realizing that I was determined to dive again, Maura and Ashley pulled out the bag containing their wetsuits from the car, though they left me in no doubt about the discomfort I was asking them to suffer on my behalf.

39

Half an hour later we were again loading the inflatable with our cylinders and the camera equipment. The wind was beginning to drop, as it does so often in the evening following a blustery day, and jagged streaks of sunlight were splitting the clouds overhead into multi-hued islands of yellow and white.

The boat was soon loaded and, as it nosed out of the slipway and into the harbor, a gray dorsal fin humped the sea ahead of us and disappeared. Our escort had arrived.

Maura went in and was trying to swim down, but as soon as she stopped moving she drifted slowly to the surface. I swam up with her and our heads broke to the surface together.

"I want to get a shot of you sitting on the bottom," I said.

"Horace, I'm too light. I haven't enough weight to do that. I forgot it was low tide now and I would need more lead than I had this morning."

"Have we any spare weights in the dinghy?"

"No. They're in the car."

"Can't you pick up a rock?"

"I'll try."

I watched Maura swim down to the seabed to search for a suitable rock. She soon found one with a frond of kelp attached to it and placed the rock, which was about the size of four house bricks, on her lap. I hovered about ten feet away to wait for the silt she had stirred up to settle.

Before it did, out of the gloom came a gray torpedo shape. It hovered momentarily, watching Maura sitting on the bottom. Then Donald moved in, pushed the kelp frond with his beak and nudged the rock off her lap. Maura floated gently up from her sitting position and maneuvered herself so that she could pick up the rock again. Clutching it to her stomach she exhaled strongly to reduce her buoyancy and allowed the weight of the rock to hold her again in a sitting position. Before she had settled Donald again moved in, pushing away the fronds of kelp with his beak. I then saw Maura move the rock from her lap and wave her legs in a finning motion to Donald, who watched from a few feet away. I could just hear her talking to him, then she picked up another rock without weeds growing on it, put it on her lap, and for the third time settled on the bottom. Donald again looked at her from a few feet away, then nodded his head and swam away to see Ashley.

I hovered nearby and waited for the silt to settle. The next time Donald swam excitedly by I took my picture. I tried to take a second picture but when I attempted to wind the lever it would not move. I had come to the end of the roll of film. I signaled to Maura to rise and we talked together as we bobbed on the surface.

"That was strange behavior of Donald's," I said.

"Why?"

"Pushing the stone off your lap."

"That wasn't strange," she said, in a matter of fact tone. "He thought I was trapped on the bottom by the stone and came to release me."

"Only twice," I said. "Not three times."

"Didn't you see me explain to him?"

"I could see you waving your legs and I thought I could hear you talking."

"I was. I was telling him that I was in no trouble and waved my legs to prove it," Maura replied, as if this was an absolutely obvious thing to do to a wild animal that could not understand English.

"When I had explained the situation to him he left the rock alone."

I had to admit that Donald did appear to understand what she was trying to impart. Donald had no hands with which to gesture, but he had expressive eyes and could nod his head. He could also make noises, some of which were in the human hearing range, though many of which were of a much higher frequency. So it is possible that he uttered dolphinese noises. But on top of all that there was something else—some kind of telepathic communication, though I hesitate to call it that—or at least a special empathy, or understanding. The relationship of Maura and Donald became more and more puzzling and fascinating.

"I've run out of film," I said.

"Shall we wind it up?" she suggested.

"No," I cried emphatically. "It's perfect now. I'll row back to shore and reload. You can stay here if you like and play with Donald. Put your aqualung aboard."

Ashley climbed into the dinghy and we rowed back to the slipway. The wind had dropped completely and the sun, low in the sky, cast a yellow path of light over the now still water.

When I looked back across the sea I could see the dark silhouetted shape of Maura's head, and occasional ripples and dark arches as Donald lazily humped the surface nearby. In that peaceful harbor the two of them were happy to be left alone without the need to pose for pictures.

I changed the film as quickly as I could, but I had to be careful that the salt water dripping from my suit did not get inside the camera. At last the job was done, but as I rowed back across the water I realized that the sun had set and the sea had lost its yellow glow. I tied up quickly and slipped over the side. Underwater it was cold and gloomy and the light intensity was too low for photography. Nonetheless I was happy. Indeed we all were.

7 · Maura and Donald

Most of the observations to date on dolphins in the wild have been made from the surface of the water, from ships. Occasionally the behavior of a school of dolphins disported themselves around a ship at sea has been recorded on film—few who have seen Cousteau's classic movie *Silent World* will fail to recall the exhilarating sight of a whole school of dolphins leaping one after another out of the water, and interweaving in the air as if in a joyous and complex dance.

Yet although it is now twenty years since I saw *Silent World,* and skin diving has become commonplace all over the world, I know of no film showing divers sporting with free dolphins in the sea. As Robert Sternuit pointed out, wild dolphins have continued to shun man underwater. Indeed, in his book entitled *Dolphins,* Cousteau describes the difficulties of studying dolphins in the wild.

In order to complete a film at all, Cousteau had to adopt a compromise solution. He captured some dolphins and restrained them in the sea with three inflated sausage-shaped buoys linked together in the form of a triangle with a net suspended beneath them. He concedes that this capture and imprisonment caused the dolphins obvious alarm and distress.

Cousteau was thwarted even when he tried to get underwater film in the sea of a "tame" bottlenose dolphin named Dolly, who had associated with the Ashbury family in Florida since May 1971. Dolly apparently made her way one day through the numerous canals that have been cut through the coral of the islands, to the pontoon off the Ashbury property, several miles from the open ocean. When Jean Ashbury offered the dolphin a fish, she eagerly accepted it, and from that moment Dolly became a regular visitor to the Ashbury dock. Dolly swam with the Ashburys' children, and would tow them through the water if they caught hold of her dorsal fin. She was so friendly that she was seen as "one of the family."

The Ashburys' inquiries revealed that Dolly had originally been captured by the United States Navy and assigned to a dolphin training base at Key West. The "study center" had then been transferred from Florida to California, so it was decided to release Dolly from military service, and she had been set free once again in the sea.

However, when Cousteau and his team visited the Ashbury family and took the dolphin out to sea in the hope of filming her, Dolly invariably returned immediately to the murky waters of the canal. Cousteau never did achieve his ambition of filming the dolphin swimming freely with divers in the sea.

I thus realized how extraordinarily lucky I had been to encounter Donald and Maura. Right from the start, however, I established one principle from which I resolved I would never deviate in any circumstances: Donald's freedom was sacrosanct. No matter how desperate I was to get pictures or underwater film, if Donald did not like what we were doing, or just felt like doing something else, he could always simply swim away. I made this private resolve independently, but I soon discovered that it was also Maura's own: to her the idea of her dolphin being constrained in any way was utterly abhorrent.

Indeed, as I talked to her about Donald, I realized that the concept of the dolphin's freedom was integral to the uniqueness of their relationship with one another. She never attempted to impose her will on Donald, as for instance trainers of captured dolphins must do when they teach them to do tricks in dolphinariums. She drew my attention to his behavior in the presence of divers as an indication of his complex and independent personality: he would remain interested in a group of divers only if they were carrying out some task of their own, not if they simply attempted to play with him. If they persisted in trying to grab hold of him he would swim away. Maura interpreted this behavior as meaning that Donald was not prepared to accept any domination by human beings. At the same time, however, he did not like to be ignored completely: he liked to have his presence acknowledged, and once this was done would take such a keen interest in what was going on that he sometimes intervened and disrupted the work altogether. If he wanted to continue the game when the divers had finished their tasks he would attempt to stop them leaving the water by pulling on their fins as they tried to climb aboard their diving boat.

Maura treated Donald as if he were a very special and sensitive personal friend. And inevitably, I too thought in terms of human characteristics when I tried to define him to myself: to me he seemed like a person of very great physical strength, happy, fiercely independent, even self-willed, but above all totally free. In the sea, Donald was so superior to both of us, physically as well as in the sensitivity of his response to environment, that Maura and I acquired considerable humility in his presence. Maura always showed great understanding and tenderness for him.

Maura was always concerned for Donald's safety, and her diving buddies would often send in reports when they spotted Donald. Maura's special diving partner was Mike Dunning. One evening Mike was driving home from work via Port St. Mary in order to check up on Donald when he saw the dolphin in a seeming frenzy, whirling around one of the buoys. Alarmed that he might have been caught up in the buoy line, Mike telephoned Maura who immediately grabbed her wetsuit, flung it in the car, and with tea forgotten raced down to Port St. Mary with her husband Pete. Mike was already suited up, and Maura and Mike snorkled out into the harbor with Pete observing from the shore. As the two snorkelers neared the moorings, Donald, who had been lying quietly on the surface, finned over to greet them. Maura was very relieved to find that her dolphin friend was quite unharmed.

Here, in Maura's own words, is what happened next.

"There followed a most rumbustious game, a right mad session. Mike became very anxious when he realized how possessive Donald was toward me and he feared for my safety when Donald got sexy. After a hide-and-seek session around the triple hull of a trimaran, Mike insisted I get out of the water for my own good, which I did."

Maura explained to me that she was sensitive to Donald's inner state, particularly as it was communicated by the expression in his eyes. If he came up to her slowly and closed his eyes it was a signal that he wanted to be loved, and Maura would cuddle him and stroke him gently. On such occasions he would remain submissive and docile to her caresses. If on the other hand his eyes were bright and full of mischief, she knew that he wanted a game, and they would romp accordingly.

I had first met Maura in August 1973, shortly after she moved to the island with her husband Peter and two sons. She came to greet me when I landed at the local airport for a diving trip and two hours later I was diving from the Mitchells' cabin cruiser into clear water amid some of the most beautiful underwater scenery and marine life I had encountered during fifteen years of diving off various parts of the British Coast. I immediately understood why Maura was so enthusiastic about her new home.

I guessed at the time that she was in her early thirties, though I later found out that her elder son was twenty years old. However, it was apparent from our first meeting that she was a woman of youthful appearance and even more youthful spirit. Moreover, she was very fit. She could carry her aqualung and heavy diving gear as well as a man and heave herself into an inflatable after a dive as easily as a seal flipping up onto the rocks. She was of small stature but with a well proportioned figure. She wore her blond hair straight and shoulder length to frame a pixie face, with bright blue eyes.

In Britain diving is still primarily a man's game. Women who make it to the top grades in the British Sub-Aqua Club, as Maura had done, are rare, and those who do so usually have very exceptional qualities indeed.

So there they were—an exceptional dolphin and an exceptional woman. And the exceptional chance that the two of them should meet in that magical underwater world that was Donald's natural environment which man was only beginning to penetrate. And I had had the exceptional good luck to encounter them both. I felt exhilarated, full of a sense that something important was happening. I was not yet clear what it was.

8 · A Magic Moment

The next day dawned full of promise. Clear blue sky. No wind. Our diving suits, which had been washed thoroughly the night before, hung lifeless and bone dry under the verandah. I am suspicious of days that begin so well. They have a nasty habit of not living up to the promises they so coquettishly offer. However, any doubts I might have had about the weather were quickly suppressed when I joined Ashley and Maura for breakfast. The sun was shining and we were all looking forward to the prospect of our next meeting with Donald.

Before our rendezvous, however, we had to repair a hole in the rubber floor of the inflatable. By the time this was done and the domestic chores had been attended to, the time was approaching midday. During the morning brilliant white puffs of cotton-wool cloud had begun to pepper the sky, and as we loaded the inflated C-Craft onto the roofrack of Maura's car the wind, which had crept into the morning as a zephyr, was already rattling the television aerials.

It was 12:45 when we drove onto the familiar jetty at Port St. Mary. The wind was blowing so strongly from the northwest that even across the small fetch of the harbor it was able to raise whitecaps. It was close to high water and waves were swishing and gurgling up the stone slipway where we had proposed to launch the inflatable. One hundred yards offshore the red, white and blue lifeboat, one of Donald's favorite haunts, bobbed up and down, snatching at its forward mooring rope like a spirited horse on a tight leading rein.

We parked the car so that we could scan the sea. The car shuddered occasionally when the wind caught the dinghy lashed to the roofrack. With the sunshine reaching us inside the car we were as cosy as embryos in a womb. But the vibrations of the vehicle and the white crests on the waves were evidence enough that my old enemy, the wind, was out there snorting, and prodding his cold sword into any nook or cranny he could find.

We could not be sure that Donald would be in Port St. Mary, and as we looked out across the harbor we realized that it would be difficult to spot him amid the waves as he briefly surfaced and exposed his blowhole to take a breath. We carefully scanned the water around the blue boat where we had enjoyed his company the day before. Even the heavy fishing boat was snatching at its mooring lines, but with a stronger, longer pull than the relatively light lifeboat which rode higher out of the water. There was no sign of the dolphin.

On the far side of the harbor a child's inflatable boat about five feet long was bobbing up and down on the sea like a buoy. It was attached to a single white mooring line that disappeared beneath the water. Two lightweight plastic oars were permanently attached to the boat with circular rubber oarlocks that were built into the tubular sides. Thus the oars projected over the sides of the boat as if held by an invisible oarsman. We hardly noticed the dinghy until a particularly vicious gust of wind picked it off the sea and held it suspended in the air, where it spun as if played on a shimmering white line by an unseen angler beneath the water. The bottom of the toy boat was colored red and the top cream. It flashed alternately red and cream as it spun before crashing back into the sea upside down. A few seconds later the wind again whipped it into the air. Like an out-of-control kite it danced in the air before flopping down again, the right way up.

Ensconced in the car we watched, fascinated by the boat's aerial acrobatics. But we were not the only ones being entertained. When the dinghy landed for a third time and briefly floated on the surface, a dark silver shape rose out of the water alongside. Cascading diamonds of dripping water from its body, it arched gracefully over the dinghy and splashed into the water again on the far side.

We all saw what happened, but it was Maura who got the words out first.

"There's Donald," she said, her blue eyes sparkling like sun on the sea. "I told you he would be here."

We all got out of the car. Maura's hair flew back like a horse's mane as she stood on the edge of the jetty clinging to the rail, waiting for the next sighting. We did not have to wait long. Seconds later Donald again performed a spectacular leap. It was as if the wind had injected him with energy. His obvious enjoyment of the wind and the waves radiated from his flashing silver body. Maura shouted and waved. Donald responded immediately. He put on a spectacular display of leaps and aquabatics as if to prove that anything the wind could do with an inanimate rubber dinghy he could do one thousand times better.

Had you asked me at that moment if I thought that Donald was even aware of our presence, let alone putting on a display for Maura's benefit, I would probably have dismissed the idea as pure poppycock. Now however, with the benefit of hindsight and a much deeper understanding of the relationship between Maura and her dolphin, I would interpret his actions differently. I would say that Donald not only saw Maura but that he recognized her, and the pleasure he derived from the wind, sea and prancing dinghy was enhanced by her presence, so that the display he now put on was not simply an expression of his own exuberance, but a sign that he was pleased to see her.

The rising of the wind had completely frustrated my objective for the day, which was to photograph Donald underwater. But my usual intense irritation and frustration at such circumstances was absent. And the reason for my unlikely good humor was one that I have since had reason to ponder on, and have had confirmed by many others who have had experience of dolphins: the fact that dolphins somehow seem to exude a special kind of joy that they are able to transmit to man. I have yet to find a man who was not happy at the sight of a dolphin. Many a ship's log has recorded that the vessel was being escorted by a school of dolphins, and to a seaman reading such a log this information immediately conjures up a vision of a happy ship—a ship going well. Even the most hardened seamen will come on deck and enjoy the sight of dolphins gamboling in the sea alongside. And there is something in this quality of dolphins that goes beyond the pleasure that most people feel when they are able to watch other animals at play, domestic or wild.

Near where we had parked, a small fishing boat was being filled up with empty scallop shells. A truck from the nearby processing plant poured its load down a chute onto the deck and returned for another cargo. When the fishing boat was fully loaded it pulled away from the jetty, turned bow first into the buffeting wind, and headed for the harbor entrance. Just before it passed out of sight we could see Donald leaping out of the water in front of it. It was time for him to carry out his escort service, a self-imposed duty he seldom failed to perform when a vessel left his territory.

We also departed. We bought some cakes and headed for the other side of the bay, where we found a spot to picnic sheltered from the wind. As we ate we looked longingly at the still clear water that idly washed back and forth over the sand and slippery green seaweed. If only it could be as flat as this in Port St. Mary we could all join Donald again. Overhead, white clouds slid across the sky like leaves floating down a fast-moving stream, and across the bay we could see white horses rearing out of the deep blue sea. But were they subsiding? I fancied they were.

Maura's husband, Peter, had decided to build himself a new boat after he had found a flagstaff thrown up on the rocks near where we were sitting. His description of this event, and how various other components for this major project had come his way equally fortuitously, had fascinated Ashley, and fired in him an immediate interest in beachcombing. This is an occupation which I openly admit I too have enjoyed since my earliest memories, so after lunch we scrambled over the rocks, turning over the flotsam with our feet and hands to see what other treasures providence might have deposited on the shore for our benefit.

From there we moved to the lee side of the harbor of Port

St. Mary. Like all working fishing harbors, it was a captivating place. The air was tinted with the smell of tar from freshly treated lobster pots, which were stacked in piles of higgledy-piggledy confusion. We picked our way among the coils of rope and fishing nets draped across the ground, and looked in and at the boats tied up to the jetty. The shapes, textures, sounds and smells harmonized into a living picture in which we were briefly moving figures. Maura pointed out a boat with the same hull structure—a Newhaven Sea Angler—as the one Peter was building. We discussed the construction, the line, the sea-worthiness, the engine and the problems and pleasures of building your own boat. We also inspected some giant blocks of concrete that had been cast on the site. Maura explained that the harbor was being modified and extended. Little did we know at that time what repercussions these harbor con-structions were to have on our lives, and in particular on that of our friend the dolphin.

As the shadows started to lengthen and the others thought of heading back for Ballasalla, my mind was gradually evolving another plan. The wind was definitely dropping. Would it weaken, as it so often does on a blustery day, to give a calm evening? If it did there was still a chance that we could dive. I put my thoughts to Maura and Ashley. They are both of a generous nature, and agreed to have one last look at the sea from the jetty where we had previously launched the inflatable for our meetings with Donald.

When we arrived it was about five o'clock. The tide had fallen, revealing a small stretch of yellow sand. Earlier the unyielding stone walls alongside the slipway had thrown the furious waves back upon themselves, in a turmoil of angry mo-tion. Now the waves had diminished. They dissipated their violence without damage into the absorbent sand, and spent the last of their energy slithering harmlessly up and down the newly-exposed beach. It certainly would be possible to launch the inflatable.

But there was no sign of Donald.

We looked out at the fishing boat and the lifeboat, his adopted homes in Port St. Mary. We could not see the charac-teristic rise of his shiny black hump.

"I wonder where he is?" said Maura. "There's no sign of him."

"I'm sure he'll turn up if we call him in the water," I said, more in hope than expectation. "Come on, let's get changed."

The sun, which earlier had penetrated our clothes and warmed us, had lost its heat and hung like a glowing tangerine in the western sky. The base of the slipway was in deep shadow. Gusts of cold wind funnelled into the slipway and pulled at the inflatable as we lifted it off the roofrack and dropped it with a bump on the stone-cold cobbles.

I pulled my wetsuit from its plastic bag and was relieved to find that it was still warm from its cosy place in the back of the car. I caught the characteristic smell of neoprene as I pulled the yielding rubber over my goose-pimpled skin.

Maura is an efficient diver and a diving instructor. Once the decision to dive had been made she disappeared behind the car and reappeared a few minutes later in her blue wetsuit. Her pixie features were exaggerated by the hood which tightly hugged her face.

The three of us carried the "Buc" down to the water's edge with the jerky steps of people walking painfully across stony ground. Ashley held the inflatable out to sea while we returned for the aqualungs and other diving gear. I returned once again to the car and opened the battered blue suitcase that contained my carefully packed cameras. Having checked that they were all in order, I closed the lid and wondered what the others would have to say about all the discomfort I had pressed them to endure, if Donald did not turn up. There was still no sign of him. I dumped my suitcase into the inflatable, where Maura was patiently holding the oars and fending off from the jagged rocks. I grabbed the transom and pushed the "Buc" into the waves before climbing into the stern. Five minutes later we were tied up to one of the old car tires hanging down over the side of the fishing boat.

We should have seen Donald by now, for he invariably came to inspect any new movement of boats or people. We peered into the cold water for a sight of a friendly face looking back at us. But we saw only the dark green uninviting depths.

"I'll go in and call him," I said to Maura as I heaved the

metal cylinder of my aqualung onto my back and buckled the yellow harness. I picked my lead weightbelt from the water swirling over the duckboards in the bottom of the boat. The lead bit into my back as I pulled it tight around my waist. I hung a camera around my neck and drew on my facemask before finally putting the mouthpiece of my regulator between my lips. I tested that it was functioning properly; when I breathed in the air hissed into my lungs. All systems were "go." I sat on one of the soft rubber walls of the inflatable and rolled back into the water.

The sea closed over me like a dark, cold, green blanket. I was surrounded by a cloud of tiny bubbles injected into the water by my entry and sucked down by my passage. I found my bearings after the two seconds of confusion that always follow a backward entry into the sea and watched the curtain of bubbles I had dragged down with me chasing one another erratically back to the surface. The dark brown seabed was only about fifteen feet beneath me. I checked that my camera was still in position, held the top of my mask against my forehead and exhaled gently through my nose. This cleared the few tablespoons of water that had leaked into my mask. I allowed myself to sink slowly.

"Donald, Donald," I called into my mouthpiece. As I sank I revolved slowly, anxiously awaiting his appearance in response to my call.

The sea was absolutely still. It must have been slack low water.

Nearby some long dark brown fronds of seaweed lay draped over a hump in the seabed like discarded flowers on a rubbish heap. I knew their presence was indicative of a rock outcrop. So I swam over to the mound and rummaged among the seaweed until I found two stones about the size of plum puddings.

I clapped the rocks together and I could hear the sharp crack of the sound penetrating the water like a gunshot. Clouds of silt dispersed when the two stones met. I stood still and peered into the encircling green wall. There was no sight of my quarry. In annoyance I crashed the two stones together as hard as I could. One of them shattered and the pieces zigzagged to the bottom.

"Oh come on, Donald, please," I pleaded into the water. The words vanished like my bubbles.

I surfaced beside the inflatable.

"He's not here," I told Maura. "At least he won't come to me. Will you come in and call him?"

"The things I do for you, Horace," she said, grinning. A few seconds later she launched herself into the cold green soup.

I could see her mouthing the word "Donald" as she descended beside me. I could just detect the distorted word mixed with the regular squeak of the air passing through her demand valve.

We swam over the mound. I picked up two more stones and banged them together. Maura found an old tin can and bashed it with the handle of her diving knife. As she sat on the hump of seaweed singing her siren song and beating time on her tin drum, I thought I could have been watching a sequence from an unlikely movie. The next event almost convinced me that I was watching a Walt Disney cartoon. For when I next saw Maura she was still sitting on the rock calling. But this time, behind her back, vertical in the water, with his nose three inches from the back of her head, was a motionless dolphin.

Donald had arrived.

I moved toward her. She looked up and raised both hands palm upwards. At the same time she tilted her head to one side and shrugged her shoulders. It was a gesture which is universally understood, meaning "It is hopeless." In the underwater world of the diver no verbal communication is possible unless special equipment, which we were not wearing, is used. Maura pointed to the surface indicating that we should return to the boat. Donald remained quite still.

I now think he was quite deliberately teasing Maura.

I revealed his game by pointing at him vigorously. Maura turned. I knew without hearing that she was talking to him. She stretched up her arm and gently stroked him under the chin. He opened his huge mouth in a gesture that looked in human terms like a loud guffaw. With a flick of his fluke he arched away and returned a few strokes later for another caress and soft words from his human friend. When he saw me raise the bright dome of the fish-eye lens attached to my underwater camera he came to inspect it, putting his snout right up against the lens, thereby making picture taking impossible. Then he stood off a few feet and opened his mouth—again as if he was laughing—before sweeping round in a circle and heading for Maura. Donald was so agile and could move so swiftly underwater that we never knew where he would appear next. He would disappear beyond our limited visibility with a few sweeps of his powerful fluke and reappeared from a completely different direction. It was as if he knew he was far superior to us in the underwater environment. He was playing with us, not we with him.

It was then that I noticed that his pale pink penis was extended and that he was attempting to stroke it against Maura as he swam past her. Maura had told me before that Donald was sometimes "fruity," and now I could see by his actions exactly what she meant. Others who have had a similar experience in Donald's company have been more prosaic and referred to him as "a dirty old man!"

I have since thought about Donald's behavior and have come to the conclusion that on that specific occasion at least it may have been completely misinterpreted. There are a number of reasons why this misunderstanding has come about.

One of the reasons is that when we look at animal behavior we almost invariably attempt to find a human context in which to put it. But by merely anthropomorphizing dolphin behavior, we misunderstand a highly intelligent animal. I suggest that when Donald approached Maura with his penis extended he was not making a sexual approach to her, but was using his penis as a tactile organ to gain a greater knowledge of her. I am proposing that in addition to its function as a tract for urine and spermatozoa, the penis of a dolphin has a third and completely distinct role: that of a limb for tactile exploration. The dolphin can use its penis for exploring, feeling and interpreting surfaces and shapes in a totally nonsexual context. In doing so he adds to the mental picture he has of the object. The dolphin, as we have already observed, is an intensely curious animal who gathers all the information he can about the world around him. So when he is in familiar surroundings and no harm threatens, he will use his most sensitive sense to gain a deeper understanding of his environment. Similarly, the blind man will feel the face of a friend with his hands to get to know him better.

How has this situation come about?

Let us consider the environment in which dolphins live. It is hostile and cold. The scars frequently seen on whales and dolphins, and which are much in evidence on Donald, bear witness to the fact that the entire surface of their bodies is subject to lacerations and violent abrasion. Thus external organs must be completely protected. But a tough protective layer will inevitably reduce the sensitivity of the underlying tissue to external tactile stimuli: imagine a nurse wearing a thick pair of gloves attempting to measure a patient's pulse rate. Thus, although the dolphin's flippers have a bone structure that is distantly related to that of the human arm, and they can feel with the tips of these fins, there can be little doubt that human hands and fingers are very many times more sensitive to touch.

Humans, in common with other land mammals, have also another part of their body which is particularly sensitive to delicate touch sensations. That part is the lips. When human babies investigate an object, they first find out about it by touching with their hands. And if it is not too hostile they then subject it to further investigation in their mouths. This is not only to find out what it tastes like, but to determine characteristics such as smoothness and hardness. In later life, the adolescent human will use his lips, because they are so sensitive to touch, to explore and discover his prospective mate.

Dolphins do not have lips. Their mouths are undoubtedly sensitive, but they lack the very supple, thin-skinned flesh that can detect very small difference in texture.

Male dolphins do, however, have a soft, flexible, thin-skinned member, rich in tactile nerves. During normal activities such as swimming and hunting it is kept safely retracted and protected. It can, however, be exposed when the dolphin wants to investigate and explore objects, including humans, in the fullest detail.

This hypothesis is supported by the structure of the penis of dolphins. In land mammals the penis becomes erect when gorged with blood. This process is controlled by hormones which are usually released by some external stimulation, such as the smell of a female of the species in heat. Thus erection and contraction of the penis is a relatively slow process compared with most other movements which involve muscular action.

A study of the histological structure of the penis of the dolphin, however, reveals that the central section is riddled with strands of tough and elastic connective tissue, with a consequent reduction in the spongy tissue present in land mammals. Thus there is little change in size upon erection, and the erect member is relatively small compared with the size of the entire body of the dolphin. When the need arises, a slit in the abdominal wall opens and the penis is flicked out by muscle action. The penis can also be rapidly retracted with the retractor penis muscle. Such muscular control, if voluntary, would obviously be beneficial to the dolphin when it uses its penis to touch and feel.

In their monograph on dolphins, Cousteau and Diolé state that a newly born male dolphin is able to have an erection only a few hours after birth. Attempts at copulation take place during the first few weeks after birth and have the mother as sexual object. They state that the mother encourages copulation by turning on her side, and that this is the baby dolphin's first lesson in sexuality. I would propose instead that the mother is teaching her offspring to feel and explore with his penis, in a nonsexual context. Not until the dolphin approaches sexual maturity years later does its penis take on the function of procreation. Throughout its life the dolphin maintains the use of the penis to feel objects, and in the same way that humans derive pleasure from touching things it probably enjoys an equivalent sensation, perhaps to a higher degree.

It is now generally accepted that men and dolphins had common ancestors about twenty-five million years ago, and that these ancestors were derived from animals that came from the sea. From that parting of the ways man and dolphin took very different paths. The dolphins returned to the sea and readopted the marine environment, but remained mammalian and continued to breathe air. During the course of evolution it is possible that the penis of the dolphin became increasingly sensitive as a retractable tactile sensor. During the same course of time our forbears evolved as upright land animals, whose hands and lips developed as their most sensitive organs of touch.

I must admit that all these thoughts were not going through my mind when I was watching Maura and Donald engrossed in their tactile, verbal and visual dialogue in the green sea off the Isle of Man. At that time I was totally absorbed in getting underwater pictures.

At one stage Maura rose to the underside of the fishing boat. As she did so I saw the propeller and the rudder silhouetted against the sun, which shone through the water like a broad spotlight. Where the beam entered the sea an amber disc of light danced to the time of the wavelets that rippled the surface. Donald swam around me and inspected the rudder in a mood of great apparent concentration. I drifted gently backward watching the scene through the viewfinder, and rejoicing at the brilliant beauty of the contrast of the dark shadows with the sparkling light. I pressed the shutter.

Donald swam away and I drifted slowly down waiting for him to return. He did so a few minutes later and I swam back toward the keel of the fishing boat to get some more pictures. When I arrived the scene had changed completely. The sea now appeared to be illuminated from inside by a pale diffuse green light. The sun had set. Dusk was falling. The magic moment of sunset had gone.

It was time to go.

9 · Masterpiece of Evolution

The animals that now inhabit the earth are the products of millions of years of evolution. They can be divided into groups which form the branches of an evolutionary tree. Each main branch, which we call an order, divides into sub-orders and families, often with wide variations.

In the course of the growth of the evolutionary tree some branches died and the species became extinct. Now only one species of man inhabits the land masses of the earth—*Homo sapiens.* His branch stands out of the evolutionary tree as a single spike, not a much-divided twig like many other orders. It has been argued that the reason why there is now only one species of man on the earth is that our ancestors exterminated similar but nonaggressive branches from our evolutionary stem. That this inbuilt aggressive characteristic, which has dominated our evolution, is still present is supported by the manner in which, even within our own species, we continue to destroy these individual tribes and ethnic groups, such as the Australian Aboriginals, who show signs of being more pacific than the rest.

Approximately two thirds of our planet, however, is covered with water, and the dominant order of animals in the sea is undoubtedly the Cetaceans—the whales. The whales range from the 100-feet-long blue whale to the five-feet-long harbor porpoise. And it has been argued that this order is so enormously diverse because, unlike men, it has in its genetic make-up a trait of nonaggression, which allowed variations brought about by the processes of evolution to survive and develop along their own lines. This trait of nonaggression is certainly apparent in the lack of reaction of whales to the hideous injustices inflicted upon them by man. With aggression so central to our own make-up, it is sometimes difficult for humans to comprehend a species in which external threats and inflicted pain do not raise an aggressive response.

The Cetaceans have evolved from mammals that roamed the land 25 million years ago. Like all mammals, they breathe air—it was for this reason that Donald surfaced regularly and made his characteristic sound, which was like a diver blowing powerfully to clear his snorkel tube. They divide into two broad groups—the Mysticetes and the Odontocetes.

The Mysticetes, which, literally translated from the Greek, means "whiskered whales," have within their membership the largest animals ever to have lived on the earth—far larger than the now extinct dinosaurs and land mammoths of prehistoric times. At the top of the scale in terms of size is the blue whale, a lifesize model of which is in the American Museum of Natural History in New York. Models may be all that future generations will see, for these magnificent creatures have been hunted to near extinction.

These largest animals in the world feed on some of the smallest animals in the world—tiny planktonic larvae in the sea. The whiskered whales sweep gently through the sea filtering off enormous quantities of krill through cartilaginous sieves composed of baleen, or "whalebone." These filtration slats are not in reality composed of bone, but are modified mucous membrane.

In the heyday of the whaling era, the baleen or whalebone found its way into many products. Perhaps best known are the whalebone corsets into which Victorian ladies squeezed their reluctant midriffs. But these animals were not hunted for their whalebone; that was a bonus. The major prize was the oil—which was used both as a food and for lighting—as much as 26 tons of it from one animal. Nowadays everything that is taken from the carcasses of these animals can be obtained from alternative sources, so it is no longer need, but man's avarice, that drives the fishermen who hunt these and other large whales to the edge of extinction. It is sad to think that two of the richest nations in the world, the Japanese and the Russians, still kill these wonders of evolution.

The same fate has befallen many of the other category of whales, the Odontocetes, which means "toothed whales." When one looks at Donald's impressive array of triangular teeth, it is obvious that he belongs in this classification, whose members range from the sixty-feet-long sperm whale to the relatively small common porpoise.

When mammals took to a life in the sea, their weight was supported by the water and they became virtually weightless. The skeletons of their forbears, which had evolved both as support structures and for movement, were now required to adapt to the needs of a swimming mammal. Over the millennia the skull changed completely from the usual mammalian pattern. The nasal bones were reduced to two small nodules, and a new passage evolved that opened to the exterior blowhole on the top of the head. There was a complete loss of the hind limbs, to facilitate streamlining. The fore limbs retained the same elements as land mammals but in greatly modified form. All trace of horny fingertips was lost. Freedom of movement was restricted to the shoulder joint, and the modified fore limbs (flippers) took on the function of controlling direction and acting as brakes. They were not used for propulsion. That function was left exclusively to the tail, which was assisted by an increase in the number of vertebrae in the lumbar region. This gave greater sensitivity and flexibility of movement to the tail. The propulsive power of the tail was also increased by the development of longer vertical processes (neural spines) for the attachment of the tendons of the powerful tail muscles.

The more I saw of Donald the more impressed I was with the dolphin's superb adaptation to life in the sea. All external protuberances which might impede the efficient passage of the dolphin through the water have been biologically modified to maintain perfect streamlining. The external ears have been reduced to two small pinholes. The eyes do not protrude. The male reproductive organ is completely hidden from view; in females the mammary glands are likewise located within the body, and the nipples retracted behind two so-called nipple slits on either side of the female genital opening. (The sex of a dolphin is thus not immediately apparent, as it is with most other mammals.)

The bends have caused the death of many a human diver. Nitrogen in the blood dissolves when he dives deep, and may reappear again in the form of bubbles of gas in the bloodstream when he surfaces. If the bubbles block blood vessels, the supply of essential oxygen to nervous tissues may be stopped, giving rise to paralysis which can be fatal. The Cetaceans, however, have evolved a complex system of oil droplets in the bloodstream with a high capacity to dissolve nitrogen rapidly under pressure. The nitrogen dissolves into the oil droplets during a deep dive and is harmlessly released again when the animal comes back to the surface.

The dolphins have also evolved a respiratory system that enables them to inhale and exhale extremely quickly. They can move five to ten liters of air in and out of their lungs during the 0.3 seconds of the active part of their breathing cycle.

However, most remarkable of all of the evolutionary processes of adaptation to a marine environment is undoubtedly the dolphin's development of a completely new communication system. Although men have spent millions of dollars on research into this system, there are still enormous gaps in our knowledge.

The need to adapt arises of course from the differences between air and water as conductors of light and sound. Whereas water is a less efficient conductor of light than air is, it is a better conductor of sound. Accordingly it is no surprise that the dolphin's primary communication system, both for collection and transmission of information, is based on sound; and his perception extends to frequencies much higher than can be detected by the human auditory senses. The external ears which serve in humans for collecting and reflecting aerial vibrations are absent. All that remains of the ear holes of the dolphin's land ancestors are two pinholes, which are extremely difficult to locate and are about two inches below and behind the eyes.

Without an air passage and an eardrum to vibrate, how does a dolphin hear? That is a question which is still being debated. Commercial divers will be aware that bones conduct sound for they will almost certainly have used "bone mikes" which are tucked inside the rubber hoods of their diving suits. A "bone mike" consists of a small loudspeaker enclosed in a tiny watertight capsule. When the signal is received by the loudspeaker (usually instructions about the task in hand), it is transposed into vibrations. These are transmitted through the case of the "bone mike" and the skin of the diver to part of the bony structure of his skull, and thence to the ear-bone complex of the inner ear. These vibrations are in turn converted into signals which are passed along nerves to the brain.

It has been proposed by one eminent delphinologist that dolphins use their jaw bones to intercept water-borne sound signals, and then transmit them to the internal ear-bone complex; Dr. Kenneth Norris evolved this theory after finding a perfect porpoise skull buried in the sand, with all of the fine bones intact.

Land mammals produce sounds by the passage of air through

the larynx during inhalation and exhalation. But although a dolphin can exhale underwater, and we have seen Donald do this on numerous occasions through his blowhole, this is not the manner in which he produces sound. The precise mechanism by which the dolphin makes sound signals is simply not yet understood. There are air cavities within the heads of the Cetaceans, and it is thought that sounds may be produced by the passage of air from one cavity to another, past tissues which vibrate rather like the reeds in musical wind instruments. The air in the upper nasal passages can be internally cycled, thus enabling the dolphin to emit sounds regardless of the duration of a dive. And one school of thought proposes that the domed foreheads, called the melons, in bottlenose dolphins act as "sound lenses" which beam the sound out in a given direction. If this is so, concentrating the sound beams in this way would considerably increase the efficiency of the dolphin's auditory system.

Man, of course, has to depend on his very restricted vision and mechanical sound aids to communicate underwater. But nowhere is his inferiority to the dolphin more obvious than when he moves. Whenever I compared my own clumsy performance with Donald's extraordinary grace and speed, I was struck by the evidence of his superb adaptation to the sea.

It is the peculiar quality of the dolphin's skin that is thought to be a key to its amazing maneuverability and ability to swim at very high speeds. It has been suggested that very small quantities of the outermost layer of the epidermis, which is composed of flat cells, actually slide off the dolphin when it swims through the water. This process is assisted by secretions of a very fine oil. Thus when it swims through the water fast, the dolphin is literally swimming out of the outermost layer of its skin, thereby virtually eliminating the drag produced by turbulence. This is typical of the subtlety with which dolphins have apparently evolved to adapt to an underwater environment.

The loss of the outer layers of skin is not of course unique to underwater mammals—it also occurs constantly in humans, whose epidermis is thicker than that of the dolphin, and consists of an outer layer of dead cells that rub off and are continuously replaced by new cells growing underneath. If you press your fingers to your forehead and move them up and down you will feel the skin moving over your skull. Can you imagine what would happen to the skin on the head of a dolphin if it were equally mobile? When the dolphin swam fast through the water the drag would tend to pull the skin back toward the tail and small ridges would form. This in turn would set up turbulence which would destroy the smooth flow of water over the skin and reduce swimming efficiency. Such an effect would not be restricted simply to the head of the dolphin but to its entire surface.

What nature has done is to effect a remarkable adaptation to eliminate this effect. The thin epidermis is keyed into the underlying layer, the dermis, by numerous fingers of tissue called papillae, which efficiently lock the dermis to the epidermis. These dermal papillae are arranged in ridges. A study of the ridges has enabled physiologists to determine just how water flows over the dolphin's body when it swims. Their research has shown that the direction of the water flow relative to the body remains the same on both the upward and the downward stroke of the tail. The upward stroke is the power stroke. This movement produces a low-pressure zone on the underside of the fluke, which draws water over the head and chest and down across the ridge behind the dorsal fin. This flow of water effectively moves the dolphin forward and downward against the hydroplaning action of the front flippers. The down stroke is simply a return stroke during which the extremity of the tail fluke is relaxed and water is allowed to spill across it.

When scientists first seriously investigated the extraordinary swimming abilities of dolphins they calculated that a dolphin would have to develop nearly two horsepower to push itself through the water if the flow of water across its body was turbulent. For a man to equal this performance in terms of muscle power he would have to be able to climb a mountain at a rate of well over thirty miles per hour. Yet an investigation of dolphin tail muscle showed it to be very similar to other mammalian muscle. Thus the investigators concluded the dolphin did not derive its extraordinary swimming performance from "super-muscle," but as the result of laminar, i.e. nonturbulent, flow of water across its body. Since that time much money has been spent on research in an effort to simulate a "dolphin skin" for submarines but so far man's technology has not matched nature's ingenuity.

10 · Boy on a Dolphin

Many of the events that have had the most profound effect upon my life have in fact been the results of mishaps that in the end have turned out well. The event on the Isle of Man on October 6, 1974, was one of those.

I had booked a return passage to Liverpool on the 12 o'clock sailing from Douglas, and was hopeful that I would have some fine pictures, particularly those taken on that last evening, just before sunset. Everything seemed to be in order until I decided to check the time of sailing.

Quite by chance I discovered during my telephone conversation that, unlike British Rail and all the aircraft companies, whose timetables were based on the 24-hour clock, the Isle of Man Steam Packet Company was still operating on a 12-hour clock. I was booked on the boat that sailed at midnight, not noon. I had another twelve hours on the Isle of Man. I stopped packing immediately and announced to Maura and Ashley that we had time to pay Donald another visit before we departed.

It was an opportunity I could not miss, and I took my 16-mm movie camera into the water to film the dolphin we had all come to love.

Donald appeared so quickly I got the impression he had been waiting for us. I framed him up in the viewfinder and pressed the shutter release. As soon as the camera motor started to whir Donald came straight for me, and pushed his snout onto the front of the camera housing. I stopped filming and tried to push him away, but as he was much larger I succeeded only in pushing myself backward.

When he had fully satisfied his curiosity he swam off to

64

inspect Ashley, who was snorkeling down to take the dolphin's photograph with one of my still cameras.

Ashley's antics then set Donald into a frenzy of excitement. From below I could see showers of bubbles as the dolphin leapt clear of the water and splashed in again within inches of my son. I continued filming from underneath, but when I saw the dolphin make a headlong rush for Ashley I feared that Donald's exuberance might override his gentle nature, and I hastened to the surface to tell Ashley to get into the dinghy. As I surfaced I saw a sight that is now etched on my memory.

Ashley rose gently out of the water.

At first his expression was one of incredulity and slight apprehension. Then when he realized what was happening he relaxed. He looked in my direction. His snorkel mouthpiece dropped from his lips and he gave me a broad grin. As he did so he held both of his hands in the air while sitting perfectly balanced on the head of the dolphin. Donald accelerated away from me with Ashley riding, legs astride Donald's head. The dolphin gradually increased speed until he was moving at an impressive rate. He took the course of an arc that swept round the harbor and then brought Ashley back to near where he had started.

Then the dolphin sounded, leaving Ashley to sink slowly in the water again like a water skier who has released the tow rope after a run.

That beautiful and spontaneous act—Ashley said afterward that it came as a complete surprise to him—left me with a joy which even now I cannot adequately describe. The power and simultaneous gentleness with which the dolphin lifted Ashley so smoothly and held him as safely as if he had been on a barber's chair forged a bond between Donald and me as strong and tender as the trust between lovers.

The mystery and enchantment of that image of the boy upon the dolphin's back had something primeval and mythological about it, and once more I turned to the legends of the ancient Greeks, who seemed to have had a love and reverence for dolphins that succeeding civilizations have lost. I found the tale about the poet Arion, who lived in the seventh century B.C.

65

and was recorded two centuries later by the historian Herodotus. Herodotus confirmed the story in Corinth and saw with his own eyes in the Sanctuary at Cape Tainaron the bronze statuette of a boy riding a dolphin.

Arion was a native of the island of Lesbos, who went to Corinth, to the court of King Periander, to win fame and fortune. Such was his talent that he became a top entertainer and went on a tour of the Greek island and colonies. But on the journey home the sailors coveted his wealth and threatened to kill him. The murderous crew would not agree to his plea for mercy but they did grant him a final wish—to dress in his best costume and sing for the last time. With his last wish granted, and the pirates for an audience, Arion tuned his lyre and began to sing.

So beautiful was his music that it attracted a dolphin who swam alongside the vessel. Suddenly, taking his would-be killers by surprise, Arion jumped overboard. The dolphin took the poet on its back and carried him to the shore at Cape Tainaron (now named Cape Matapan). Arion made his way to Corinth and told his story to Periander who was skeptical and asked for proof. When the ship arrived back in its home port the sailors said they had left Arion behind. But when Arion presented himself their guilt was proven. In gratitude Arion offered a bronze votive figure of himself astride the dolphin to the temple of Tainaron.

Another story about a boy and a dolphin was told in about A.D. 200 by Oppian, in his poem "Halieutica." The poem tells of the love and friendship that developed between a boy who grew up in the port of Porosolene and a wild dolphin. According to the story the boy was the fairest in the land and the dolphin surpassed all the creatures in the sea for its good nature and grace. The young man would row his boat out into the middle of the bay and call the dolphin by name. The dolphin would gambol to his friend, leaping from the water as he made his way toward the boat. He would raise his head beside the boat and the boy would stroke it tenderly as they greeted one another. Then the boy would leap into the water and the two of them would swim side by side, touching one another gently. The boy would often climb upon the dolphin's back, and the dolphin, understanding the child's wishes, would take him wherever he wanted to go.

The story of Arion and the poem by Oppian are two romanticized accounts of boys riding dolphins. But though they belong to a golden age, some two thousand years ago, I have seen a boy ride upon a dolphin, and my concept of what is possible has changed accordingly.

When we climbed aboard the midnight ferry in Douglas I told Maura that Ashley and I would be back to see her and Donald as soon as we could in 1975. As the ferry sailed across the sea, which was as flat as the Serpentine, there was no wind and the moon rose high in the sky. I thought of Donald resting in the dark, still waters of Port St. Mary.

I stood beside the ship's rail watching the black water rushing past the hull and listening to the muffled swish that it made. When the chill of the night air started to filter through my clothing I made my way below deck, stretched out along one of the seats and pulled a blanket over myself. I was too excited to fall asleep but was lulled into a state of semiconsciousness by the regular throb of the engine. As I drifted contentedly into the limbo between sleep and total awareness I compared Donald's life with my own. I had a vague sense of an identity between us, a connection between his fate and mine.

His early misadventure with the man with a gun seemed to have been completely forgotten and the ride he had given Ashley was a sign that he was prepared to associate even more closely with humans—especially ones he knew.

I felt satisfied, and at peace. I had a successful career in medical and veterinary research and had reached a position in the senior management of the pharmaceutical company. My hobby of underwater photography and a deep interest in all aspects of sea life, particularly dolphins, provided me with the relaxation I needed to escape occasionally from the pressures that all people in demanding professions experience. I was happily married with a son of thirteen and a daughter of sixteen. I had a nice house, could afford to run a modest car and enjoyed my job. Yes, my life was stable and my future secure. With this sense of wellbeing, I slipped contentedly into a light sleep.

It is perhaps as well that we do not know what the future holds in store for us. For Donald's life and my life were by no means as secure and peaceful as I thought.

11 · The Volcanoes Erupt

One of my titles at work was Veterinary Services Manager, and part of that function involved lecturing to veterinary surgeons on a very powerful animal immobilizing drug I had investigated in detail and introduced into the market along with its antidote. I was enthusiastic about the product because it was a strong analgesic in addition to being an immobilizing drug and so could relieve stress in domestic and farm animals in pain and in need of surgery. In November 1974 I spent an evening in Chelmsford with a regional association of veterinary surgeons and showed them the two films I had made on my research into the drug and its effects on both large and small animals. Most of the audience had used the drug and the evening developed into one of lively debate. It was after midnight before the last veterinary surgeon left the meeting place.

The following morning I caught a very early train from Chelmsford in order to spend a few hours in my office in Hull before returning home. In the warm comfort of a first class compartment on an intercity train I wrote up some notes and enjoyed the satisfaction of knowing I had done a good job. In his closing remarks the chairman had thanked me warmly and said the drugs I had pioneered were now regarded as indispensable by veterinary surgeons. I had made a major contribution to veterinary medicine and I was proud of the achievement.

It was November 28, so Christmas decorations were beginning to make their annual appearance, and a general spirit of bonhomie was in the air. Life was good. I sat back and pondered the stimulating events of the night before and looked forward to the festivities to come. There were no dim rumblings to indicate the imminent eruption in my life.

For Maura, Christmas was a happy time. It was the season when she briefly dried out externally. Throughout most of the months of the year she spent hours every week on or under the water, fishing, sailing, water skiing, snorkeling or aqualung diving. But these activities were at a minimum from November to March, and she and her family became caught up in the swirl of local parties and social events. As Maura enjoyed cooking, Christmas was a time for producing large quantities of mince pies and other goodies. The winter months were also the time when the wine that she had made the summer before, and the summer before that, was broached.

Her younger son was at home and he brought into the house a stream of friends who enjoyed the uninhibited hospitality of the Mitchell household. Her elder son had just married and was busy setting up his new home. Maura had fashioned a lifestyle that embraced her children but was not centered on them. She was happy to see all the members of her family making their own way in the world and leading full lives.

So the winter of 1974 promised to be a happy time. There was, however, one thing that worried her. She had a feeling, deep down, that all was not well with Donald. She tried to discover what it was in moments of quiet contemplation. But the questions she asked herself could not be answered in precise terms. All she could identify was a rather vague feeling of unease.

On my return trip from Chelmsford the train was late arriving at Doncaster station, and I missed the connection for the last leg of the journey to Hull. I telephoned my office to let them know that I would be delayed, and one of my colleagues told me that the medical director had been asking after me. There was nothing unusual about that. Anticipating that he might require an account of my activities, I marshaled my thoughts for a report on my meeting.

Eventually the small local connecting train arrived and rattled its way to Hull. I arrived in the medical department offices in good spirits, and was told that the medical director wished to see me as soon as I came in.

I pressed the appropriate digits on the intercom on my desk and announced my arrival. A minute later I was in the medical director's office being told that my job had been "made redundant."

I was dumbfounded.

A situation where jobs are threatened and cut is like one of war; it brings out both the best and the worst in men. It raises the question of survival, and there is nothing like that to reveal the true characters of men. And it brings into play that potential for vindictiveness and corruption that can come with power—particularly the power to control one of the most vital elements of a man's life—his livelihood.

As I evaluated and re-evaluated my situation, in the context of the changes that were taking place within the company, I found myself not only distressed by my own dismissal, but sickened by the struggle I saw going on around me. I seemed to be tangled in a net, enmeshed in a system which played on avarice and envy simply to survive. The men of power were manipulating stress and tension—their own and others'—for gain. The whole social system, geared to more and more consumer production, more and more greed, suddenly disgusted me. "Affluent" or not, it was no happy place for the majority.

The contrast between the fraught situation in which I now found myself and the freedom I had enjoyed in the sea with Donald a few weeks before was never greater. I thought of Donald, without possessions and responsibilities, leaping for joy in a blue wind-tossed sea, the waves capped with white foam. And I began to feel that somewhere within me a choice had to be made.

I had no way of knowing that Donald too was in distress. And that the source of his distress was not his own kind, but man.

I felt no resentment toward those of my colleagues who had been spared the axe and who would take over the work I was doing when I left. I worked out my four weeks' notice to the full. Christmas came and went, and I joined the ranks of the unemployed.

During this period I had no news about Donald from Maura, and felt some slight unease about him. Then the thought was pushed to the back of my mind by my own preoccupation in losing my job. Maura's Christmas card made no reference to Donald, which stirred my suspicion that all was not well with him, but my concern was overwhelmed by the

Christmas festivities which proceeded with their customary energy in the Dobbs household.

I decided not to rush headlong into any new job but to let events take their own course for a while, so I started to make contact with friends and acquaintances who could give me more work as a freelance lecturer, writer, film-maker and photographer. Eventually I telephoned Maura and told her what had happened. She immediately tried to console me, stressing how much happier she and her family had been since her husband had given up his motorcycle engineering business and adopted a more relaxed life-style on the Isle of Man.

When I mentioned Donald I sensed that Maura was reluctant to add to my problems, but she did tell me that she was worried about Donald. She said that he was acting differently, spending more time away from land and harbors. He had taken to rushing from place to place, and could no longer be seen regularly in Port St. Mary.

I was by now aware that Maura was exceptionally sensitive to Donald's moods, and that she had an uncanny ability to communicate with him by a means that I could not identify precisely but which I thought of as some kind of sympathetic understanding. I asked her if she knew anything about why he should be behaving so strangely. Then she broke the news to me that underwater explosives were being used in the course of work to deepen the harbor at Port St. Mary, to enable more fishing boats to come alongside the harbor wall.

The method used was to drill ten to fifteen feet into the rock bed of the harbor with a compressed air drill mounted on a pontoon. The drill, painted with red oxide and black bitumen, was called Tarroo Ushtey—which is Manx for Water Bull, a legendary creature with flashing red eyes and a shining black coat that came out of the sea to cause trouble and stress on land. Sausages of explosives were dropped into the holes, the tubes removed and the wires connected. About ten holes were drilled and prepared per session. Two banks of charges were detonated per day, the first usually at about midday. Bill Ash was the man who carried out most of the work, and early in the project he had seen the dolphin watching the noisy drill biting into the rocks under the sea. On one occasion Donald had nearly become tangled in the connecting wires. A white dinghy fitted with an outboard engine was used in an attempt to entice the dolphin clear of the harbor before the explosives were detonated.

Work on the harbor improvement started in November 1974. Complaints received from the residents of Port St. Mary indicated that the explosions were sufficiently violent to rattle the cups on their sideboards.

We both knew what a traumatic effect all this would have on Donald, who had a supersensitivity to underwater sounds. We also realized that if he happened to be close by when a charge was detonated he would be killed. Knowing how curious he was and how he loved to investigate new objects placed in the sea, the thought that he might actually have his inquisitive face close to a charge when it exploded was a prospect that filled both of us with horror.

The days passed. The day of March 18, 1975, was not of great significance to Peter's mother, who lived on the Isle of Man. She went for a walk in the afternoon and saw a dolphin swimming fast, occasionally leaping out of the water, offshore from the jagged coastline of Langness. She noted the incident in her diary, and gave the matter no more thought. But hers was the last sighting of Donald on the Isle of Man.

The following day Maura and Peter were having a drink in their conservatory, which was warmed by a weak March sun. Peter was drinking coffee from a mug with a dolphin motif on the side that Maura had bought specially for him. The mug slipped from Peter's fingers and crashed to the floor, breaking the handle. Maura felt so cold she started to shiver uncontrollably.

"Peter," cried Maura, "something has happened to Donald."

"Don't be daft," said Peter. "What could happen to him?"

"I know it's silly," she said as she started to regain her usual composure, "but I feel inside me that something has happened to Donald."

"It's just your imagination," said Peter, "he'll be in Port St. Mary tomorrow—you'll see."

"Perhaps he's been injured by the explosives."

"I'm sure he hasn't," said Peter.

72

Not wishing to invite more ridicule than necessary, Maura said no more about the incident, but she still felt uneasy as she picked up the handle, thinking it might be possible to mend it with adhesive.

Many of those who live on the Isle of Man are very superstitious, and Maura's Manx ancestry would not let the thought that the incident with the dolphin mug was some sort of portent slip from her mind. She remembered an incident a year earlier, when she found that a plant that had been given to her by an aunt was broken. When she saw it her skin had prickled. And two days later she learned by letter that her aunt had died. Maura was relieved that the mug was not shattered, for that, she felt, might signify that Donald was dead—with the handle gone, it probably meant that a link was broken.

The feeling that something was wrong stayed with her all through the night, although she said no more about it to her husband. The next day as soon as Peter had left for work, she put her wetsuit into her car and drove to Port St. Mary. From the jetty she looked out toward her dolphin's favorite resting spot beside the lifeboat. There was no sign of his hump rising in the water and blowing. She looked carefully at all the moored boats. They all lay quietly bobbing in the water. None of them were moving out of harmony with the others.

The days passed and still there was no sign of Donald. Her anxiety grew. She knew he would not be able to resist investigating any divers laying charges. Surely, she argued with herself, none of the divers would let off the charges with the knowledge that the dolphin was nearby? On the other hand, she reminded herself, commercial divers have a hard job and they are not the sort of people to let things stand in their way when they have work to do.

She knew that shock waves travel considerable distances underwater, and that a diver may feel the impact of even a comparatively small explosive charge fired underwater over a mile away. Donald, with his supersensitivity, would be much more severely affected if he were anywhere in the vicinity of Port St. Mary when a charge was exploded.

The effect would of course be related to the distance between him and the explosion. If he were far enough away it might cause him only momentary discomfort, but if he were close by it could cause pain and risk of internal injury. If he were very close, the explosion would kill him. She read the local newspapers every day to see if there was any news of a dolphin's body being washed ashore. No such news appeared. On the other hand, if he had been injured by an explosion he might have rushed away from Port St. Mary in fright and even now be lying lonely and wounded off a remote part of the island far away from the sight of man.

"If he is still safe and sound and as intelligent as I think he is, what would he do if the peace of his adopted home was shattered by explosions?" she asked herself. The answer seemed obvious. Move somewhere else. That raised the question: Where?

She telephoned her friends at the Marine Biological Laboratory at Port Erin, but they had no reports of dolphin sightings. She asked her friend and diving partner, Mike Dunning, to maintain his lookout for their mutual friend, as she was to be off the island for a while.

She was reluctant to leave, but on April 19, 1975, over four months since she had last been in the water with Donald, and still with the fear nagging her that some disaster had befallen him, she left for the Shetland Isles on an expedition which was part of David Bellamy's project "Countdown." She had been in the Shetlands a week when a package arrived addressed to her. There was no note inside, just an inflatable blue and white plastic dolphin. It was a sign from Mike to tell her that Donald was gone.

Spring matured into summer. With the coming of the warmer months came the basking sharks. These gigantic fish, often more than twenty feet in length, cruised just below the surface, sweeping the sea with their colossal mouths, scooping and sieving the plankton. Following the sharks came the Scandinavian fishing boats, with harpoon guns mounted on the bows. The men aboard harpooned the sharks as they cruised along on the surface of the sea. The oil and vitamin-rich livers were removed, and the carcasses were then tossed back into the sea to rot.

The prospect of Donald being killed by a harpoon filled her with horror. She thought how he might go out to a vessel to play in the bow wave, and the agony he would suffer when the harpoon cut into his sensitive body. She shuddered at the thought of his pain as he sounded. When he surfaced for air, would he spout blood from his blowhole, as countless others of his cousins, the whales, had done at the hand of man? How long would it be before he finally died? The picture gnawed at her mind. She knew full well that if such had been Donald's fate, she was unlikely ever to hear the truth.

12 · Reflections on Men and Dolphins

When I was laid off I realized that external events had taken hold of me. My encounters with the wild dolphin had caused me to begin to formulate questions about the quality of my life, but they had been kept in the back of my mind by the pressures of my job. Now, suddenly, those pressures had evaporated. I found myself with time to look at my values and decide what it was that I wanted from living. I asked several people what they would do if they were suddenly given a completely free choice. To my surprise none of them knew. When I asked myself the same question, I realized that I too had no answer.

In those uncertain days I took to cycling along the banks of the River Humber which flowed past the village of North Ferriby where I lived. During these rides I thought about the days in my youth in the early postwar years, when I spent hundreds of hours on my bicycle exploring little known paths in Sussex, Surrey and Kent. I reveled in the solitude of the river bank, the lapping of the dark brown water as it eddied round the banks at high water. I loved to watch the wild geese and the seagulls rise from the reed beds. I would sit on the bank, enjoying the subtle warmth of the early spring sunshine, and let my mind wander, while tugs and cargo boats chugged past on the tide.

Slowly the mists around the answers to my questions started to clear. One incident which helped to drive them away was an unexpected meeting on the river bank. Very few people made the journey along the riverside between Hessle and North Ferriby, and I was surprised one day to encounter a man in his fifties, wearing a bowler hat and sitting on an upturned crate. He was brewing an enamel kettle of what appeared to be tea on an open fire, and tinkering with a clock he had found on a nearby rubbish heap. I stopped and said "Good morning" cheerfully and noticed that he had established a camp. His bedding was hidden under a nearby bush and various objects he had collected from the rubbish heap were placed at strategic positions around his campsite. At first he said little, and clearly did not welcome my presence as I leaned on my bicycle and asked him about the river and the weather and the ships and barges sailing upstream. He did not reply to my questions, but he asked me abruptly where I worked. When I told him I was unemployed he immediately became more responsive and told me that he also was between jobs—although my guess would have been that he had had his last job at least twenty years before.

Our first meeting was brief, but as the weeks passed they became longer. He was not always there. One day, as I stood looking down at the charred sticks that remained of his fire, I realized that he was free to wander according to the whim of the moment. I did not envy him his hard existence, but with it he certainly had a kind of freedom that is a rare commodity in our society.

The words "tramp" and "vagrant" do not conjure up the right picture. He was always clean-shaven; he usually wore dark clothes and though they were not smart, they fitted him well and were not ragged. From a distance he looked like a slightly down-at-heel London business man. He was well built but not at all flabby. He had a good set of teeth, which were stained and wearing down, like those of an aging horse. He appeared to be fit and strong, and after seeing him pedaling furiously along the road I concluded that he was also of good wind.

Gradually our conversations got deeper, and he informed me he was writing a book. Then he launched into a diatribe that at times was crystal clear, but then would suddenly become unintelligible. If normal prose is a photograph, then he put his words together like an abstract painter. A splash of metaphor here, a turn of phrase there blended together in sentences that were individually coherent yet when added together left me searching for a meaning. He could have been a scientist giving a brilliant paper on nuclear physics to a lay audience. As he rattled on fluently, and my brain tried to reorganize the words into something I could comprehend, I realized how thin is the line between genius and madness. I also accepted how little we understand the nature of the distinction. Until we could bridge such gaps among ourselves, it occurred to me, how could we hope to cross the much wider gap between the brain of man and the brain of a dolphin?

Thus it was that the encounter with the stranger on the banks of the Humber brought me back to Donald, and helped me to recognize that whatever I was going to do with my life would have to make room for my obsession with the dolphin, and in particular for my interest in how the dolphin perceives and communicates.

Dolphins are known to hear and emit sounds underwater. Many investigations have been carried out to discover what roles sounds play in the lives of dolphins, and the results have sometimes been surprising. Scientists have found that dolphins emit sounds with frequencies up to 153 kilocycles per second. Thus much of the sound emitted by dolphins is at a considerably greater frequency than the twenty kilocycles per second which is the highest pitched sound that can be heard by most men.

It has been discovered that dolphins use this high-frequency sound to pass information to one another, and they are thought by some scientists to have a whistling language. However, despite very sophisticated research involving the use of computers, nobody has so far succeeded in unraveling the mysteries of delphinese—which is what the whistling language of dolphins has been called.

What is clear is that enormous amounts of information can be passed in the form of high-frequency sound signals. Just how much the dolphin's large brain is able to utilize this potential is something scientists will speculate about for years to come, but most of them are already agreed that if dolphins have a language, it would make our speech by comparison appear like a recording played at a very low speed. That is, our deep verbal rumblings would probably register as dull and tediously slow to the dolphin's lively mind. Indeed our own brains are capable of taking in and comprehending information at a faster rate than through normal speech: our reading speed, for instance, can be much faster than the spoken word.

What is perhaps even more intriguing is the evidence that the dolphin uses sound to provide an "acoustic picture" of his surroundings. It was found in one set of experiments that a blindfolded dolphin could locate a target as small as one inch in diameter with unerring accuracy across a tank thirty-five feet wide. The sounds used by the dolphin for this purpose were analyzed and shown to consist of clicks about one thousandth of a second long.

The manner in which dolphins interpret the sounds bounced back by the objects around them has been likened to underwater sonar. Sonar is used by trawler fishermen to detect shoals of fish. The images the skipper sees on his sonar readout result from the changes in the signal when it intercepts the air bladders of the fish in the shoal beneath the boat. Thus the telltale signal is produced not just from the exterior of the fish, it also comes from their internal structures. On the basis of this analogy it has been suggested that dolphins can use their sonic vision to see *inside* objects. If this is true, then the dolphins have evolved a sonic sense which gives a three-dimensional sound picture of the internal as well as the external features of the object they are "looking at." Although we have compared this sense with our sonar systems, it is probable that we will never fully comprehend it because our brains have not evolved to interpret such nerve impulses directly. Our mental quandary can perhaps be understood if we consider the plight of a person with normal color vision attempting to explain the qualities of color to another person who has been blind since birth.

As a scientist I too have speculated on the possibilities of the dolphin's proven ability to differentiate between objects of different density but the same external appearance. I recalled seeing one of the first demonstrations of a hologram at a Physical Society Exhibition at Alexandra Palace. An object was illuminated with light from a laser, which was split into a reference beam and an object beam. The reference beam was directed at a photographic film and the object beam reflected off the subject was reflected onto the same film. Where the beams met and overlapped interference was produced and recorded. When I looked at the processed film illuminated with a beam of coherent light I saw a totally three-dimensional reconstruction of the subject. To my eye and brain, conditioned to the fact that light travels only in straight lines, the experience was a little short of uncanny.

Could the acoustic image seen by a dolphin come about by a process similar to that by which holograms are formed, I asked myself? If a dolphin emits a coherent beam of sound waves, and then compares the phase difference between the output beam and the reflected beam, I concluded, it is indeed possible that this would form a sonic hologram image which would reveal internal as well as external features.

I took my riverside speculations a stage further. Armed with the knowledge that dolphins have a brain equal to our own, on a weight for weight basis, and that they have traditionally a special empathy with man, I tried to imagine what it would be like to think like a dolphin and to see sonic pictures like a dolphin. To do this I set out to put my own brain inside Donald's head, as it were, to relive that first fateful encounter with the diver Henry Crellin in Port St. Mary on March 26, 1972.

This is the story, as I told it to myself.

Donald was first attracted to the site by the sound of an anchor going overboard—a sound with which he was familiar and which had always interested him. It was part of the world of sound in which he lived and which always surrounded him. But when a new shape appeared on the radar of his brain his insatiable curiosity was aroused beyond repression. What was this new animal that had come into his sea? Was it the mammal he was looking for: an animal with clumsy movements that breathed air like a dolphin, but was neither a dolphin nor a fish?

His instinct for survival told him to stay out of visual range and first investigate the newcomer with sound. He beamed a short burst of sound at the unfamiliar animal and his brain immediately translated the reflected sounds into a three-dimensional picture indicating the internal structure of the new animal.

The sound picture revealed an animal with two very large air sacs, surrounded by a relatively thin-walled body. There were more air cavities in a bony structure—the head—and the mouth was very small with few teeth. The new animal did not adopt the usual horizontal attitude of a fish. Indeed, it behaved in a very unfishlike and undolphinlike manner. It appeared to have two tails which ended in fins that were used for propulsion. The two tails were very inefficient at moving the animal through the water when compared with his own single tail or even those of the fishes, which were a lower order of animal than himself altogether.

All of these things were unusual to him. But the most unusual features of all were the parts of the body that corresponded to his own front flippers which the dolphin used for steering. The flippers of the new arrival were long and could be articulated in any direction. They ended in long paddles that the new arrival used for moving the chain, when the dolphin would have used his mouth. The clumsy newcomer was not much of a swimmer but his ability to manipulate the chain was most impressive.

Another thing that puzzled the dolphin was the major dense thin-walled air sac from which the two-tailed mammal drew an apparently everlasting supply of air. When swimming the two-tailed mammal used its air supply at a prodigious rate compared with the dolphin's respiration rate of about once every two minutes.

Having established an image of the inside structure of the two-tailed mammal, the dolphin considered the danger the new animal presented. It was apparent that it was very poorly adapted to live in the sea. An inefficient swimmer with a most interesting respiratory system, and manipulative flippers that divided into separate limbs, did not appear to pose much of a threat.

Curiosity urged him to move in close enough to obtain a visual picture of the outside of the animal. He swam slowly past and briefly saw that the intruder had a black skin, which he knew from his sound picture was cellular and about one quarter of an inch thick. It was very much thinner than his own layer of blubber, and a far cruder method of reducing the heat loss from the mammal than the dolphin's combined blubber and vascular system of temperature control.

Through the water he could hear the two-tailed mammal's heartbeat. The information fed into the memory bank of his computer-like brain. Just as he came into visual range the heartbeat of the two-tailed mammal raced and the water carried the alarm signal to the dolphin as quickly as a telegraph message. Then the panic-stricken newcomer rushed to the surface in a frantic flurry of its fins and was followed by the exhaust bubbles it had left behind.

The dolphin was both amused and saddened that he should have caused the two-tailed mammal such a fright. The frightened mammal had climbed into the flimsy transporter that had brought him to this part of the dolphin's new territory. Through the rubber floor of the inflatable came the deep slow sounds of the mammals communicating with one another. He observed that the language of the two-tailed mammals was very much slower than the dolphin's high-pitched information transmission system. Although he knew otherwise, it seemed to the dolphin at that moment he could have little to fear from the air-breathing animals.

They were physically close, but were separated from him by twenty-five million years of evolution that had dictated that he should stay on one side of the air–water interface above his head, and they should remain on the other. Now they were invading his environment, which would give him an opportunity to study them more closely. That was what he wanted, but he would not be able to do so if he frightened them.

He decided to surface gently near their transporter in order that they could visually identify him. Once they knew he was a dolphin they would surely be aware that there was no cause for alarm.

*   *   *

That, for the moment, was as near as I could get to imagining myself into Donald's first encounter with man. But I was pleased with my piece of fantasy. It seemed that I had made the first steps toward bridging the gap in consciousness between myself and another species, and I felt somehow that I had also taken an important step in defining my own life.

13 · Moment of Decision

Having failed to introduce Luciano properly to the thrills and hardships of British diving in the summer of 1974, we agreed to try again in August 1975 when I was scheduled to run an underwater photography course at Dale Fort. Dale is an attractive village that lies on the furthermost southwest tip of Wales, in a county that once had the romantic name of Pembrokeshire but has now been renamed Dyfed.

The fort at Dale is situated at the extremity of a high peninsula and is an obvious defensive position for the deepwater harbor of Milford Haven. It was built in the mid nineteenth century from huge blocks of stone as a defense against a possible foreign invasion, and has none of the classic castlelike lines of many of its romantic predecessors in Wales. It was designed to house guns, not human-propelled missiles, so it was therefore given a low profile that blends in with the natural line of the headland.

In 1975 Peter Hunnam was director of diving, and he welcomed Luciano and me when we arrived by car. We had engaged an old steel-hulled boat, the *Conshelf,* owned and skippered by an Australian. She was a working boat and looked it, painted black and with no frills on her. She was used as a general work boat and as a diving boat. It was easy to jump overboard fully suited-up with diving gear, as her deckline was close to the water.

This time the weather was kind and Luciano sampled his first real dive from the *Conshelf* off the Island of Skomer. There were strong contrasts between the underwater worlds of the Bristol Channel and his native sea. Even when it was flat calm, the maximum visibility was thirty feet (in the Mediterranean the underwater visibility is often in excess of 100 feet). Where we swam near the bottom clouds of silt were stirred up at the slightest disturbance by our hands or fins, and remained suspended in the water. It was also much colder.

We swam down over a forest of kelp. Kelp plants are like miniature palm trees with dark green leaves attached to long rubbery stalks that cling to the rocks with rootlike structures called holdfasts. We examined the holdfasts, which provide a home for a host of small organisms, and continued down. At a depth of about thirty feet the kelp disappeared and we entered a completely new zone populated by sponges, sea urchins and many other small organisms, including the tiny Devonshire cup corals. Flash guns fired as our group drifted down into the quiet depths. A three-pound crawfish, which Luciano immediately identified as a relative of the Mediterranean langouste, inspected us with its long antennae banded with alternate light pink and dark pink stripes. I hovered as quietly as I could to take a picture, but found I was not quite in the right position. I attempted to reposition myself with a gentle movement of my hands, but the turbulence caused a flurry of silt particles to float up into the water. During the one-thousandth of a second in which the flash fired I saw it illuminate the particles like stars in the night sky. For the merest fraction of a second the dark underwater world had burst into color, but that was time enough for it to register on my mind, as on the film. Then the light was gone and the scene resumed its blue-gray tone.

After twenty minutes Luciano signaled, clasping his arms together across his chest as a man does on a cold day. We headed back toward the surface.

The following day there was no wind and the sea was flat calm. Our class again headed for Skomer. Conditions should have been perfect for diving, but we were frustrated by the idiosyncrasies of the British climate. This time it was fog. Thick gray swirling mists that would have blown away with a puff of wind engulfed us. The temperature dropped. It seemed that Luciano's diving in British waters was again to be blighted by the weather. The waters around Skomer are very treacherous and visibility was so bad that even if we had anchored off the island we could easily have lost sight of a diver if he or she had surfaced very far from the boat. We abandoned the dive and headed back for the mainland, planning to hug the coast as we made our way slowly toward Dale.

"We could dive in Martin's Haven," said Peter Hunnam, eager to see that our group of divers would not be completely disappointed. Although the fog horn was still blaring regularly, the fog had indeed lifted slightly when we nosed quietly into Martin's Haven.

I was in the stern of the vessel chatting to the other divers about photographic techniques prior to our dive, when suddenly I heard a familiar loud puff alongside the boat. I rushed to the side to see a dark shape disappearing into the green water. I couldn't believe it. We had a dolphin alongside. My bag of diving equipment was with me and in a few moments I was in my wetsuit. I leapt into the water, and Luciano followed close behind.

What I saw next was almost unbelievable, for out of the misty waters came the cheeky gray face of Donald. I recognized my old friend from the Isle of Man immediately. He came to inspect me briefly, nodded his head and flashed away. From his movements there was no mistaking him, though who would believe me? We were over 200 miles from his old haunts.

There was one way of making a positive identification—the dreadful wound on the top of his head caused by the skeg of the outboard. So the next time he appeared I swam over the top of him so that I could clearly see the crater on the top of his head. Skin had now covered the wound, which earlier had been raw red, and the new scar tissue was a vivid white. Close inspection revealed that the edge of the crater had become pigmented a dark gray color. Eventually the pigmentation would cover the entire cavity. Then the only external signs of his encounter with the boat would be another dent in his otherwise smooth contours—like the one on the side of his head from his gunshot wound.

The visibility was poor, ten feet at the maximum, so even when face to face with Donald, when I looked down the length of his body, the end of his tail disappeared into a green fog. It is virtually impossible to get first-rate pictures under such conditions, but knowing that Luciano wanted a photograph of a diver and Donald in the same picture, I passed him my fish-eye lens attachment and viewfinder to fit to his underwater camera. Then I submerged to the propeller and rudder of the *Conshelf* and started to tap on the hull with the handle of my diving knife, hoping that Donald's curiosity would bring him in close. It did. As I tapped away I was aware that the end of his beak was just a few inches from my hand.

I talked to him as I tapped, and for a few minutes he hovered, watching what I was doing with his bright inquisitive eyes. I knew that Luciano was getting his pictures. After a few minutes, however, Donald tumbled to the fact that I was not doing anything more interesting than tapping, and he swam away. I looked up at Luciano. I could see his eyes alight in his facemask and knew he was thrilled.

Luciano expressed his delight in the only way he could. He touched the tip of his forefinger with the tip of his thumb—the diver's sign for OK. Luciano made the sign three times in quick succession, indicating that he was not just OK, but trebly OK.

Later, back on board the *Conshelf,* Luciano was still excited. He had dived only four times in British waters, at two locations 200 miles apart and one year apart in time, yet on both occasions he had had an encounter with perhaps the only truly wild friendly dolphin in the world.

"It is like winning first prize in the football pools not once but twice," he announced happily. "I think I am Lucky Luciano." From that moment everyone on the boat referred to Luciano as Lucky—and that is how he was recorded in the diving log.

For me the totally unexpected appearance of Donald would turn out to be the deeply significant event needed to crystallize my thoughts about my own future. I had by now been out of full-time employment for eight months, and during that period had undertaken various freelance jobs. As time had passed I had enjoyed my new life style more and more. It was certainly precarious financially, but the variety more than compensated.

And above all else I had at last gained a feeling that I was in control of my life. I was no longer a digit to be manipulated by a computer in a multinational company.

I was me, I was exultant, and I was free.

And I would no more give up my freedom again than would a wild animal, as I surmised, exchange his die-or-survive situation for the constrained but well-fed existence in a cage in a zoo.

At first I had been hesitant, but now I knew what I was going to do. I was going to run for freedom. When the decision was finally made I felt a great sense of relief. Twenty years were lifted off my shoulders. I felt as excited and as eager as a young man stepping out to conquer the world, and confident that I could do it.

When I told my wife, Wendy, that I had decided not to seek full-time employment again, and that this would introduce a high degree of financial uncertainty into our lives, she said she had complete faith in our ability to survive.

My wife is a pragmatic person, not strongly religious or given to belief in the occult, so her next comment came as a surprise. Fate, she said, had decreed that I should devote at least part of my life to understanding dolphins.

She could not explain her conviction; it was just a feeling that sprang from somewhere within her. To back up her theory, however, she argued that I was really admirably equipped to take advantage of the unique position for studying the dolphin in which chance had placed me, pointing out that I combined diving ability with a great deal of special experience in handling animals both large and small, acquired during my research in veterinary medicine.

I had to admit that the chance that had brought Donald and me together on two occasions with Luciano was so extraordinarily farfetched as to invite a mysterious explanation of some sort.

I telephoned Maura on the Isle of Man to tell her of my unexpected reunion with Donald. I also had to give her the less pleasant news that he was by no means safe in his new home.

Before my return from Wales I had set about the task of finding out as much as I could about Donald's presence in

86

Pembrokeshire. Once I made my interest known and was able to throw some light on Donald's previous history, several people came forward and told me stories about the newly arrived dolphin. He had already aroused in them the same kind of affection that he had inspired on the Isle of Man, and he had been named by the local people "Dai." But it emerged that some friends were concerned that his life was being threatened by the fishermen. One local fisherman had claimed that when he was shooting his herring nets the dolphin had swum right through them, tearing great holes in the mesh. The same man had also complained that when he was working on mooring buoys the dolphin would continually rise and sink between the work boat and the buoy chain, blowing bubbles as he went. To this fisherman, Donald was simply a great nuisance, and he proposed a simple solution to the problem—to shoot the dolphin.

Once I had told Maura all the news I could have predicted her next question.

"How quickly can I see Donald?"

I explained that I had only just come back from Wales and that Dale Fort was about as far away from my home as any part of Wales could be.

"But I've got to see him," she persisted.

"I knew that's what you would say," I replied, "so I have made loose arrangements for us both to go back to Dale Fort and stay there."

"How soon?"

"That depends upon how soon you can get away."

14 · Maura in Martin's Haven

A few days later I collected Maura from the Douglas Ferry at the docks in Liverpool and we headed southwest, the car loaded with cameras, the boat and diving equipment. It was approaching noon the following day when I drove up a steep, narrow high-hedged road from Dale village to the fort. I parked the car just outside the entrance to the Field Center and we disembarked at the head of the steep path leading down to the jetty. We looked down on to Dale Roads spread beneath us. It was a chocolate-box view. The day was crystal bright and there was not a breath of wind to disturb the oil-flat surface of the sea. The *Lord Hircomb,* the redundant lifeboat now used as a diving and general service boat by the Field Center, sat on the water as still as a souvenir on a mantleshelf. Only the edge of the sea moved, as it slid gently back and forth over the wrack-covered rocks with the slow gentle rhythm of a waving cobra.

We looked expectantly down toward the water, hoping to see an arch of silver that would indicate the presence of Donald, but nothing stirred the surface. We had hoped that we would spot him immediately upon our arrival, because I had been told on the telephone the night before that he had been around the lifeboat. The group from the Field Center had been trawling a plankton net off the jetty, and had had some difficulty completing their studies because of Donald's antics. Apparently he had done everything he could, short of actually grabbing it in his teeth, to obstruct the passage of the net. Having failed to stop the study he had rounded off the evening with a spectacular display of aquabatics. Now there was not a sign of him. We stayed at our lookout for ten minutes, enjoying the tranquility but disappointed that Donald was not there to greet us.

"He's probably over at Martin's Haven," I said as we discussed his whereabouts with Peter Hunnam.

"I'll bring the Zodiac around," said Peter, "I want to collect some samples from Martin's Haven anyway."

So we drove round the twisting roads to the tiny inlet and pulled into the parking lot at the head of the track leading to the sea.

The fact that a friendly wild dolphin was sometimes to be seen in Martin's Haven had been reported in the local paper, *The West Wales Guardian,* and the resultant extra influx of cars carrying hopeful dolphin viewers clearly did not please the parking lot attendant. When I enquired about Donald the man's reply was matched by his abrupt manner. He softened slightly, though only slightly, when Maura spoke to him, and we concluded that he really did not know whether Donald was in the vicinity or not, and would have been happier if we had kept our questions to ourselves and happier still if we had not inconvenienced him by coming.

Somewhat taken aback by our rebuff we decided to investigate for ourselves. We walked down the road and then clambered high onto the headland which commanded a view of Martin's Haven and the surrounding area. The island of Skomer, lichen-patched and seabird colonized, floated on a deep blue sea. A small boat carrying birdwatchers, reduced to toy size by distance, was edging its way into an anchorage. Had Donald followed the ferry out to the island? I strained my eyes to see if I could detect any signs that would indicate his presence, but could see none. Northward, St. David's hovered on the far horizon. A small fishing boat glided silently toward the open sea followed by the white tail of its wake. If Donald was out there playing with the fishing boat I knew there was no chance that I could see him. Maura said she would go down and talk to the few people on the beach at Martin's Haven while I climbed to the end of the headland to see if I could detect any signs of him from a higher vantage point. As I walked alone over the heather I breathed the air deep and thanked the circumstances of life that had brought me to such a beautiful place on a self-appointed mission. From my seagull view I looked down onto the turquoise-green water below. The mooring buoys lay on the surface of the sea like orange balls on a lawn-bowling green. To one of them was attached a small wooden dinghy, to another a small sleek cabin cruiser. I looked at each of the moored boats in turn, hoping to see a dark gray lump appear alongside, but nothing happened. I remembered Donald's habit of pushing moored boats until the mooring line was stretched taut and then letting them slide back again to resume a balanced position. But none of the boats moved.

A verse from "The Ancient Mariner" flashed through my mind:

> *Day after day, day after day,*
> *We stuck, nor breath nor motion;*
> *As idle as a painted ship*
> *Upon a painted ocean.*

Changing my viewpoint to cover every corner of Martin's Haven, for fifteen minutes I continued my vigil. But not a single sign could I see, so eventually I scrambled down to join Maura. She had been chatting to Terry Davies, the boatman who transports visitors to Skomer Island. He said Donald was not around.

It seemed that our luck was out. Donald was neither at Dale nor at Martin's Haven. Just as we were about to depart, however, an inflatable loaded with a group of divers, their black wetsuits still shining with water, rounded the headland and ran their boat ashore. They were university students who had been out collecting specimens.

"Have you seen the dolphin?" asked Maura.

"Yes," replied one of them, "he's been swimming around us while we were collecting specimens."

"Where was that?" asked Maura.

"Just round the headland, close inshore," he said, pointing to the very headland on which I had been standing. I had not seen them because they had been so close inshore. While we continued our interrogation of the man who appeared to be in charge, the remainder of the group carried their equipment and specimens onto the beach in plastic buckets.

"What happened when you left?" I asked.

"He got hold of one student's fins and tried to pull him back into the water."

"What happened next?" I pressed.

"He followed us in," he said.

"Where is he now?" asked Maura.

"Out there under a boat," he said, pointing to one of the moored vessels with a cathedral hull.

"Will you take us out to him?" pleaded Maura. "Please."

By this time the boat was empty and the divers were ready to haul it ashore.

"OK," said the black-clad figure, "in you get."

He backed the inflatable slowly away from the shore, taking care that the propeller did not hit any submerged rocks. Once clear he accelerated forward, swinging round in an arc toward the moored boat.

Before we reached it there was a puff alongside. Donald had come to see us.

"Stop!" cried Maura and our boatman put the engine out of gear. The lightweight inflatable came to a halt almost instantly. As soon as it did so a dolphin face appeared alongside.

"Hello, Donald," said Maura and then she started to talk to him in a quiet, very relaxed and happy-to-see-you voice.

For a full thirty seconds Donald remained stationary, with his body vertical in the water and his head back in the air just about one foot away from the side of the inflatable. He looked at Maura and then looked inside the inflatable. He shook his head a few times and opened his jaws as if replying to her conversation. Then, when he had finished welcoming her, he dived and a few seconds later appeared on the other side of the boat and again raised his head above the water and looked in. It was the first time I had seen him do this, although Maura had seen him do it several times before. After a further brief conversation he dived and swam away for a quick circuit of the boat moored twenty yards away from us.

We could keep our boatman away from his companions no longer, so he put the engine into gear and headed back to shore. All thoughts of lunch were forgotten and we hastened back to Dale Fort to tell Peter Hunnam to bring the Zodiac for a proper reunion in the water. One hour and a half later the Field Center's Land Rover with the trailer behind was bouncing its way down the steep rocky approach to Martin's Haven.

As soon as the boat was launched Donald came alongside and escorted us to one of the moorings. When we stopped, he again put his head right out of the water to inspect Maura. It was a pleasantly warm sunny afternoon and Maura, who was wearing a bikini, leaned over the side and talked to Donald whenever he surfaced. Once, still only in her bikini, she slipped over the side of the inflatable and I took some pictures, but the water was very cold and she soon climbed back inboard.

Since his arrival in Wales, Donald had quickly made a name for himself, and all of the divers who had encounters with him had stories to tell of his behavior. Some of them said that he had a definite preference for female divers and that he had made uninhibited advances of a directly sexual nature to some of them. Virtually all those who dive in British waters wear wetsuits complete with hoods, so I felt that if females attracted his attentions more than males it was probably because female divers were gentler and more understanding toward Donald, more motherly if you like, than male divers.

Having taken some still pictures we went ashore to pick up the 16-mm camera in its underwater housing, for I wanted to shoot some film of Donald and Maura for television. By the time we had loaded the wooden box containing the camera into the inflatable, and Maura had put on her wetsuit, she was warm enough for another immersion. During our trip ashore other activities in the Haven commanded Donald's attention. However, as soon as we were waterbound he swam alongside, we slipped into the water and I began filming Donald and Maura swimming happily with one another. But their session together did not last long; after a few minutes Donald disappeared. I surfaced and we both looked around. Fifty yards away was a very sleek white cabin cruiser. A girl with blond hair, her black wetsuit unzipped to her waist, was draped over the cabin catching the rays of sun while her male companion in a wetsuit longjohn was frantically pulling at the starter of the outboard engine. As he did so a dolphin face appeared alongside to watch the performance. Donald was obviously delighted at the new form of entertainment. When the man took the cover off the outboard and started to tinker with the engine the sound picture of tools clumping into the fiberglass hull would have been transmitted into the sea very clearly and were obviously of great interest to Donald. He dived and circled the boat, leaving us swimming in an empty sea, getting cold even though we were wearing wetsuits. We needed a counter-attraction.

"Peter," I called out. "In my bag there is a can full of stones with a handle on it. Would you please find it and give it to Maura?"

Peter rummaged in my diving bag and produced the "dolphin rattle" we had used on the Isle of Man.

Maura took the handle and shook my home-made rattle under the water. In a few seconds—as inquisitive as ever—Donald appeared and inspected the source of the new noise. His stay was short-lived, however. Having got his engine running, the man in the cruiser was hauling up his anchor. Even from where we were we could hear the sounds of the chain rattling and true to form, Donald again disappeared to investigate.

I realized that if Donald followed the boat out of the harbor I would not be able to shoot any more film. So as the boat cruised out I got Maura to shake the rattle vigorously. Whether it was the attraction of Maura or the rattle I know not, but Donald did remain in the Haven. However, he soon became restive again and would appear out of the sea only for a few seconds before speeding off again. Although I am sure he was pleased to renew his acquaintance with Maura he was exhibiting a side of his character that I was only now coming to understand: his passion for activity, and his need for constant mental stimulation. Unlike that of dogs, who seldom seem to tire of fetching a ball, Donald's attention was very difficult to command for long periods. Like a child with a lively mind, he needed new interests.

We were getting cold and tired so I decided to wind up the operation, and handed Peter the heavy camera. I next removed my weightbelt and was handing it into the boat when one of the weights slipped off and dropped to the seabed thirty-five feet below. I asked Peter to lower a weighted line overboard so that I could follow it down and retrieve my lead weight. So I put on the weightbelt again, deflated my life jacket completely and swam down. At a depth of about ten feet I became negatively buoyant, and allowed myself to sink very slowly, waiting for my ears to clear—which always took a considerable time. As I neared the bottom I saw a tail fluke, and there vertical in the water with his tail uppermost was Donald, carefully inspecting the weighted line. Donald was stationary and was in a perfect pose for photography. The frustrating thing was that all of my cameras were now in the boat above. I gave him a friendly stroke under the chin and told him I had come to look for my lost weight. The seabed was flat and sandy and I spotted a scallop, its eyes peering like an even row of bright marquesites in the water. As I was over it the two shells slammed shut. I swam in ever increasing circles about the scallop, followed all of the time by Donald. Then I spotted my weight and triumphantly picked it up, still watched by the dolphin. As I swam back slowly to the surface he must have decided that that was the end of the action, so with two powerful flicks of his tail he disappeared into the blue-green horizon.

The following morning I drove into Haverfordwest to put

the film on a train to the BBC, and to mail an article I had sat up most of the night completing for the magazine *Photography*.

It was noon before I got back to Martin's Haven. When I arrived I could see the Zodiac out in the haven with Maura aboard. Peter Hunnam was obviously diving. As I walked down I spotted another Land Rover, and upon peering inside saw some packages of 100-foot spools of 16-mm film. I must admit that I did not welcome the prospect of competition from what appeared to be a television unit. I identified the group from the Land Rover at the water's edge, and went over to find out who they were. It turned out that the new arrivals were not from television, but from the Dale Fort Whale Research Unit and Institute of Oceanographic Sciences of the Environment Research Council. A member of this expedition explained that the Pembrokeshire parks warden had told them about the unique wild dolphin who befriended divers along the coast around the islands of Skomer and Skokholm. The group had been so intrigued by the report that they had come to Wales to study and film the dolphin above and below water, as part of their general research information program.

I explained my own interest in—or more accurately my obsession with—"my" dolphin Donald. I realized that it would be in neither of our interests to compete with one another to film Donald that afternoon: although it might be highly amusing to Donald, if there were two camera crews in the water he would simply get so excited, and flit from one to another with such speed, that we would both find it difficult to obtain usable photographs.

The leader of their expedition, Christina Lockyer, agreed that I should go in first and that they would come out later. As we spoke I watched the Zodiac and could see Donald surfacing regularly. Then I saw Peter surface, climb aboard the Zodiac and a few minutes later he and Maura were on the beach.

"We've had a lovely time," said Maura.

"Donald has taken a keen interest in my collection of specimens," said Peter, who was carrying out a survey on very pretty tiny creatures called nudibranches.

"I've spent ages playing with him," Maura said.

I was eager to find a better way of "calling up" Donald when we visited his territories. To date I had been extraordinarily lucky, but I knew if I could find a way of attracting his attention and identifying myself without getting into the water it could possibly save some future frustrating immersions. I reasoned that the call should be interesting from Donald's viewpoint. For an animal that lived mainly in a world of sound my call sound would have to be subtle enough to compete with whole orchestras of other fascinating noises. The most effective method I had found to date was to rattle a can full of stones.

My reasoning was to a certain extent vindicated by some later studies by Dr. Robert Morris, who attempted to attract Donald with a series of single-frequency notes known to be audible to dolphins and played into the water with hydrophones when Donald was near. Donald showed no visible response to the sounds. My interpretation of the dolphin's apparent lack of interest is that sound of a single fixed frequency is not sufficiently arresting to warrant his attention. On the other hand, the sounds from my dolphin rattle or the clockwork motor in my underwater movie camera, which he came to inspect at very close quarters whenever I ran it in his presence underwater, were variable in frequency and therefore far more interesting.

After a brief picnic lunch, we loaded the Zodiac rubber boat. I picked up the dolphin rattle, which until then we had used underwater only, and shook it vigorously. Almost immediately Donald surfaced in the sea and looked in our direction. I continued to rattle the can and Donald gazed at us. Then he turned around and headed toward the shore.

I wanted to study how Donald responded to visual images, so the last thing to be packed into the Zodiac before we moved away from the shore was a mirror mounted in a wooden frame. Donald, who had been idly cruising around the Haven while we were loading the inflatable, surfaced briefly alongside as soon as we were in deep water. I slipped over the side with my still camera and Maura followed immediately. Donald appeared and disappeared in his usual manner. When he had been away for a longer period than usual, Peter gave Maura a small brass bell which she tinkled under the water. When I was close to her I could hear it quite distinctly. So did Donald. He came, had a very quick look at it and disappeared again. Despite further efforts on Maura's part, the bell seemed to be of only very fleeting interest to him.

To explain this lack of interest I tried once more to put myself inside the mind of a dolphin. I remembered how on previous occasions I had watched Donald's fascination with the regulator on Maura's demand valve, which being of the twin-hose variety was located on the top of the air cylinder she carried on her back. The regulator had a few moving parts, which controlled the escape of the air from the very high-pressure cylinder into the inlet breathing tube. When she exhaled, the exhaust air flowed out in a spurt via a oneway valve into the water, making the characteristic plumes of bubbles that will be familiar to those who have seen films of divers underwater. Maura's exhaust valve was also situated behind her head. I asked myself what, as a dolphin, I would have found more interesting: the tinkle of a bell, or the noise of a demand valve which was composed of a mixture of sounds including the flutter of the rubber diaphragm, the movement of levers and the reverberating sounds made by the passage of air through a tube? The answer seemed obvious, and to confirm Donald's own preference for the valve. But proving this in a scientific manner would call for controlled experiments which I was not prepared to contemplate, for I was determined that I would never attempt to reduce the relationship between Donald and myself to the level of researcher and guinea pig. Controlled experiments were out. Nothing whatsoever was to interfere with the dolphin's total freedom, so the choice about whether or not he would cooperate in my studies was always to be his. If he did not like what I was doing at any time, or became bored, he could simply swim away. Anything I learned about him was to be only a bonus on top of the friendship he had with Maura and me.

I did not know what reaction to expect when Maura took the mirror into the water. On a number of occasions territorial fish have had mirrors placed within their boundaries. Upon seeing their own reflections the fish have adopted aggressive attitudes toward the images, which they have taken to be intruders. Filmed sequences have shown fishes attacking the illusory invader in an attempt to drive it away. I suspected that Donald would not be so easily fooled, and he wasn't. Indeed,

This picture, taken in October 1974, shows the severe wound inflicted on the top of Donald's head when he was accidentally hit by the metal skeg beneath the propeller of a powerful outboard motor traveling at speed. *Horace Dobbs*

The human-dolphin connection is made with a wild dolphin off San Salvador in the Bahamas. *Chris McLoughlin*

Donald swims down quietly to take a look at a picture of himself drawn by a schoolboy. When the picture was removed and the mirror behind it was exposed, Donald became very agitated. He knocked the mirror from Maura's grasp and would not let either of us go near it. *Horace Dobbs*

The camera moves in to film Maura and Donald in a quiet mood. *Horace Dobbs*

For committing the crime of eating fish, dolphins are executed by Japanese fishermen off the island of Iki. *Dexter Cate*

although Maura tried to position the mirror so that he could see himself, he appeared to take no notice of the small part of his own image that I thought he could see. Instead he nibbled at the wooden frame with his teeth—his way of establishing its texture—then shook his head and swam away. (Later events showed how completely wrong it is to draw conclusions from a single observation. His behavior on the later occasion when confronted by a mirror was violent, and so disturbing that I was really scared with Donald underwater.)

By the time we had finished with the mirror it was time to let the Whale Research Unit make their observations, and they came to join us in their inflatable. Donald was delighted to have more action and immediately took an interest in the newly arrived vessel and its occupants. One of those on board was Arnold Madgwick of the Institute of Oceanographic Sciences, who was eager to obtain surface movie film of Donald.

When the inflatable swung around in an arc Donald followed. The person at the controls opened the throttle. The inflatable responded immediately and rose onto the plane. As it did so the water parted at the keel and formed two waves that followed the course of the boat as closely as a shadow. Donald positioned himself just ahead of the waves, so that he could be pushed forward by the water rising continuously behind him. As the inflatable swung into curve after curve, Donald rode the waves like a surfrider, reveling in the mastery of his element, and the innate sense of balance and movement through water, that enabled him so effortlessly to keep himself in the correct position to benefit from the man-created wave. The sensitivity with which he maneuvered with his tail and flippers reminded me of a seagull delicately fingering the air with its wingtip feathers as it soars high on the upwelling air created by an onshore breeze deflected by a cliff.

From our Zodiac we watched fascinated as the other inflatable passed by.

As the boat raced past us we could clearly see Donald just below the surface, riding the arm of one of the V-shaped waves that followed the boat. We noted that he rode the waves that followed, and did not position himself to ride the bow waves. Perhaps he remembered the incident in the Isle of Man when he was hit by the outboard skeg.

When the inflatable again pulled up alongside us, Donald swung away and performed a couple of spectacular leaps to show his appreciation. He moved at such speed and was so unpredictable that attempts to photograph and film proved very frustrating. Running the 16-mm camera all the time was out of the question—the 100 feet of film it contained would run for only two and a half minutes at twenty-four frames per second. So with Maura acting as dolphin spotter I tried to follow her pointing hand as she desperately attempted to indicate his position when he was rushing along just below the surface. Anticipating when he would surface and perhaps leap was almost impossible. So I watched Maura's hand with one eye and attempted to keep the camera pointed in the right direction, while peering through the viewfinder with the other eye. When I saw him surface I would slam on the shutter button in an attempt to get the most spectacular sequences I could with the limited amount of film I had available. I longed for the use of a camera with a 400-foot magazine, and for the resources to enable me to make a really good film of Donald in one of his exuberant moods. And not being in the fortune-telling business, I had no way of knowing that the stars were set right for this ambition to be realized someday.

From our conversation with members of the Whale Research Unit, it was apparent that Maura and I had a lot of information on Donald that would help them fill in background details on their new subject. So when they heard that we were to leave the next day, Christina Lockyer suggested we all get together during the evening. A few hours later we approached The Griffin, still not quite sure what to make of the sudden interest in Donald by a group of professional scientists.

The Griffin is in the middle of the village of Dale. The entrance opens onto the road, a low wall and beyond that the sand and the sea. In the summer months the patrons flow out of the pub door and spread over the road and along the seawall, and as we approached in the car the crowd parted and closed behind us again.

Inside, a juke box in one corner pumped out the latest pop tune, competing with the hubbub of raised voices and making conversation all but impossible. In one corner I recognized the

Dale Fort people, among them some of Britain's acknowledged authorities on Cetaceans. I suspected that they were likely to be rather wary of me, and perhaps slightly resentful that a mere enthusiast, with no recognized expertise on whales, should engage in their specialized field of study.

I for my part was certainly suspicious of them, for I had heard rumors that they intended to capture Donald and fit instruments to him. Having just completed ten years of research in human and veterinary medicine, I appreciated very well that research workers might regard Donald as an ideal subject for a host of scientific studies. I knew also that every effort would be made to ensure that he came to no physical harm; but I was certain that if they interfered with him, they would greatly change, if not destroy altogether, the purely spontaneous relationship he, and I emphasize that it was *his* choice, had established with humans in general and with Maura in particular. I wanted to know the purpose of their visit.

Shouting at the top of your voice in a packed public house is not an ideal way of conducting a diplomatic exchange in which each side is attempting to uncover the intentions and aspirations of the other party. I think we were all relieved when "time gentlemen, please" was eventually announced and Annette, one of the young lecturers from the Field Center, invited us all to her room for coffee.

Her room was in part of the fortifications and it had a high vaulted brick ceiling. The men and women assembled there were all keenly interested natural historians, and throughout the two hours we spent sipping coffee and eating freshly made shortbread the conversation hardly deviated from dolphins and their related species. As the minutes unwrapped themselves, to reveal unknown upon unknown, I realized how little information the experts really had about the life of the dolphins and whales in the sea. It was obvious that a lot of research material had been gathered on captive dolphins, but on wild dolphins living free in the ocean man clearly knew extraordinarily little. What I found perhaps even more surprising was how limited was the information on whales: an entire worldwide industry had been based on whales for over a hundred years, had thrived and declined; yet that enterprise had been so totally commercially based and conducted in such a free-for-all manner that it was not until the 1920s that any real attention was paid by those directly involved to the life history and the survival of the hunted species.

Nonetheless, research work in the present century has made some contribution to our knowledge of the sea's largest inhabitants. Some whales were tagged with stainless steel markers in the 1930s and this work has continued ever since, the information gathered from these and other studies being analyzed to indicate that most species of whales make annual migrations. It has been shown, for instance, that distinct populations of southern humpback whales feed in the summer in the plankton-rich waters of the Antartic, then migrate northward up the coasts of the continents of South America, Africa and Australia as the winter sets in. In the shallow warm water they mate and give birth to their young. We do not have similar information on whales in the northern hemisphere, and details on the populations and movements of dolphins are even sparser. Even the apparently simple question "What is the world population of bottlenose dolphins, and where are they to be found?" cannot be answered with any degree of accuracy.

The main source of data has been that gathered from reports of strandings, that is of animals washed ashore, or dead animals found on beaches. However, deductions made from such observations must obviously be cautious: numbers may reflect for instance a tendency of a particular species to become stranded (or a preference for a shallow water habitat) rather than population density. Species that steer well clear of the coast when migrating will appear to be less common than those that may exist in relatively small numbers, but hug the coastlines when they migrate.

Another major source of information is of course the sighting of the species in the wild. Here again we must ask ourselves "How accurate are the data?" How many of those who see wild dolphins in the sea are able positively to identify the species from a brief glimpse as the dolphin surfaces or leaps out of the water? Knowing of Donald's love of following boats, just how much does the frequency of bottlenose dolphins' sightings depend on a bottlenose dolphin species characteristic: the tendency to associate with vessels that move through the waters?

These were just a few of the problems we debated that night in Annette's room at Dale Fort. And when we came to considering the social behavior of bottlenose dolphins in the wild, we concluded that the information from which valid deductions can be made was even more hopelessly sparse. The reason is simply that men have never been able to get in the water and study dolphins at close quarters, as they have on land with wild animals such as lions.

Since man first sailed the seas he has observed that dolphins sometimes congregate in groups or schools. And a few incidents have been reported which indicate that a dolphin school is a mutual aid society in the wild. One such incident was described by two trained observers, members of the staff of the Living Sea Gulfarium at Fort William Beach in Florida. They noticed that an underwater dynamite explosion had injured a bottlenose dolphin in the bay. The animal rose to the surface in distress and then sank. Immediately two other dolphins came to his assistance. They positioned themselves on either side of their wounded companion, put their heads under his flippers, and carried him to the surface for air. In this position they were unable to breathe through their own blowholes. They therefore had to let go of their casualty from time to time to catch a breath themselves. They returned to their first-aid stations the moment they had filled their own lungs.

The incident in Florida was one of the rare instances where observations have been made on spontaneous dolphin behavior in the wild. On the other hand, many studies have been made on the social behavior of dolphins in captivity. But any conclusions drawn from this source must be viewed with circumspection. Confinement in a dolphinarium may impose such severe conditioning on the captive dolphins that their behavior may bear little resemblance to the social order of a free life in the sea.

Thus the presence of Donald off the coast of Wales was of special interest to the Whale Research Unit: it presented a very rare opportunity for close observations on an unrestricted animal.

As the shortbread biscuits disappeared from the plates and the coffee vanished from the cups, I came to realize that there was no conflict between Christina Lockyer's group's interest and ideals and mine. They merely wanted to observe and record Donald's behavior and movements. I was assured that these studies would not involve Donald's capture, or any interference with his freedom, and my apprehension melted. And when they realized that Maura and I were primarily concerned for Donald's wellbeing, I think any reservations they might have had concerning our contact with the dolphin were also dispelled. Indeed, we found that our respective pools of information were mutually beneficial. The members of the Whale Research Unit had considerable knowledge of the scientific work that had been conducted on other dolphins, in which both Maura and I were keenly interested. Maura and I on the other hand had a great deal of background information on Donald, especially dates of incidents and sightings, which was of interest particularly Christina Lockyer, the team member assigned to compiling a record of Donald's past.

It was well past midnight when we all eventually left the Field Center. The Whale Research Unit expedition party were camping nearby. Maura and I were staying in a guest house in Dale, and I crept into the silent house to collect an album of photographs of Donald that had been taken in Port St. Mary, to show Christina. The headlights of the Land Rover were switched on and we squatted on our haunches in the road leafing through the book. Christina Lockyer was also interested in the rate of healing of wounds in wild dolphins, and we examined the photographs to see if we could identify any of his old scars and relate them to existing marks. She was particularly interested in the wound on Donald's head, which we could date precisely. When I had first seen the photographs taken shortly after the incident, I had been distressed because the wound detracted from the beautiful smooth line of his shape and made him look rather battered. Now however, on a road in Dale in the early hours of the morning, I looked at the pictures of the ugly wound from a new viewpoint. First, they provided incontrovertible evidence that Donald and Dai were the same dolphin—a question we were often asked. Second, by comparing Donald's present condition with that indicated in the photographs we could see how well the wound had healed, spontaneously, without any interference from man. We anticipated that over a period of a further year or two the entire area would be dark gray and the only external sign of the accident would be a permanent depression about six inches behind and slightly to the right (looking forward) of his blowhole. Third, the photographs confirmed my view that we could learn a great deal about dolphins in the wild without subjecting Donald to the rigorous controls usually assumed to be necessary by research scientists. We would gather our information merely by observing and photographing him.

A friendly meeting with scientists from the Institute of Oceanographic Sciences and the Whale Research Unit was a rewarding way for Maura to end her reunion with Donald. We agreed to exchange information and photographs freely. When the Land Rover eventually departed and the red rear lights disappeared around the bend into a black Welsh hillside, we departed happily to our respective beds, happy that so many people were taking a friendly and above all protective interest in our dolphin.

The next morning we collected our wetsuits, sopping wet after an overnight downpour, from the clothesline at the Dale Fort Field Center. We thanked Peter Hunnam for his help and headed for Harlech Television Studios in Cardiff. One of the films I had shot underwater was processed while we had lunch, and during the afternoon we videotaped a news feature. It was Maura's first visit to a television studio.

A few days later when she was back in the Isle of Man, she was able to pick up the item when it was broadcast. For a few minutes she relived the pleasure of being underwater with Donald, sad that he had left the Isle of Man, but pleased that he appeared to have settled happily into a new home.

15 · Call to Cornwall

The circumstances that have brought Maura, Donald and me together have often been linked by curious contacts and coincidences.

Quite by chance I sat next to a very attractive young woman with long brown-blond hair at lunch at the British Sub-Aqua

Club's Diving Officers Conference in London. We were introduced by a mutual friend and I was told her name was Hazel Carswell. She had clear natural English beauty. I was not surprised when I later discovered that for part of her young life she had been a shepherdess. As we chatted at the lunch table, I learned that she and her husband Bob now made a living running a boat called *Aquanaut* which they chartered for diving trips out of the tiny Cornish fishing village of Mousehole. When not taking out divers they collected sea urchins, the tests (shells) of which were sold to tourists. As I had just been appointed conservation officer of the British Sub-Aqua Club and had made an appeal requesting divers to restrict what they took from the sea, she naturally was a little apprehensive as to how I would react when I found out that she was denuding the sea bed of some of its sea urchins. So on the principle that the best mode of defense is attack, she took a slightly aggressive attitude toward me. However, I have always taken the view that rules are mostly for guidance and not necessarily for strict observation, and had no inclination to condemn her for what I knew was a very hard source of living from the sea, especially when she told me she had given up gathering gorgorian coral, which was a lucrative business, when she learned of its very slow growth rate.

I recognized her immediately as one of those special women whom I had met occasionally in the diving community, and who, once they take up the sport, stick to it come hell or high water. Those who believe in astrology will not be surprised to learn that her birthday was March 10, the same day as Maura's. And the coincidence did not end there. Both their mothers had the same birthday, March 6—all under the sign of Pisces—the fish. I told her that I had often dived in the Plymouth area but I had never dived in the far west of Cornwall, and we discussed the possibility that perhaps one day I could arrange to dive from the *Aquanaut* if I could fit it in with a trip to the West Country.

What I did not know as we sat eating lunch together that November in 1975 was that a few weeks later I would receive a letter from Penzance telling me that a wild dolphin had arrived in the area. I was told that Bob and Hazel Carswell had befriended the dolphin and if I wanted to see it I should contact them.

Just how long it took for Donald to make the trip from Dale Haven to Cornwall I do not know. The first person to observe his arrival was a man called Geoff Bold, the mechanic of the Penlee lifeboat.

He had spotted a fin between the breasting buoys which are used to guide the lifeboat back up the slipway after a launch. At first Geoff thought it was a "basker"—a basking shark—but then he realized that they are seen in the area only in the summer. A small whale? The following day there was a lifeboat exercise, and when the new arrival was attracted by the sounds of rattling chains and the activities of the launching and came to gambol in its characteristic way about the lifeboat, Geoff recognized it as a dolphin. He kept a log of some of the activities and movements of his newfound friend. Thus the date of his arrival is precise: January 10, 1976.

Geoff was born in London and became a highly skilled tool maker. He earned good money, ran a fast car, had a wife and a son. Everything should have been fine. But Geoff was someone for whom the pressures of city life irritate and corrode like an abscess in the mind. He grew so embittered and so short-tempered with his wife and the son whom he adored that the family eventually split up. Freed from home ties he was given a job in Cornwall, which he completed in record time. The man for whom he was working said, "Why don't you take some time off?"

With nothing but sad memories to attract him back to the city he explored the area of Cornwall west of Penzance, fell in love with it and decided never to go back to London.

He met a dark-eyed Cornish girl called Liz, married her and took the low-paid job of lifeboat mechanic which carried with it a cottage in the beautiful fishing village of Mousehole. Again, everything seemed set fair for him. But as the years passed Geoff discovered that as a stranger he was not readily accepted into the tightly knit community of the fishing village, and that the claustrophobic atmosphere of the village could be as stressful as the anonymity of the city. His wife wanted to travel but Geoff had had enough of traveling. His wife, whom he adored, became very discontent and the strain was telling on Geoff. It was then that Donald sailed into his life.

From the way he himself described the experience to me later, it would be no exaggeration to say that Donald's arrival transformed Geoff's life in much the same way that both Maura and I felt he had transformed ours. Geoff is a man with an acute sensitivity to his environment and to the people around him. It had brought him much mental pain but it had also made him aware of the indefinable emanations that appear to come from Donald and that experience, from the beginning, made Geoff happy.

When he tried to describe what he meant, Geoff gave as an example one day when he was feeling particularly depressed. He was greasing the steel runner down which the lifeboat slides when it is launched, and was wondering why he, a skilled mechanic, should be doing such a dirty, unskilled task. Then suddenly the gloom that enveloped him lifted, and he found himself continuing with his work in an unusually cheerful frame of mind. As he became aware of the change, he looked around and noticed that Donald was watching him from the water a few feet away. Geoff made the point strongly that he was quite unaware of the dolphin's presence until after his depression lifted, and that he saw his feeling of wellbeing as springing directly from Donald's arrival. When Donald was near the slipway of the Penlee lifeboat station, Geoff Bold was a happy man.

Right from Donald's first appearance Geoff studied the movements and behavior of the dolphin, much of which he recorded in a log book.

He had a keen interest in natural history and was in a unique position to observe Donald's behavior. As the days passed Geoff noticed that Donald had settled by the right-hand buoy which he seemed to use as a territorial marker. Geoff evolved a theory that Donald used the buoy chains as sonic reflectors which enabled him to set up a kind of sound fence in which he could trap fish when he was feeding. When the fishing boats from nearby Newlyn approached on their way to their mackerel fishing grounds, the dolphin would become very active and would frequently break the surface, though he seldom followed the boats out to sea. The fishermen for their part often deviated toward the lifeboat slip from their homeward course especially to see Donald, and toss him fish, which he appeared to accept. (Maura and I later made observations underwater, however, that suggested that he did not in fact eat them, but let them sink to the seabed.) Westward Television got wind of the story and sent a cameraman to the lifeboat station to record the scene.

In due course news of the dolphin's arrival at Penlee reached Malcolm Cullen, a warden of the Pembroke National Parks, who was missing him from Martin's Haven. Malcolm was anxious to identify the new friendly dolphin as Donald, so he requested Geoff to check on his markings and scars, and Hazel and Bob Carswell were called upon to dive with the dolphin off the slipway and observe him at close quarters. Their report left absolutely no doubt that Cornwall's gain was Wales's loss.

As before, Donald was making new friends, and in addition to Geoff Bold one of his favorites turned out to be Hazel Carswell. Hazel was as near to the kind of human friend he had had in Maura as Donald had met since he left the Isle of Man. Since Hazel and Bob took the boat out of Mousehole harbor nearly every day, his encounters with them were frequent and he joined them on many of their dives. And it was from Hazel and Bob that I learned most about the dolphin's adventures in Penlee, and about what I was to come to see as his ever-deepening relationship with human beings.

One of the incidents that most moved Hazel took place off the Carswells' boat, *Aquanaut,* when a group of divers from Colchester had chartered it for a day. In the morning they were practicing a lifesaving drill in the water. Such aquatic activities bring out the mischievous spirit in Donald—who had been christened "Beaky" in Cornwall—and it was not long before he was totally disrupting the exercise by putting his nose between the divers to separate them, and on occasions actually pushing the "victim" in the opposite direction to that in which the "rescuer" was trying to tow him. Donald's involvement in the practice exercise was so energetic and disruptive that the lifesaving drill had to be abandoned. However, on the same afternoon, the group were diving near a wreck in Mount's Bay when one of their number, a student teacher named Keith Monery, got into difficulties and surfaced. His lifejacket was punctured and full of water, so it failed to function. Keith shouted for help and started to sink. Hazel, who was acting as safety lookout, was then horrified to see Donald swimming toward the diver. Would the dolphin behave in the same manner as in the morning, and push the distressed man around, making his plight even more serious? She threw herself into the water and swam toward the drowning man.

Although Hazel is a very experienced diver, she admits she is not an exceptionally strong swimmer, and as she made her way toward the victim she realized that although she could cope with the man she would be quite unable to save him if Donald interfered. When she reached Keith Monery she found that Donald was indeed with him. But instead of teasing him, the dolphin was gently supporting Keith from beneath. Hazel grasped the coughing and spluttering student from behind, calmed him and towed him back toward the *Aquanaut*. As she did so she found that he was being gently supported from below by Donald, who also managed somehow to help Hazel tow him back to the boat. And when she stood on the diving ladder helping to get the man aboard, Donald did not pull at her fins, as he often did when she was leaving the water after a dive and he wanted her to stay and play longer. Instead he stayed beside the boat with his head out of the water watching the scene. Keith Monery made an uneventful recovery.

When Hazel told me the story afterward, she said she was absolutely convinced that Donald knew that the diver was in distress—that he had been able to differentiate between a real emergency and a mock operation. She concluded that the dolphin was able in some way to "sense" that the vibrations made by the diver were genuine distress signals.

Certainly other aquatic animals have this sense; I witnessed it in operation myself in the Persian Gulf when I was floating on the surface watching a snorkel diver about sixty feet below me spear a fish with a harpoon gun. I had seen no sign of sharks for the entire morning, yet within two seconds of the spear hitting a fish two eight-foot-long sharks arrowed in out of the blue. One "bumped" the fish, the other swam straight at the fisherman and bumped him with its snout. Then both sharks disappeared again as quickly as they had appeared. There was certainly no time for the blood from the fish to diffuse through the water toward the sharks.

I would expect the dolphins, with their exceptional sensitivity to sound, to be even more alert to distress signals. And if a dolphin is able to sense a human's personality, which is what our experience of Donald already suggested, then why not also his moods?

Bob Carswell subsequently had an experience with Donald which he saw as further evidence of Donald's ability to "sense" human temperament.

When Donald encounters or, more often, is approached by a group of unfamiliar divers, he may not want their company for very long, and after allowing them to play with him for a few minutes he usually moves away. With divers with whom he is very familiar, however, he likes to play for long periods, and he resents it when they pay no attention to him. He also has a keen interest in underwater activities in which the divers may be engaged, and ideally he likes a combination of work and play, with the divers periodically breaking away from the job in hand to take notice of him. One day Bob was diving in about sixty feet of water collecting sea urchins, and Donald was swimming around him. Bob, preoccupied with the need to make a living, concentrated exclusively on picking up the urchins and putting them in his sack. After about ten minutes of being ignored, Donald swam over him and pinned him firmly to the bottom for what must have been a few seconds, but which to Bob seemed like a long time. Although he was surprised by the dolphin's actions, Bob was not unduly upset, and did not struggle or behave in a distressed manner. He told me that he realized the dolphin was only taking him to task for neglecting him.

If however Donald had done this to a less experienced diver, or had pinned a diver with a more excitable temperament to the seabed, the outcome might have been different. Bob suggested, though, that the dolphin can hear heartbeats through the water, and that he associates a high heart rate with distress. If this is the case, it is unlikely that he would have persisted in pinning a frightened diver to the seabed.

Bob Carswell stressed that at no time has he felt any fear when Donald has been in the water with him, and indeed that for no other creature in the sea has he felt the same warmth and affection. He has often been in the water with basking sharks up to twenty feet long, which are plankton eaters and therefore not considered dangerous, but he has no such warm feeling toward them as he has for Donald.

With news that Donald had found a new home and a new set of friends, Maura and I were naturally eager to visit him. Our opportunity came following a short broadcast I did for an early morning radio program. Details of my interest in Donald reached Yorkshire Television, who wanted something special to include in the first of a new series of "Don't Ask Me" programs. Having failed to get a large live shark into the studio, they opted for what they considered to be the next best thing— a live dolphin in the studio. When they heard about the relationship that Maura and I had with a wild dolphin in the sea, they pulled out all the stops to include a feature on Donald and Maura to link with studio sequences. By the time the full television crew was mobilized, however, I was leading an underwater photographic safari in Kenya, and it seemed that my entire journey along the coast of Kenya was accompanied by a series of telephone calls, each of which took an extraordinarily long time to reach me. There was always some confusion at the switchboard when the calls arrived, and someone else with a name similar to mine would be hunted for while the transcontinental telephone minutes ticked by. When the mistake was eventually discovered I would hasten to the telephone to answer such impossible questions as "How long will it take you to find the dolphin?" and "Do you think you will be able to get any really good underwater footage?" I replied that Donald was a totally free wild creature living in the sea, so I could guarantee nothing, but I would do my best. It was the sort of situation that gives nightmares to a producer with a budget and a deadline to meet.

Meanwhile it was left to my wife Wendy to carry the administrative role from my home. She contacted Maura and the

Carswells, and the entire operation was geared up for my return from Kenya. As soon as the jumbo jet from Nairobi touched down at Heathrow I said a rapid farewell to the members of my safari and was whisked away to where the Yorkshire Television helicopter was waiting to fly me to my home in Yorkshire to collect my underwater movie camera and diving equipment.

I sat next to the pilot and as we rose in the air I felt as if I was sitting in a magic chair high above the countryside. It was April and the weather was cool and showery. The green landscape below contrasted vividly with the dun-colored expanses of the game parks of central Africa through which I had been traveling a few hours before. We flew at a height of about one thousand feet and at one point passed over Woburn Abbey. From my kestrel-eye view in the sky, I could see the tracks and the animals in the Safari Park. It looked minute compared with the 12,000 square miles of the Tsavo Game Park over which I had flown two weeks earlier, and the sight raised once more in my mind the question of the morality of confining animals whose natural habitat is the vast plains of Africa to the confines of English parks, or even worse, the tiny cages of a zoo. The same question was to come right into focus later when I saw the dolphin in its pool in the television studio.

I looked down on my village of North Ferriby, which is still dominated by its church, and savored that "it's nice to be back" feeling that one has after a long journey away from home—no matter how exciting the expedition has been. As we flew over my house I noticed a strange apple-green car in the drive beneath the trees I loved, which were in their new spring foliage. The grass of our landing field flattened and bits of straw were whisked into the air as we touched down. News of our arrival had spread through the village and a small crowd had gathered in the drizzling rain at the edge of the field. My seventeen-year-old daughter, Melanie, rushed up to the helicopter before the blades had stopped rotating and flung her arms around my neck as soon as I stepped out.

Wendy had prepared a superb homecoming lunch, eaten amid excited talk about the trip I had just finished and the new one I was about to make. I was introduced to the owner of the strange car in the drive, Yvonne Ingham from Yorkshire Television, who was to take me and my equipment to Cornwall.

Two and a half hours after my homecoming I waved farewell once more to the family and we sped to Manchester Airport where Maura, who had flown over from the Isle of Man, was waiting patiently for us. Yvonne was a vivacious blond whom Maura liked immediately, and they later became firm friends.

It was nearly midnight when we eventually arrived in Penzance. I was exhausted.

The next morning dawned a sullen gray. I rose early before the rest of the crew were awake, and walked along the deserted seafront. The sea lapping quietly against the wall outside our hotel was the color of lead.

Arrangements had been made for Bob and Hazel Carswell to bring their *Aquanaut* across from Mousehole to the quay in Penzance, near where the *Scillonian* was due to depart for her daily run to the Scilly Isles. Compared with the *Scillonian*, the *Aquanaut* was minute. She was a typical fishing boat of the region, about thirty-five feet long and painted the traditional blue. The influence of Donald on the Carswells was already to be seen; there was a bold dolphin painted in silver on the forecabin. As we began to bring our diving equipment and underwater camera onto the *Aquanaut* it started to drizzle; conditions for photography—above or below water—were far from ideal.

I was a little distraught, partly as the result of the long journey and a general lack of sleep, but mainly because of the uncertain outcome of the expedition. I watched the white mass of *Scillonian* start to move gently out of the harbor and could see the dark water turning in whirlpools round the stern as her powerful propellers bit into the sea. Then suddenly a small black hump broke the surface and disappeared in a second. The *Scillonian* inched forward. The hump appeared and disappeared again. Donald had arrived for the filming—on cue. The television crew watched excitedly as the dolphin frolicked around the vessel which was slowly moving away from the quay. My anxiety started to evaporate, but the day was not yet won.

The one thing that now concerned me was whether Donald

would maintain the daily pattern of movement our research had shown he had established, or whether he would choose today to go out with the *Scillonian* and join the fishing boats far out to sea. We watched him disappear as the *Scillonian* sailed quietly across Mount's Bay. It was still drizzling, but I was in high spirits, delighted to see my friendly dolphin again.

The arrangements for our rendezvous with Donald were complicated by the fact that the team from the Whale Research Unit and the Institute of Oceanographic Sciences, with whom we had made contact in Wales, were also in Penzance for a brief stay to continue their own observations of Donald. Dr. Robert Morris of the Institute wanted to investigate what sounds Donald would react to. Each of the teams was anxious not to upset the other, and none of us wanted to interfere too much with Donald's routine, so we agreed to limit our filming session to the morning only, leaving the afternoon free for the scientists to pursue their interests. We also offered them space in the *Aquanaut* for any observations they might care to make, and Christina Lockyer and Arnold Madgwick came aboard. Once these negotiations had been completed we were faced with the not inconsiderable task of tracking a wild dolphin in the English Channel and then getting both above-water and underwater film of him—in the space of a few hours.

I had been told that Donald sometimes went out as far as St. Michael's Mount. As we waited for our aqualung cylinders to arrive I looked across the bay at the famous landmark. It stood out of the sea like a picture in a fairytale book—a rugged triangular island topped with a castle. That day it was gray and just visible through the mist. There was the whole vast expanse of Mount's Bay in which Donald could hide himself. Our main hope was that he would go straight to the Penlee lifeboat station.

So when our fully-charged aqualung cylinders arrived we set off for Penlee. Maura and I got into our wetsuits while the rest of the crew huddled under their parkas. It was a far cry from the scorching sun and heat of the tropics I had recently become accustomed to.

I could soon see the two parallel strips of gray concrete that make up the Penlee slipway rising out of the sea to a lifeboat station nestled close to the rocky coastline. Offshore from the slipway were two buoys. This is where we were told Donald might be. But there was no sign of him.

Maura did not put on her aqualung but slipped quietly into the water. Miraculously, within half a minute Donald appeared. Their reunion was very gentle. Donald was quiet and the two of them swam slowly side by side. Maura put her arms around Donald and crooned to him in a quiet voice and told him how glad she was to see him again. Donald lay quietly, his eyes tightly shut. "I could see his eyes, under the lids, rolling in ecstasy," said Maura afterward. She continued, "He lay alongside for a while, then we finned along gently together, with one of my arms across his neck."

I followed Maura into the sea with my cameras, and swam very quietly toward the two of them. Donald took no notice of me, which was most unusual; he normally inspected every person entering the water. I had never seen him so relaxed before. Later, Geoff Bold, the lifeboat mechanic, explained to me his theory that Donald had adopted the buoy outside the lifeboat station as a territorial marker. He pointed out that if any boat headed directly for his buoy, Donald would become excited and swim vigorously toward the vessel, as if to deflect it from approaching too close to his territory. I was myself to see this behavior pattern exhibited very clearly at a later date, when Donald had moved to a new site and adopted a new territory. This place was his haven, a place of security. His peace of mind was in no way disturbed by the *Aquanaut* because it was a very familiar boat in his adopted territory, and an old human friend "dropping in" could be welcomed with confidence.

I glided quietly past and looked closely at his eyes. Maura put her arms around him and cuddled him and he shut his eyes in bliss. Those eyes really were extraordinarily expressive. The eyes of fishes are permanently open and cold, but a dolphin has eyelids which can be opened and closed like those of most other mammals. The eyelids are parts of the small area of a dolphin's body where the skin does not have a thick underlayer of blubber.

Donald stayed with us for a few minutes and then dived quickly and disappeared. We waited in the cold water for his

114

return and called him. When he did not reappear we swam back to the *Aquanaut* where the television cameraman wearing a wetsuit was standing on the lower rungs of the diving ladder with his feet submerged. Donald was just beneath him looking at the rubber booties dipping into his territory. Then he darted away, swung in a tight circle and returned to the steps again to see what was happening.

The cameraman was a young Jordanian named Mostafa Hammuri. What I did not know was that I was witnessing the first steps in the formation of another quite positive relationship between Donald and a fellow human being. (Fate had decreed that Donald and Mostafa would meet again, and this in turn would lead to Mostafa and me becoming firm friends.)

The entire television crew was excited at seeing the dolphin so close, and having got his above-water shots Mostafa insisted on joining us in the sea. He was not wearing a hood on his diving suit, and the water must have felt very cold. He swam as if the devil were chasing him, finning rapidly and sweeping his arms vigorously through the water. He swam diagonally down, then raced up again. He was breathing at an incredible rate, the air rushing from his exhaust valve like a steam locomotive at full speed. A diving instructor would have gone into a state of apoplexy if he had seen a novice diving in such a manner.

In contrast, Donald was delighted with the newcomer's company and the two of them were soon embarked on a whirlwind of underwater activity. Which of the two was more excited I could not say.

Mostafa was a law unto himself. We were told later that he had a reputation halfway around the world for disregard of his own safety. On one occasion, it seemed, hand-holding his heavy camera, he had stood on the pillion of a motorcycle going at full speed in order to get a film sequence. People like Mostafa are few and far between, and it is not surprising that they are often regarded with a little envy by the less venturesome among us.

Mostafa's stay in the water was brief, and he handed his aqualung back into the boat a few minutes later. His encounter with Donald was in complete contrast to that of Maura, who was now wearing an aqualung. She swam over to the buoy for me to get a sequence of Donald by the chain, which was covered in interesting marine growth. Donald appeared for a few seconds, then disappeared again. We waited patiently for his return but the cold was beginning to get through the synthetic rubber of my wetsuit and I started to shiver. When Donald did not reappear I signaled to Maura to surface.

I looked across at the boat. I could see that the cameraman was still on the ladder with his feet in the water. It was obvious from what he was saying that Donald was just beneath him.

I yelled over to the director, "Would you please get Mostafa right out of the water."

The director asked the cameraman to climb aboard and I again sank beneath the sea into the gray depths. Then Donald reappeared and circled us. My camera whirred satisfactorily. When Donald again swam away and did not return I gave Maura the sign to surface and we made our way back to *Aquanaut*. I was cold but Maura still felt warm enough and energetic enough to go for a final snorkel. So while I clambered aboard she swam over to the lifeboat station to talk to Geoff Bold.

When it was time to leave I called Maura back to the boat. As she snorkeled across from the slipway she was unaware that Donald followed her all the way, with his snout about two feet behind her gently oscillating fins.

Having got both the underwater and above-water film footage of Donald that they required, the television film crew departed from Penzance. But Maura and I wanted to learn more about Donald's experiences in Cornwall. Armed with a couple of bottles of wine, we made our way to the Carswells' house in Mousehole.

Their home, locked onto the steep ground above the harbor, was one of a row of tiny houses built of local stone and weathered into harmony with one another and with the surrounding land and seascape. The room into which we squeezed ourselves was full of trophies the two of them had collected from the deep in the hundreds of dives they had made together from *Aquanaut*. However, much as we enjoyed the tales of their adventures on wrecks, it was their stories of Donald that

116

interested us most. By now we could anticipate their account of their surprise at their first encounter with Donald. But how, I wondered, would two people who spent their working lives, day in and day out, winter and summer, in Donald's own environment, view their experience with him? I had a keen interest in whales and dolphins for many years and had read widely on the subject before I ever encountered Donald. So my views on his behavior may to some extent have been influenced by what I had read. I was anxious to listen to Bob and Hazel Carswell, who perhaps had not had a special interest in dolphins before they first met Donald.

As the hours passed it was apparent that their views and attitudes were very similar to Maura's and mine. Indeed it was almost as if Hazel had taken Maura's role and Bob had taken mine. They both now regarded Donald as "their dolphin" and both had developed a deep love and enormous respect for him. Bob commented on the great understanding that Donald had for what was going on around him, and Hazel was sensitive to his gentleness and affection. When we heard this, and about the relationship the dolphin had established with Geoff Bold, the lifeboat mechanic, we were delighted that he had found the company of such sympathetic people. We felt that if he was otherwise undisturbed Donald was likely to stay in the area for some time, an idea that pleased Bob and Hazel enormously. As it turned out we were wrong and Donald's peace was to be shattered once more, but that was to come later.

The underwater film I had taken of Donald for the television program was to be linked with sequences of a captive dolphin in a tank in the studio, and a few days later Maura and I were in the Yorkshire Television studios in Leeds with my old friend David Bellamy who was the human star of the show. The animal star in this instance was to be Pixie, a young female bottlenose dolphin who was confined to a small tank. She had been tranquilized and brought from a local zoo. The poor creature was daubed with violet antiseptic along her body and on the leading edge of her dorsal fin where the skin had been damaged. Before Maura and David got into the tank with Pixie I studied her carefully and quietly from the side. Although she had the right shape for a bottlenose dolphin, I had to ask myself if she was really of the same species as the creature we had seen and enjoyed in the open sea. Where was the zest for life we knew so well? Where was the emotional warmth that we could feel when we were near Donald? I could just sense it, but it was to Donald's fire like the dull smoldering of a pile of damp burning leaves. Where was the bright mischievous eye of Donald? Pixie shut her dull eyes and opened them again listlessly. I touched her skin, expecting to feel the silky texture of oiled velvet. It was slippery and unpleasant—more like the skin of a fish than a dolphin. She swam in a never-ending circle, wheel upon wheel of dejection.

My God, I thought to myself, what have we done to you?

The morality of keeping dolphins in dolphinariums for public display is a subject worthy of consideration. If, as I believe, dolphins are creatures with a brain and sensitivities different from but of an order as high as man's, if not higher, then what right have we to imprison them in tiny pools? Consider such subjection from the dolphin's point of view. He is an animal that lives in a world of sound. The sea is full of natural sounds, probably as diverse to the dolphin as are the shapes and colors of the wild flowers in a meadow to us. Some of these sounds we can hear underwater when we are diving—ranging from the rasping sound of a crawfish, or spiny lobster, to the roar of the waves advancing and receding over a pebble beach. In some areas the sea has a constant background of crackles and clicks, the source of which we cannot identify. Any new sounds interest Donald immediately. Those made by man he finds particularly fascinating: the rattle of chains, the throb of an engine, and probably many more which we cannot hear or give no thought to, but which he listens to attentively.

But what sounds does the dolphin imprisoned in a dolphinarium hear?

The dolphin is also aware of textures and shapes—of that we are certain. We also know that he has a very highly evolved brain. What happens to his higher senses when he is confined to a concrete box and totally deprived of sensory experiences? We know that man, in situations of extreme sensory deprivation, risks madness.

It is thought that migrating fish such as the salmon find

118

their way back to the rivers in which they spawn by the taste of the water. This too must indicate a sensitivity of a very high order. Do dolphins have a similar sensitivity to the taste of their environment? Man is prepared to spend considerable money and effort in producing tastes to please his palate. Does the dolphin enjoy the different tastes of the sea? If so, what does a dolphin taste in a dolphinarium, the water of which, if it is not filtered and changed at a considerable rate, will contain above all an unnaturally high percentage of the dolphin's own excreta?

Anyone who has seen dolphins in the sea cannot fail to observe how thoroughly they appear to enjoy the freedom of the seas about them. Their bodies are superbly adapted to moving through water and they spend much of their time traveling. That same instinct to travel is certainly present in many men, and we all suffer immensely if we find our movement severely restricted. Do dolphins have an inbuilt urge to move on, see new places, experience and enjoy new tastes and sounds? If so, what happens to those urges when the animal is confined?

An observation made by many dolphin trainers is that dolphins tend not only to learn tricks by mimicking the behavior of other dolphins, or of their trainers, but that the dolphins invent tricks themselves. In other words the dolphins themselves—not their trainers—create their acts. If this is so, who is training whom? Are the dolphins manipulating their captors? Imagine a highly intelligent man drafted into the lowest ranks of the army, where all scope for thinking things out for himself is removed. Such a person may well deploy considerable effort, both mental and physical, to devise ways of avoiding duties. He will often put more effort into avoiding a duty than fulfilling an order, merely for the intellectual satisfaction of "beating the system." Would a captive dolphin, finding itself faced with the irreversible prospect of confinement to a dolphinarium, adopt a corresponding attitude? And if so, how would it act? Would it for instance explore the limit of possible experience within the confines of its new environment—which we would interpret as learning new tricks? Dolphins will certainly not perform the same tricks endlessly. Dolphin trainers have found that it is necessary to change routines and to "rest" dolphins after a series of shows. And this need for rest is not seen as related to physical exhaustion. Sometimes dolphins simply refuse to perform. So who is the master—man or dolphin?

Dolphins, like humans, have different personalities and some will adapt to a captive life more readily than others. However, it is not widely known that in fact many dolphins do not survive long in captivity. Maura has heard that the average life expectancy of a captured dolphin is only about six months. Gastroenteritis is common—which may be due to the fact that the animals have to eat dead fish which are not fresh. (Before humans eat fish they cook them and kill any harmful bacteria.) But in many cases there is no sign of disease and the dolphins do not die for want of proper food.

If dolphins have even some of the mental and emotional needs and sensitivities I have outlined above, confinement to a small tank may compress their minds to such an extent that they die of intellectual and emotional starvation—a cruel but, alas, not yet unusual punishment.

16 · Ride a Wild Dolphin

Barry Cockcroft, a freelance film director under contract to Yorkshire Television, is a busy and successful man who always has a full schedule ahead of him. When he was asked in 1976 whether he would like to make a film about a man who had lost his job and had become friendly with a wild dolphin, he agreed to look over the possibility. I told him my story over lunch at Rowley Manor. My son Ashley joined us, and Barry Cockcroft introduced me to his production assistant, Julie O'Hare. I found Barry a charming and sympathetic person, and by the end of the meal we had decided to go ahead with the project and agreed on a contract. I made it clear from the start that at no time should we consider restraining Donald in any way—he was to be left free to swim away at any time. Cockcroft agreed. He knew that making the film would be a gamble. So did I.

I felt reasonably sure that we could get underwater footage, but I could not be sure that it would be spectacular. Barry Cockcroft's chosen cameraman, on the other hand, was none other than the amazing Mostafa Hammuri, whom I had seen in action in Penzance. Balanced against the fact that we might not get spectacular underwater footage was a track record. Barry Cockcroft, director, and Mostafa Hammuri, cameraman, were a very successful team with a string of television awards to their credit. I had also heard that Barry was incredibly lucky when making documentary films.

There was a possibility that Donald could disappear at any time, so immediate arrangements were made for a full television camera crew, plus Maura and me, to visit Penzance.

Telephone calls between us were not frequent, so one day when I rang Julie O'Hare after I had sent her a list of possible film sequences, she answered the phone with the abrupt question:

"Have you called to tell me what I already know?"

"What's that?"

"The dolphin has moved."

"Oh, no," I groaned.

"The last report was that he is in St. Ives—I am just going to check up on that."

"What does Barry think of the situation?"

"He thinks we should go ahead."

"So do I."

The die was cast.

That was the last I heard from the television center in Leeds before I set off to collect Maura from Manchester Airport in the middle of what turned out to be the longest, hottest summer Britain had known for 200 years. It was June 30, 1976, and the countryside in the Midlands and southwest already looked arid. The drive to Penzance was more like a drive through the South of France than through England. The sun shone down from a sky of unbroken blue. I wore shorts, and the backs of my legs were sticky with sweat where they touched the plastic car seats. We stopped for tea after we had passed Exeter and ate freshly picked strawberries still warm from the sun and smothered in delicious Devon cream. Although it was six o'clock in the evening the sun still felt fierce on our bare skin when we stepped out of the log cabin café to resume our journey to Penzance.

The following morning we were awake early to make the journey over the big toe of England from Penzance to St. Ives, where Barry Cockcroft was staying and where we hoped to meet up with Donald again.

Bob and Hazel Carswell had brought the *Aquanaut* around Lands End from Mousehole, and were as pleased to see us again as we were to renew our acquaintance with them. I did not realize just how many people make up a full television crew, and when we were assembled all together I was reminded of the old nursery rhyme:

> When I was going to St. Ives,
> I met a man with seven wives,
> Each wife had seven sacks,
> Each sack had seven cats,
> Each cat had seven kits,
> Kits, cats, sacks and wives,
> How many were there
> Going to St. Ives?

Unlike the catch solution to the nursery rhyme (there was only one man actually going to St. Ives) there seemed to be a multitude of us. It was obviously a very expensive operation, and Yorkshire Television had clearly gambled a not inconsiderable sum of money on the prospect of finding and filming an animal that was free to roam anywhere in the English Channel.

Barry Cockcroft is the antithesis of the autocratic film director. When we met him in St. Ives he was cheerful, dressed in casual holiday clothes, and looking relaxed.

"Any signs of Donald?" I asked as we walked together toward the stone jetty known locally as The Pier.

"Oh, yes," replied Barry reassuringly. "He's around all right."

He was right. Donald was there just outside the harbor entrance, surrounded by a crowd of small rental boats with out-

122

board motors that we immediately nicknamed "buzz boats."

Bob Carswell told Barry the tide was falling and he would have to get his crew on board the *Aquanaut;* otherwise it would be grounded until the evening. It was then that I realized the benefit of having a large well-coordinated team, for in a very short time we were all on board and nosing out of the harbor with an inflatable boat towed by a rope at the stern. Donald obviously still followed his previous habit of acting as escort to boats moving in and out of his territory. He appeared as soon as we were clear of the harbor wall and we could see his dark silhouette moving from side to side under the inflatable. Our dolphin stayed with us until we were well clear of the harbor and then he left us to sport with the buzz boats that swarmed around him like wasps around a jam pot. The open sea just outside the harbor of St. Ives was calm and as busy with small craft as the Serpentine on a Sunday afternoon. With so many distractions I had a feeling that filming with Donald was going to be difficult. And I was right.

Maura and I were soon suited up and Donald joined us immediately we jumped overboard. However, he was in an excited mood and swam quickly between us. His reunion with Maura was quite unlike their previous encounter off the Penlee lifeboat slipway, when the dolphin had been completely docile and relaxed. He allowed himself to be stroked a few times and then darted away to play with the buzz boats which kept coming uncomfortably close to us. Knowing that the drivers of the boats were vacationers, who were probably unaware of the hazard their whizzing propellers were to divers, I was anxious for our safety as well as that of Mostafa, who was having difficulty with his diving equipment and the cumbersome underwater camera he was attempting to film with.

While we were in the water the wind started to rise and the sea became choppy, making it even more difficult to film. As the sea became rougher, those on board the *Aquanaut* began to feel the effects of the rolling motion of the boat. The buzz boats were recalled by a man who came out in a speedboat fitted with a very powerful outboard. Donald disappeared. So after consultation with Barry we decided to abandon filming.

The harbor of St.Ives had dried out completely and we were rowed ashore by a local fisherman while Maura snorkeled in through the waves, leaving Bob and Hazel Carswell alone on their boat, which would have to remain at anchor and ride out the waves in the open sea until the incoming tide allowed them to sail back into the harbor.

Remembering our experiences on the Isle of Man, when Donald was usually in his most cooperative mood in the evening, and counting on the habit the sea had of calming down late in the day, we postponed our next attempt to film until five o'clock.

As the afternoon progressed the wind started to abate and the sea crept slowly back into St.Ives harbor. The running lines of green, algae-covered ropes and chains that stretched across the sand were again awash with salt water. The boats heeled over at the harbor entrance started to rise. The sea that slid into the harbor was crystal clear and the sand was the bright yellow of a railway poster. Gradually the wind died, leaving the ocean as flat as ice.

We rejoined Bob and Hazel aboard the *Aquanaut* and Bob told me that on a number of occasions he had attracted Donald's attention by blowing on his foghorn with the end of the trumpet submerged. He tried it and within a few minutes Donald appeared. He was in a very happy and playful mood. He seemed to particularly enjoy playing with our dolphin rattle and nibbling at it.

It was sheer joy to be in the water with him and I soon shot the 100 feet of film in my camera. Then, after I surfaced to hand in my 16-mm camera and start taking stills, Donald disappeared. We called him again and again in vain, we tried the dolphin rattle and the foghorn, but he did not return. So we headed back for the harbor and berthed alongside the pier. Events had not gone perfectly on our first day, but we had made a start, Barry was happy with our progress and we were optimistic as we dined together that evening in his cottage in the back streets of St. Ives.

We agreed on an early start the following day to gain maximum benefit from the tides. It was a gray day and right from

124

the start I felt uneasy. Maura, who is normally very cheerful and easygoing, was on edge.

I had a premonition that something was going to go wrong.

By the time we got to sea the buzz boats were again out in force and we decided to attempt to entice the dolphin beyond the buoy which was supposed to indicate the limit of the hire boats' excursions into the open sea. The *Aquanaut* was crowded and we had an additional cargo of two young ladies lured aboard by a couple of the camera crew—no doubt with promises of stardom. Bob tried attracting Donald by rattling a chain overboard just as we were about to dive. His ruse worked, but as soon as he had inspected the chain the dolphin swam off again, before we had a chance to get into the water and carry out an observation I had planned.

As a result of an article I had had published in the *Sunday Times,* a class of seven-year-old school children had sent me letters. Many of them had drawn pictures of Donald, and one of them had shown my son Ashley sitting astride the dolphin's head. I was curious to see how Donald would react to this picture of himself, especially in view of the past historic associations between dolphins and children. I always felt that as the minds of children are less conditioned than those of adults, they are better able to transcend the gulf between dolphin and man. And if dolphins have the intellect I suppose them to have, it was possible that Donald might appreciate the primitive caricature of himself.

I had placed the drawing in a transparent plastic bag and attached it to the wooden frame of a mirror in such a way that the reflections from the mirror were completely hidden. When she launched herself into the water, Maura was carefully carrying the picture mounted on the frame. However, to assess Donald's reaction I needed his presence. So I tried to attract him first by blowing through the foghorn, then by using our dolphin rattle, but he did not respond to our calls.

I reasoned with myself that as Donald was intelligent he already knew we were there, but that just swimming around would be boring to him so he would not return unless we could offer him a new experience. Then I remembered that Donald

125

always took a keen interest in divers actually performing a task underwater. I sank down to the seabed, which was flat and featureless apart from a large congregation of spider crabs wandering across the sand in an apparently aimless manner, took the diving knife from its scabbard strapped to my leg, and attempted to see what I could dig up from under the sand. I had not got very far with this project when I was aware that I was being watched. I carried on digging and within a short time a dolphin snout was six inches from my hole. Donald had arrived and his eyes sparkled with curiosity.

I stopped digging and Maura diverted his attention to the picture stuck to the mirror. He eyed it intently and I could hear Maura talking to him and telling him about the picture. He seemed to understand what she was saying and to take an amused interest in his likeness.

What, then, I wondered, would be his reaction to his real likeness? So when Donald had finished looking at the child's drawing of himself I took the mirror from Maura and removed it from the plastic bag. Maura called Donald back and this time held the mirror up so that he could see his own reflection.

Up until that moment I had dismissed from my mind the premonition that all would not go well. But the instant Donald saw his own reflection his mood changed completely. He became extremely agitated and knocked the mirror out of Maura's hand. As he did so the edge of the mirror struck Maura a glancing blow that dislodged her facemask and bruised her face. The mirror fell to the seabed and landed reflective side down.

Maura was intensely upset by Donald's frightening and sudden change.

By the time Maura had returned safely to the boat Donald had disappeared. I went below again to collect the mirror, and as I returned to the surface with the mirror tucked under my arm I realized that Mostafa, who had been around part of the time when I was filming Maura and Donald, was no longer in the water, but I suppressed any further feelings of unease in my concern about what had just happened between Maura and Donald.

126

It was Barry who called me quietly over and told me that Mostafa had had to go ashore. I agreed that we should suspend all diving activities and take the *Aquanaut* back into the harbor while there was still sufficient water for us to get alongside the pier. At the time I thought it strange that Mostafa should take it into his head to want to go ashore. I had heard him refer to an acid stomach, and simply assumed that he was suffering a little from the motions of the boat and probable ingestion of seawater.

I found out later that Mostafa had run out of air and had surfaced rapidly, holding his breath at the same time. When he surfaced, his facemask was half-filled with blood, much to everyone's alarm, including Mostafa's. Fearful that he had done himself some serious injury, Barry had called Julie on shore with the intercom, and she had immediately arranged for Mostafa to see a doctor as soon as he landed.

The news of this event was broken to me over a drink in the Schooner where we were having lunch, only minutes before Mostafa himself made a dramatic entrance, bright and breezy as ever. But his brave countenance was a front. The doctor had told him that he was not to dive again for a week. It looked as if the famous Cockcroft luck had run out.

Mostafa objected furiously to the doctor's advice, and made clear that he intended to ignore it. Barry consulted me, as the most experienced diver in the group, and I told him that one of the first laws of aqualung diving is that one should never hold one's breath and rush to the surface, because the air trapped in the lungs expands and may rupture the alveoli. If the bubbles then get into the blood system the results can lead to death. However, it seemed from Mostafa's complete absence of symptoms that he had not suffered an embolism—it was more likely that some fine blood vessels in Mostafa's nose had burst and bled. Some people are prone to nose bleeds, which are quite common amongst divers—even experienced ones—and a little blood in the water that invariably gets into a facemask looks much worse than it really is. Having heard what tests the doctor had performed I was satisfied that this is what had happened.

Even so, Barry decided to get a second doctor's opinion and was adamant that Mostafa would not dive again on that day at least, despite his protests. Barry said he wanted a long shot of the sunset with the *Aquanaut* in the bay, and by discussing this at length he gradually took our cameraman's mind off the unacceptable prospect that he would do no more underwater photography.

In view of the chain of events that followed I can only comment that had it not been for Mostafa's nosebleed we might never have gotten some of the most exciting sequences in the film.

It was 5:30 before we could get the *Aquanaut* out of the harbor, and again after a slightly blustery day the wind dropped away in the evening to become a zephyr. As the *Aquanaut* moved out into the bay we caught occasional glimpses of Donald playing around a buoy with two buzz boats. He swam over when we left the entrance to the harbor, but disappeared again in a few minutes. Maura and I suited up and jumped into the water. As we had agreed to concentrate exclusively on above-water shots I did not wear an aqualung and did not take any cameras into the sea with me. We tried to get Donald to join us, but no amount of calling or rattling of our can of stones persuaded him to leave the boat with which he was playing.

I had taken on board the *Aquanaut* a small aquaplane, a board with handles that is towed behind a boat on a long line. The diver holds onto the handles as he is pulled through the water, and by deflecting the plane of the board he can adjust his course above or below the surface. An aquaplane is usually used by divers to survey large areas of the seabed at speed with the minimum consumption of air. I suggested that I be towed near Donald in the hope that he would find my new mode of transport interesting. Barry agreed.

I took hold of the handles of the aquaplane, and raised one hand in the air, making the circular movement which was the agreed signal for the helmsman to put the engine into gear and slowly increase the revolutions of the propeller. I felt the sudden tug on my arms as the rope went taut, and then, holding the board so that I would stay on the surface, I felt the water surging past my body in a flurry of bubbles. The boat settled to a comfortable speed, at which the rush of water past my head would not sweep off my mask, and I was adjusting to the exhilaration of being towed when I felt a presence. I looked to my right and could see Donald's head cutting through the water at exactly the same pace. I could also see that he was watching me intently. In the stern of the *Aquanaut* Mostafa was pointing his camera at us.

Taking a quick breath I dipped the blade of the aquaplane downward and immediately went into a dive. At a depth of about five feet I leveled out for a few seconds and then deflected the aquaplane upward. This caused me to rise to the surface very rapidly and I was immediately breasting the waves again. I began to feel I was capturing some of the joy of being a dolphin. I took a quick breath and pointed the handles down again.

When I was under the water I looked to my right and could see Donald keeping pace with me—this time completely submerged. So again I pointed the board toward the surface and we both rushed upward and surfaced in unison. It was a superb sensation. I felt I was a dolphin and the feeling was good. After several more thrilling minutes the boat slowed. Mostafa had run out of film.

When the camera was reloaded the sound crew and Mostafa moved into a small boat with a powerful outboard engine. The outboard motor was started, and Mostafa was ready to photograph the aquaplane sequence from a new angle—alongside me.

As the *Aquanaut* set off I again experienced the thrill of riding the waves like a dolphin. However my joyride was short-lived. As I moved through the water I felt a gentle nudge on my right side. I looked to see what was happening and Donald was prodding my arm with his jaws as we sped through the water. At first I took no notice. Then he swam up to my elbow and bit it. I let go of one handle and managed to steer the aquaplane with the other as I yelled an account of what was happening to those in the inflatable. As I did so, Donald came up underneath me and tried to push me off the aquaplane. I did not wish to appear unfriendly to my dolphin friend, but I was determined to enjoy my ride and again grabbed both handles. Donald, however, was equally determined to get me out of the driver's seat and nipped my right elbow painfully hard.

I knew then that Donald was not going to give up until I let go completely, so not wishing to lose my arm I released my hold on both handles of the aquaplane, which skimmed away from me, bouncing over the surface. It was followed immediately by Donald who grabbed the board in his teeth and had a free ride across the sea behind the *Aquanaut*. I could not help laughing into my snorkel tube as I saw him disappearing in the distance.

Mostafa was again out of film so the boat slowed and circled back to me while the aquaplane was pulled inboard.

Donald was delighted with this new turn of events and played around the boat waiting to see what action would take place next. If he was working out some way in which he could repay me for his free ride it did not take him long to think up a solution. He swam underneath me and his dorsal fin broke surface just in front of my face. I put both of my hands gently around it and held on. Donald moved off, slowly at first. I gripped tighter and then tighter still as he increased speed. His dorsal fin rose and fell slightly, to counterbalance the action of his tail. Faster and faster we went. Soon he was going full speed, and I was still clinging to his dorsal fin, the sea swirling up in white foam around my facemask and shoulders. On and on we went in a huge loop. Then Donald decided it was time to stop. He spun around in a very tight circle and barrel-rolled at the same time, churning up the water like a powerful ship turning its propellers at top speed. I had no option but to let go as his fin was wrenched from my hand by the roll. I looked down at Donald through the swirl of bubbles that were rapidly dispersing. It was the end of an express ride to end all express rides.

Later we were joined by Maura in the water and Donald gave both of us rides, with me hanging onto the fin and Maura clinging to me, then vice versa with Maura on the steering end. He then towed Maura in short bursts of great acceleration round the inflatable, turning sharply, Maura being flung out like a bucket on a string.

During the evening the sky had cleared and the sun started to sink, painting an orange-red line across the still sea. So Mostafa got his sunset shots. Not from high on the land as he had planned—but shots packed with action close to the sea. I commented on this to Barry as we made our way back to St.Ives.

"When there is action," he said, "forget the pretty-pretty stuff, and film the action."

In Barry's case he had achieved both the action and the pretty-pretty stuff, as he called it. What was more it had all happened almost by accident. It seemed his record for luck was holding out. I liked him, and I was coming to like Mostafa Hammuri more and more. There was something about the man's spirit that was hard to resist, and Maura too was clearly enjoying his irrepressible vitality.

17 · Donald Shatters His Own Image

After my exhilarating ride on Donald it seemed that everything came together to make the film a success. When we wanted Donald we would send out the inflatable and ask the appointed dolphin organizer to bring Donald to the boat or entertain him until the *Aquanaut* arrived. Somehow we never failed to find him. It was almost as if Barry Cockcroft had only to say "Cue dolphin" and up Donald would pop. After our first two days we were aided in this respect by one of the experiments we carried out in front of the cameras.

We were absolutely convinced that Donald had never been in a dolphinarium or associated with man in any way before his arrival on the Isle of Man. Our major reason for this conclusion was that when we had first encountered him, although he was not timid, he would not allow himself to be touched with a bare hand. As the years passed he had developed closer

131

and closer associations with Maura and myself, and his unwillingness to be touched in this way disappeared. However, we felt we would like to test on film his reactions to the kinds of playthings that dolphins are given in dolphinariums.

Most dolphin trainers admit that dolphins learn to play games very rapidly, and some trainers, aware of the extraordinary intelligence of the animals in their care, have suggested that it is the dolphins who program their trainers, not the trainers the dolphins, to respond to certain signals. It is also widely accepted that dolphins have very good memories, and there are a number of cases on record, reported by well-known scientists, to support this conclusion.

So to investigate our hypothesis that Donald had never been in captivity we decided to present him with some of the toys he probably would have encountered in captivity. To start with Maura and I threw a ball, in the form of a plastic buoy, to one another. Donald followed the ball, swimming to each of us in turn and watching our movements from under the water with his usual curiosity. However, after five minutes' play, even when we presented the ball directly to him, he did not take an active part in our game. He just watched.

We then threw the buoy back into the boat and started to play with a small rubber quoit which quite by chance was attached to a length of rope. We splashed it in the water and then tossed it to one another, again watched by Donald, who swam back and forth toward whichever of us was holding it. Then I waved it underwater at Donald and called to him. As he came up to take it in his beak I raised it out of the water and he raised his head well clear of the surface to grab it. I tossed it to Maura, who did likewise. At last we allowed him to take it, then pulled it away from him and continued our game. Donald became more and more excited and was clearly getting the idea of the game. He began to take the ring from us and to hang onto it tighter and tighter. Then, when Maura held up the ring with both hands, he poked his beak into it and accelerated away with Maura desperately trying to hold on. She yelled to me and I too grabbed the rope. But so powerful was his pull that our combined efforts could not restrain him and we had to let go. For a brief moment we thought that we would be entangled in the rope and dragged after him.

I am sure from the way in which he behaved that he had never played with a quoit before.

The next time he took the ring in his mouth, instead of swimming on the surface he sounded and pulled the rope through my hands so rapidly I let it go because it burned. We thought that was the last we would see of the quoit. But a few minutes later he reappeared with it still in his mouth, and after two more high-speed tows he left us, the inflatable with the camera crew on board chasing after him. Then someone on board managed to grab the trailing line and, much to the delight of everyone, he towed the inflatable with two of the camera crew at breakneck speed across the bay. Eventually the rubber ring could stand the strain no more and broke. Mostafa had loved every second of his ride.

Thereafter, if we wished to attract Donald's attention and he did not respond to our calls, we trailed a rubber quoit through the water.

Once Donald had been located and his interest engaged with the quoit, it was necessary to entice him to the area where we could film him. However, one of the disadvantages of the quoit technique was that if Donald was in a boisterous mood he was likely to tow the inflatable away from the *Aquanaut*, which was our floating base for filming operations. In this event we used the trump card in our deck of dolphin baits. That card took the form of the bare legs of an ex-rugby player named Jack Rogers, who was the chief electrician in the camera crew. We discovered Donald's predilection for Jack's legs one day when he was swimming with the dolphin after a filming session. Jack was wearing a bright blue "shortie" wetsuit jacket. Several of the crew were swimming, but it was Jack whom Donald singled out for particular attention. Donald's penis became erect and he used it to stroke Jack's legs. It was as if the act gave the dolphin sensual pleasure—although as I have indicated before I do not regard this as having an exclusively sexual meaning, and I think that Donald simply liked the smooth soft warmth of Jack's legs and used his most sensitive tactile organ to experience it.

However, whatever the reason why Donald liked Jack's legs,

we established the fact, and Barry used his electrician as human dolphin bait when appropriate. Jack was a little apprehensive when Donald made his first approach, as anyone would be in the circumstances, but he soon came to enjoy his new role in the film.

Here again, Donald was having his mysterious effect on human relationships. Crews in commercial television are often staunch union members and closely observe job demarcations. Yet I was intrigued to observe how often these demarcations were ignored when Donald was present. Barry Cockcroft's adroit diplomacy, coupled with Donald's magic, imbued the entire crew with a remarkable enthusiasm for the film, which overrode all of the barriers which could so easily have disrupted progress. And if ever Jack is asked to account for his role as "dolphin bait" to his union, I only hope that his colleagues will take the view that one hour when work is fun is worth ten hours when it is a burdensome duty.

Having aroused Donald's interest in quoits, we thought we could use it to discover whether or not he had a preference for color. Cathy Rooney, one of the production assistants, bought a set of hollow, smooth plastic quoits colored respectively red, blue, yellow, green and white, and a sixth quoit made from a yellow corrugated tube. I passed them one by one to Maura who presented each of them in turn to Donald during one underwater session, and he playfully bit them all. When I held them up to him in my hands, he showed no preference for any single one. He did however seem to have a preference for the first ring we had played with, which was made of sponge rubber, not hollow plastic, and I got the impression he preferred it because of its texture. The color appeared to be irrelevant.

We also tried feeding Donald with freshly caught mackerel. Although he would take them from our hands when we held the fish in the air, he treated them in exactly the same way as he had the rings when we offered them to him from the surface. He took them in his mouth, went underwater and then let them go. This episode cast doubts on the reports we had had earlier from the fishermen who thought he had eaten the fish they offered him. They would not have seen him releasing them from his mouth underwater, of course. This was also another small pointer to the fact that he had never been in captivity.

I was still puzzled by his reaction to the mirror. I asked Maura if she would take it down again, but she refused point blank, saying that it antagonized him. So I decided to show it to him again myself. I took the mirror, mounted in its strong wooden frame, to the seabed and pointed the reflecting surface toward the dolphin. Donald immediately attacked it, knocking it out of my hand. It zigzagged to the bottom where it remained facing upward. I went down to recover it, but every time I approached Donald swam over and pushed me aside with his head. I hung on the anchor line until he had gone out of sight, but as soon as I made my way back to it he swam up and pushed me aside again.

On the next dive, accompanied by Maura, I took another mirror with a thin plastic frame, and as I descended I held it with the reflecting side toward my body. When I reached the bottom, which was only about twenty feet down, I held it above my head and turned it around so that Donald could see his own image. He spun around and swam nose first at the mirror at full speed. It disintegrated with the impact and the water glistened with a shower of mirror fragments that spun in all directions as they settled toward the bottom. Afterward Maura said, "I will never forget the look on your face, eyes popping with surprise, surrounded by glittering confetti."

When I recovered from the shock of that very disturbing moment, we discussed this episode at considerable length. It was probably the only moment when I had ever been fearful of Donald in the water. Yet I do not think his gesture had been meant as an act of aggression against me. We tried to look at the situation from his point of view.

First, we considered that vision plays a small part in the dolphin's perception of objects around him. His most important sense is his "sound vision," and this would have told him that the object was a simple solid sheet. Yet he was being confronted at the same time with a visual image which indicated part of a dolphin-shaped object. This information clearly conflicted with that of the "sound image." This confusion could have caused Donald's agitation. When he was unable to account for this new creature he was seeing with his eyes but could not perceive with his sound, he no doubt became concerned for our safety and tried to keep us away from it. Finally, when we persisted in our apparent indifference to this potential source of danger he attacked it as he would have done a shark, by swimming straight at it snout first. It is well known that dolphins attack and kill sharks in this way, and the technique could well be an instinctive defense mechanism. In the case of the mirror it certainly worked, for when he made his final attack it disintegrated into smithereens. He had destroyed the unknown threat.

In between our sessions with the mirror we also showed Donald a plain piece of Plexiglass. Maura was not wearing her hood at the time and she could hear him examining it with his "sound vision." She noticed he made a continuous sound, whereas when he was playing with us his sounds were intermittent. He showed no agitation. He was simply interested. Maura placed the Plexiglass sheet over a crab on the seabed. Donald went down to examine it but made no attempt to move the Plexiglass. Maura then placed the crab on top of the Plexiglass and balanced it there as the crab attempted to crawl off. Donald immediately came down and nosed the crab, and the dolphin then shook his head in his usual gesture of amused curiosity. At no time did he display any of the hostility he had shown toward the mirror.

During our one week's filming, Mostafa's diving improved noticeably, and just as both Maura and I got to like him, Donald did also. If ever Mostafa hung on the ladder Donald would hover just underneath biting at his fins and waiting for him to come into the water for the next round of highjinks.

Barry Cockcroft's luck persisted for the entire week. On the final day, when he was taking some long shots of me calling Donald with my dolphin rattle from the very top of the cliffs, Donald astonished us all by appearing around the headland right on cue, leading the fleet of small boats going out to fish for mackerel.

As the television crew put the wraps on their mass of equipment and stowed it in the van, it started to rain for the first time and it became noticeably cooler. The heatwave had come to an end and so had the filming.

Maura and I stayed in Penzance for an extra couple of days, and we had one great pleasure left to us. We had dinner one night with Bob and Hazel Carswell, two of the television crew who had remained behind, and Geoff Bold and his wife Liz. The setting was The Lobster Pot at Mousehole.

Geoff told us then that he had been visited by some members of the Whale Research Unit, with whom I too had exchanged much information on Donald. While Donald was in Penzance, it seems, members of the team had managed to measure him and found his length to be 3.6 meters (eleven feet ten inches) from the tip of his beak to the end of his tail. From this and other measurements they had estimated his weight to be between 300 and 400 kg (approximately 660 to 880 pounds). A full-grown bottlenose dolphin reaches a maximum size of about twelve feet, though like humans not all animals grow to the same size. Thus we could take it that by the time Donald reached Cornwall he had reached his maximum size.

That raised the question: Was Donald fully grown when he reached the Isle of Man in 1972? Estimates of Donald's length when he was off the Isle of Man varied considerably, up to a maximum of fifteen feet. When one takes into account the fact that objects seen underwater appear one third larger than their real size, that would make his length about eleven feet. The difference between this estimated figure and the real length is probably insignificant, so it seemed reasonable to assume that if Donald was not fully grown when he reached the Isle of Man, he was probably close to it.

This conclusion is interesting because it throws some light on the question that I am most frequently asked: How old is Donald?

It is thought that bottlenose dolphins live to an age of about thirty years in the wild, and that they reach full size and maturity at about the age of seven. Thus we can deduce that in 1972 Donald was between six and twenty-six years old.

I got a more accurate estimate of his age by doing some detective work on his teeth, in collaboration with Christina

137

Lockyer of the Whale Research Unit. Unlike humans, the Odontoceti do not shed their first set of milk teeth. Their teeth have only a single root and the central pulp cavity is fairly small. After a time no further dental growth takes place and the pulp cavity gradually disappears. Like the teeth of most other mammals, man included, the bottlenose dolphin's teeth consist of dentine, surrounded with cement and covered with an enamel cap. In older animals the crown is often worn down, sometimes so far that the enamel disappears completely and leaves a row of dentine stumps. A dolphin's teeth will probably show distinct signs of wear from the age of twenty on.

One of the photographs I took on the Isle of Man showed that one of Donald's teeth was broken, but the remainder looked to be in prime condition. In 1976 Donald's teeth were still in good condition, though they were perhaps showing the first signs of wear. So we concluded that in 1972 he was under sixteen years of age.

It has been found possible to estimate the age of a dolphin by removing one of the teeth and etching it, which reveals a series of annual rings. However as such a procedure would be unthinkable with Donald, we can only conclude that he was probably born somewhere between 1956 and 1965. If asked to pinpoint a specific year for Donald's birth I tend for no good scientific reason to plump for 1960—which happens to be the year my son Ashley was born.

Among the other subjects we talked over that evening in The Lobster Pot were Donald's feeding habits and his daily food requirement. Here again we found our knowledge to be derisory. Nobody had actually seen him take fish in the wild.

In addition to pelagic fish, the stomachs of bottlenose dolphins have been found to contain cuttlefish, and it is reported that when eating this food they spit out the cuttlefish bone (familiar to owners of parakeets) and retain the edible portion. We know too that dolphins use their teeth only for capturing their prey, not for chewing it, and that the fish they catch are swallowed whole. A dolphin is able to swallow in such a manner that very little sea water finds its way into the stomach. Seaweed too has been found in the stomachs of bottlenose dolphins. However, it is likely that Donald feeds mainly on fish such as mackerel, pollack and whiting, because these are common in the areas he frequents.

We do not know exactly how much he eats during the course of a day. But we can make an informed guess, based on some work carried out by Russian scientists who measured the food requirements of the Black Sea bottlenose dolphin and found that the intake was 5.6 kg fish (mackerel and mullet) per 100 kg of bodyweight. Thus, if we estimate Donald's weight as being in the region of 350 kg, his daily consumption of food could be about 20 kg, or 44 pounds per day.

Much of the food that Donald eats is required to keep his internal body temperature higher than that of the sea around him, for like all mammals he is warm-blooded. If we consider that still water conducts heat away from our bodies about twenty-seven times faster than still air, and that a normal human being loses consciousness after three hours in water at 60°F, and after only fifteen minutes in water at 32°F, we can appreciate what problems the dolphin has overcome during his evolution into the marine environment. The answer nature has provided, for all of the whale family, is a thick layer of insulating blubber under the skin. This layer of blubber accounts for between thirty and forty percent of Donald's weight. The thickness of the blubber varies with different parts of the body, as does the human layer of subcutaneous fat. In a dolphin it is thin around the blowhole and the eyes, and this is almost certainly related to the need for flexible movement of the eyelids and the walls of the blowhole.

One of the characteristics of nearly all mature bottlenose dolphins found in the wild is that their skins are crisscrossed with scars. This was another of the many mysteries I sought to unravel. The skin of a dolphin is very thin and therefore easily scarred. But why should an animal like Donald, capable of very precise movements, become injured in this way? The question is compounded by the observation that numerous Cetaceans have been found to have signs of fractured ribs that have healed. In the Brussel Museum a skeleton of a bottlenose dolphin has indications that the third, fourth, fifth and sixth ribs have been broken and that the fractures have healed in the form of pseudo-arthroses.

In British coastal waters, however, Donald should have few natural enemies apart from man. So it would seem unlikely that the scars are the results of encounters with species such as the giant squid which are thought to do battle with his larger cousins in the deep ocean. From my observations of Donald I knew that even deep wounds become pigmented to match the surrounding tissue once they have healed. I guessed, therefore, that Donald's crisscross scars were only superficial and were the result of self-inflicted abrasions caused by over-enthusiastic "buoy bashing" and similar activities when he was in his more exuberant moods.

As dinner progressed Geoff told us more about his relationship with Donald, and the special feeling he had for him. He confided that his great ambition was to dive with the dolphin, and that Bob and Hazel had already given him one lesson on snorkeling. Geoff had been very upset when Donald moved away from Penzance, because he felt the opportunity to get close to the dolphin was irrevocably lost. Maura and I had just one day left, so I suggested that the following morning might be a suitable time for Geoff to have an underwater introduction to his dolphin friend after all. Geoff was nervous and undecided so we left the invitation open. Next morning while we were having breakfast he appeared in our hotel. He had decided to join us, so we set out for St.Ives.

We were greeted warmly by the parking lot attendant on the pier, who announced that Donald was just outside waiting for us. Geoff pulled on the jacket of a wetsuit he had borrowed and I loaned him one of my facemasks. He and Maura went into the water first and I followed some five minutes later. We rattled the can full of stones but Donald did not appear. So we swam out to a buoy about 400 yards offshore. Geoff was not a strong swimmer, it was his first snorkel dive in the sea, and he was apprehensive when he saw himself getting further and further out of his depth. We looked down into bright yellow sandy seabed that was peppered with spider crabs. There were no other visible forms of animal life. We clung to the buoy and rested. There was still no sign of Donald. As Geoff was getting cold we decided to swim back to the shore, still calling and shaking our rattle.

Throughout the return journey Geoff, who was not wearing a diving hood, could hear what he thought was the sound of a small outboard. My wife Wendy, who was watching our activities from the top of the pier, told us afterward that Donald followed us all the way back, keeping about twenty yards behind us. The outboard noise that Geoff heard was obviously Donald sounding us out. Then, when Geoff and Maura were just about to go ashore, the dolphin surfaced a few yards away. In a few seconds he cruised up to me. I called out to Maura and Geoff, who forgot the cold and came to join us in only about five feet of water. Donald kept swimming past so that I could stroke him and for ten minutes he stayed to play.

Geoff found the size of Donald awe-inspiring. Donald was not slender and his considerable length was matched by an equally impressive-looking girth. Geoff himself was a big, very strong man who kept himself physically fit, and when he saw the dolphin glide past so effortlessly underwater he realized the immense power that was locked up inside the dolphin's body. He marveled too at the silky texture of Donald's skin. Nervously and delicately he caressed Donald's head and the dolphin responded by brushing his belly against Geoff's bare legs. As the two made physical contact for the first time and the gap between air and water that had separated them was closed at last, I found myself deeply moved by the great tenderness of the meeting. I could sense that for Geoff it was an overwhelming experience.

I was certain that Donald knew that Geoff was a little scared, for the dolphin made no moves that could frighten the novice snorkeler. Only when he switched his attention to Maura did his attitude change. He became more active and the two of them had a farewell cuddle and rolled around together like two lovers in a haystack. Then when Donald swam to me I gently grasped his dorsal fin between my hands. It was as if I was a jockey who had just mounted a spirited horse. Donald accelerated out toward the sea. It was low water and I could see the dark green kelp and bright yellow sand passing in a blur underneath me as I set off on another switchback ride that set me tingling with pleasure and excitement. Faster and faster we went. Then came the inevitable barrel roll and turn which would send me into a flurry of waves and bubbles. It was the moment when Donald told me that he was the master.

I left the water delighted that we had been able to bring Donald and Geoff together in this way at last. I could see that the experience had made a deep impression on Geoff, and the obvious emotional bond between him and Donald set me to thinking again what a unique animal Donald was, and what a profound influence he had on people. In his odyssey round the coast of Britain he had already changed many lives, making them in some magic way richer and happier.

18 · Flight into Fantasy

Shortly after I had finished filming with Donald in Penzance I left for a diving holiday in Sardinia with my entire family plus my daughter's boyfriend, Steve. We were Luciano's guests in a villa near Stintino at the rocky northern extremity of the island, an area renowned for exceptionally clear water—and therefore spectacular diving.

But upon our arrival in Sardinia it was apparent that Luciano was in the middle of a crisis. It seemed that only a few weeks before a reaction had got out of control at a chemical works in northern Italy and spread a dangerous compound over the adjacent land and countryside. The accident was soon to be news all over the world as the "Seveso affair," and Luciano was concerned with the long-term effects the toxic substance might have on human beings. We discussed the implications of the disaster with intensity and at length. Luciano was of the opinion that mankind had now reached a stage where there was no way forward without high technology. He maintained that in order for civilization to survive, and to preserve aesthetic and human values, we had to accept this fact and evolve a new culture which would take into account the natural environment and the technology which threatens to destroy it. He called his philosophy "survival culture."

At first I thought it strange that his lines of thought should have been running parallel to some ideas in fantasy form I had developed concerning the reason for Donald's association with man. On further consideration, however, I was less surprised because of certain sensitivities common to Luciano and myself.

Inevitably, we talked about Donald. On the basis of their known behavior, and the fact that dolphins, like men, have a large cerebral cortex (the part of the brain that in man is associated with the higher levels of mental activity, such as appreciation of music, for instance, creative thought, and deep emotion) we argued the possibility that dolphins have a level of consciousness on a par with, or even higher than, that of man. Although it is known that human brains have plenty of spare capacity, could we assume that the cerebral cortex of dolphins, which is roughly the same size as man's on a weight for weight basis, and bigger in terms of total mass, has a similar function? Exactly what role the cerebral cortex plays in dolphins is still very much open to speculation, but Carl Sagan has considered the possibility that the intelligence of Cetaceans is channeled into the dolphin equivalent of epic poetry, history and elaborate codes of social interaction . . . .

With these thoughts in mind I told Luciano that I had been trying to understand Donald's way of thinking. There were many aspects of his behavior that I found intriguing. It is well known, for instance, that dolphins, like man, are gregarious animals. Why, then, was Donald always on his own? Why had he associated so closely with Maura and me? I told Luciano that in order to find the answers I had tried metaphorically to put my mind inside Donald's head. I had tried to perceive the world through the ears, eyes and frontal lobes of a dolphin. Before I told him about my flight of fantasy, however, I wanted to examine another mystery about Donald that was bothering me.

I knew that it is extremely rare for dolphins to become entangled in nets by accident. Indeed, it is extraordinarily difficult to capture any dolphin against its will. When dolphins were first put on exhibition in the United States in the 1950s, a number of methods of capturing them were tried. Deliberately netting them by conventional methods invariably failed, no matter how many ruses were used. With their sonic vision the dolphins were able to detect the nets from afar, to deduce what their would-be captors were about, and to take evasive action long before the nets were closed.

The technique eventually developed was to utilize the dolphins' delightful habit of swimming alongside and in front of boats. When the dolphins and the vessels were both moving at the same speed, the dolphin catchers plunged nets mounted on circular frames down into the water just ahead of the dolphins. Once they left the hands of the catchers the nets were virtually stationary in the water relative to the directional movement of the dolphins, and as the dolphins were making rapid forward progress they swam into them in a fraction of a second, before they could take evasive action.

Thus, although I knew that during his stay in Wales Donald would be in a region where there were inshore fishing boats, I had little fear for his safety. However, he was captured—not, as it happened, in a fishing net, but in a buoy line. I had heard about it afterward. Quite how it happened was an enigma that I felt I had to unravel. But before I could answer this and the other questions I was posing myself, Luciano was called urgently back to his research institute in Milan.

The Seveso disaster was now an international scandal. Luciano appeared on the front pages of newspapers and on BBC television. I could see a remote analogy between the plight of man threatened by his own technology and the continuing plight of the Cetaceans.

When Luciano returned he was eager to hear me expound the dolphin's-eye view I had promised him of the events that caused Donald's departure from the Isle of Man and followed his arrival off the Welsh coast. I suggested that Luciano imagine that I was Donald, and that my words were Donald's words, spoken from the dolphin's own mind.

Here is the story I told him.

144

Since I left the seas where I first met the two-tailed mammals with the fast respiration, I have been fortunate. I have found another part of the sea which has made a good home for me, a place where there are many interesting sounds and movements. In many ways this new home I have found is like my previous one, and here too I have two places where I can rest and play.

Nearby is an isolated land mass that causes the water to flow very rapidly between the tides. When the water is running fast the fish wait behind the rocks for their food to be swept by, and when they are gathered there I can easily feed myself. When the tide races through, the water surface is rough. All of the other water beings take shelter behind the rocks and the two-tailed mammals who float on the top of my world with their noisy machines stay away. They are afraid; I am the master. When all the other animals are hiding, I have my sea to myself.

(Port St. Mary and Port Erin, two of Donald's favorite resorts on the Isle of Man, were separated by a distance of about seven miles by sea. The presence of an island—the Calf of Man, close to the land and between the two resorts—causes a dangerous tidal race which runs at its fastest between the periods of slack high water and slack low water. Likewise in Wales Donald "adopted" the two harbors of Dale Haven and Martin's Haven which are separated by about ten miles if a sea route is taken. The island of Skomer, just off the headland between the two havens, also creates a dangerous tidal race through Jack Sound.)

I can race through the water and I can dive up through the air. When I hit the air I feel the sensation of weight and gravity that I cannot feel when I am in my own en-

145

vironment—the sea. The air feels much harder than the water.

When I leap into the air and I am pulled back down again into the soft welcoming water with a splash I realize how lucky I am to live in the sea. Feeling gravity for a few seconds is fun, but feeling gravity for all time must be dreadful, as I remember when I was stranded on land two years ago. The two-tailed mammal comes from the land above the sea where the gravity forces make him extremely heavy. Moving fast with such enormous forces on his body must demand great strength and use up much energy. Perhaps that is why he needs to breathe so fast. I wonder what it feels like when he comes into the soft cushion of the sea where he has no weight? If he is so strong as to move on land why is he so slow in the sea?

Are the two-tailed mammals as slow in their own environment as they are in the sea? They are by far the most intelligent creatures I have encountered, but they are very slow in what they do and how they communicate.

There is, however, one feature of a two-tailed mammal that I do admire. It is his flippers with which he can catch things and move things better than I can with either my mouth or my flippers. In that one respect he is superior to me.

The two-tailed mammals appear to have little appreciation of the sounds of the sea. The sea is full of natural vibrations that I can hear and they cannot. Some of the sounds have distinct meanings, such as the scream of a wounded fish. Such vibrations are primitive, with a single meaning. The seals, warm-blooded mammals like me, make more meaningful sounds than the fish. They use some of their sounds for echo-location. I sometimes play with the seals in the water, and I enjoy that. They are far less interesting than my first cousins the toothed whales and second cousins the whiskered whales. I can exchange complex information with my fellow Cetaceans by the use of sound. Each of our species has its own exclusive culture based on sound. Indeed, that is why I now lead this lonely life.

I remember when I was selected by the mentor dolphin of my school for my task. He told me that the sea, which had been ours for millions of years, was being invaded with so many new sounds that our survival was at stake. He told me that four dolphin generations ago our big cousins the whales made the loudest noises in the sea and that they could talk to one another over great distances. The sounds made by the two-tailed land mammals were very, very quiet—a few splashes near their own environment. When they traveled over our environment on floating wood blown by the wind the noise was local and no more obtrusive than that made by the sea foaming up a sandy beach.

Then the two-tailed mammals changed to more elaborate vessels that could transport them across the sea. The new vehicles were pushed through the water with tiny tails that made unusual continuous rotational movements. They made a fascinating sound which penetrated deeper into our environment, and the noise continued for the entire time the transporters were moving on the surface of our undersea world. The two-tailed mammal must have a very great desire to move like us dolphins, because many of their water transporters hit the hard seabed where it rose into the air, and their transporters sank into our world with the death of many two-tailed mammals.

Then two dolphin generations ago they started making many more sounds, not just interesting sounds but painful sounds that would kill our kind if they were nearby. Many of the hollow, high-density transporters were broken by the powerful new sounds. Hundreds of the transporters came down into our sea with the loss of many two-tailed mammals. At first we could not understand what was happening. They appeared to be deliberately killing their own species, not just the old, infirm and deformed specimens, but many young fit specimens. They were behaving in a manner we had not before experienced even among the lowest orders of sea life, the sharks.

The sounds the mammals made, however, were only a small part of the world of sound in which we live. A very few dolphins were also killed. We were puzzled, but the sounds did not disturb us too much and we took no action. However, worse things were to come.

A much bigger invasion of our sound world came during the course of the last dolphin generation, and since then the situation has progressively deteriorated. The sounds they now make are very much more penetrating. When their transporters are on the surface they send out sound beams that penetrate deep into the sea. In addition they have built stationary objects that emit a continuous noise. The noises they make are now reaching a level where in some places they are interfering with our own communications.

In addition to sounds my sea is full of tastes. When a shoal of mackerel have passed nearby I can taste their presence in the water. But in many parts of the undersea world the natural tastes have now changed. In some areas where fresh water flows into the sea the taste has become bitter and noxious. We dolphins suspect that the two-tailed mammals have brought about this change. So now we have two types of pollution in our world, sound pollution and taste pollution. That is why I volunteered to isolate myself from the school to learn something about the two-tailed mammals who are threatening our present existence.

The mentor dolphin was wise, and told me that the dolphins must evolve and develop a new survival culture which will take into account the two-tailed mammals' culture of kill, destroy, and pollute. To evolve our survival culture we must find out more about the two-tailed mammals. We had already learned a lot about the ingenious devices they manipulate with their remarkable flippers. Now we need to know something about what motivates them toward apparent self-destruction. In other words we need to know about the vibrations of their minds. To do that I was to attempt to let my own mental vibrations overlap with theirs.

My mentor warned me that my mission would be dangerous, because the thing that characterized all information so far about the behavior of the two-tailed mammal was that it is a very unpredictable species. He told me that I must always be on my guard. When he sent me on my mission he knew I would be gone for a long time, for in order to accomplish it I would have to isolate myself completely from close contact with dolphin vibrations. Only by doing so would I become sensitive to the sound vibrations of the two-tailed mammals, and the information that would be contained in their complex interference patterns. Occasionally a messenger dolphin would be sent from the school to get news of my progress. I was to communicate with the messenger only briefly.

After my first encounter with the two-tailed mammals I felt that I was doing very well. First I sensed fear—acute fear—but then that vibration gradually diminished and I sensed friendship. Then came the female with whom I had the maximum overlap. Not only did I receive her vibrations, she received some of mine and I was lulled into a sense of security, false security as it turned out. I thought all the two-tailed mammals were basically friendly once they had overcome their fear. But my mentor proved to be correct. The next male I tried to communicate with and help when he was catching salmon emitted first fear and then the new vibration I had never before experienced, but what the land mammals call hatred. I felt that mind vibration reach a maximum the moment before the explosive sound that tore into my flesh and sent me crazy with pain. For that brief moment I knew both the mind vibration and sound vibration made by the two-tailed mammals on their course of self-destruction. My cries went unheard because the dolphin school was far away. So I kept clear of the two-tailed mammals until I had recovered. When the messenger came and I told him of my experience he told me to carry on my work and that he would carry my information to the mentor dolphin. So the next time I encountered the two-tailed mammals I sought out only those with friendly vibrations. With their help I gradually built up the courage I needed to continue my mission.

149

The complexity of the problem I had been sent to help resolve was brought home to me with startling clarity when I was stranded. With no water surrounding me, my full weight pressed me with increasing pressure harder and harder into the newly uncovered seabed. I was becoming hot and finding it almost impossible to expand my chest to breathe. I knew I would die if I could not get back into the water and again sent out my dolphin distress signal. Fortunately one of the two-tailed mammals nearby received my vibrations and immediately I sensed faint but familiar dolphin-like response vibrations. The mammal called upon the small school of other two-tailed mammals for help as he would if he were a dolphin, and I was saved as I would have been if I had been drowning and was near a school of dolphins in the sea. The next time the messenger dolphin came I gave him the new information and he said he would pass this good news to the mentor. He also informed me that I was to continue with my mission.

As I reported my experiences to the messenger dolphin I realized that the two-tailed mammals can be both cruel and kind. This I still cannot understand. First they tried to kill me, not just for food but for another reason which does not occur in our culture. Then, when I was stranded, they behaved in a dolphin-like manner and rescued me.

I was pleased to report to the dolphin messenger my relationship with the two-tailed mammal who has visited me frequently. She is the one I have come closest to understanding and she seems to be the best of the two-tailed mammals at entering my world. I like it best when she is on the interface between our two worlds because there she can be most active and controlled. When she communicates with me in her own sound pictures they are limited to the long-sound part of my sound vision, which does not give me information on shape and density. Her sound is very deep, as if a dolphin voice has been slowed down many times, and the information it contains comes to me equally slowly. Sometimes I feel so good when I am with

150

her I wish she could speak delphinese and then we could exchange much more information.

I liked her visits so much that I would have stayed in one place near her for a long time.

Then I heard a strange, very loud noise that I had not encountered before. I came suddenly, without warning, and stopped. I was frightened, and did not know what to do. For tide phase after tide phase* I swam, not knowing what to do and where to go. Then there was another single very loud noise—the same as before. The noises continued for several moonphases** and I became more and more distressed. Then one day when I was near my favorite place, I was hit by an explosion.

The gigantic vibrations thumped into my body as if I were being beaten on all sides but with a single blow. I was so dazed I screamed for help but my two-tailed mammal friends did not come. My distress call was not heard by my own school of dolphins. Or if it was they did not respond as they would normally have done. Then there was another enormous sound and a crushing vibration. I cried as loud as I could but again my distress call went unheard. I sank to the seabed and could barely remember that I must surface to breathe. Again and again I sent out my distess call but neither dolphins nor the two-tailed mammals came to assist me as I expected.

Then I remembered why I had been sent on my mission, to try to understand why the two-tailed mammals were polluting our environment with sound. Now I understood fully what my mentor dolphin had told me about the sound that the two-tailed mammals used to kill one another, and I realized that I needed to gather much more information. I was not going to die, but still crazy with the shock I left my familiar seabed territory and swam and

---

*The time between one high tide and the next—about 12½ hours.
**The time between one full moon and the next, i.e. one lunar month—about four weeks.

swam all through the dark moon-phase,* over deep water which I had not crossed for many moon tides. On and on I went skimming through the water until the shock damage was healed by the vigorous movements of my body.

When the dawn came I found myself exhausted and close to a high seabed which stretched up into the air. Near to this mass I found a hollow object floating on the surface. It was attached to the seabed by a rope and I was thankful to find a place to rest. Although my entire brain was exhausted I knew I could only rest half of it—that the other half must be kept alert for danger and to make me breathe. So with the buoy to protect my resting side I stayed quietly all day recovering, first resting one side of my brain and then changing position to rest the other side.

When the evening came I was feeling better, but my body was aching from the long unaccustomed exercise and I swam slowly around the seabed peninsula in which I found myself to record all of its details in my brain. Whether I stay or go I will always remember this place. There is just a single floating ball to which the two-tailed mammals attach their hollow transporters but there are none of the transporters here and none of the mammals have come. It is good here. It is peaceful. I can be alone quietly until I recover.

Two moon tides** have passed and I am completely recovered. I think I shall stay here. I have explored the isthmus of seabed nearby through which the water flows when the tide is set fast, and there is plenty of food. Beyond that is a promontory of seabed with more buoys and I have found a sea transporter the same shape as the one I often used as a resting station in my previous island. It is comforting to stay with it over my head. When I am

* Night.
** A moon tide corresponds to a cycle of the moon's phase from new to full moon or from full back to new moon, that is, fifteen days.

alongside the dense part that comes deepest into the water I feel protected and can rest one side of my brain.

As the moon tides have passed I have had encounters with more of the two-tailed mammals. Some have come to visit me in my own environment. One day when I was near my feeding isthmus I sensed a familiar two-tailed mammal on one of the transporters. The overhead world was thick with water vapor, which is dangerous for the transporters, so I escorted it to the sea island I have made my base. As soon as the transporter stopped the two-tailed mammal with the interesting box in his adapted flippers came into my environment.

I was delighted to see him and told him time and time again to take a message to the female two-tailed mammal who was often with him before. He does not understand me like the female, but I hope he got the information I tried to convey to him.

As the moon tides have come and gone and the water has become warmer the two-tailed mammals have become more active and have brought their transporters to my small peninsula of water.

Each day after sunrise I hear a two-tailed mammal arrive. He moves awkwardly over the land above the water to the beach. Then he starts his interesting routine. I like routines. First there is a general clatter, and then he pulls a small wooden transporter down the land toward the water. It makes a lovely sound as it bounces over the rocks and mixes with the regular rhythm of the sea swell running back and forth joining his world to mine. He splashes into the sea and pushes his small transporter ahead of him. Then he climbs into his vessel and moves it over the water with a wooden fluke which he moves with his adapted flippers.

The sound picture now changes. I hear clicks and groans coming from the transporter as it is stressed by the push of the wooden fluke, which sweeps like a tail movement over the stern. That sound is mixed with the subtle swish of water as it hurries past the rippled sides of the transporter. I swim to greet him. I cartwheel high out of the water as I take a breath. He talks to me as he stands in his transporter propelling it over the water. When he arrives at the larger transporter, he climbs aboard and leaves the small one for me to play with when he goes on his journey. I push my head up into the heavy air and look at him with my sight vision. He talks to me again with his deep slow voice as he starts his next routine.

Next, after a vigorous movement, comes the sound I know will eventually make the small fluke at the back of the transporter start to rotate. Once the sound commences it settles to a regular thud that comes through the water like a very powerful heartbeat. I dance through the water around the transporter when this happens because I know shortly will come the sound I like most of all. Then it happens. Clunk, clunk, click, click, clunk in quick succession; pause, then clickety clunk, clickety clickety click. I dive down to the seabed and watch the anchor chain bounce on the seabed before the hook which is partially buried finally breaks free. It is a delicious mixture of shapes and sounds and movement. I follow it up through the water as the chain links slide over the side of the transporter. Clickety, clunkety, click, pause.

Then it is taken out of my world and there is a final session of random sounds before the heart-throb increases and the transporter moves to the edge of the land to collect its load of the two-tailed mammals. They clamber awkwardly over the dry seabed and then the transporter sets off for the big pool of land above the sea that is the home for many birds. I escort the transporter halfway to the island and then swim back to base, to see what other activities are commencing.

As the sun climbs into the air over the water it is time for me to rest and lie gently beside the small transporter left by the two-tailed mammal who has gone to the bird island. There is little danger here but I must always be on the alert. I rest beside the transporter and close one eye, pretending the transporter is another dolphin protecting my sleeping side. My outer eye stays alert and that part of my brain tells me when I must gently surface to breathe.

If another interesting sound comes to my brain when I am resting I awake in an instant and go to investigate. Often there are two-tailed mammals who come and visit the underwater world. I always go and see what they are doing. At first I keep out of sight, as I have been trained, and examine them with my sound vision. Then if the vibrations are good I go to investigate and let them see me. Some come regularly and emit good vibrations. When I see them I let them touch me and I enjoy that.

The two-tailed mammal who always has a box in his flippers took the message to the female and I was very pleased to hear her sounds again. I was delighted to have the female back in the sea with me and we exchanged many messages. I like her to touch me all over because she is so gentle. I was sad when she left the sea, but just over one tide later I heard the signal she and her partner make with stones in a tin on the high land above water. I rose out of the water and then they saw me. They waved their modified flippers and made mouth noises. I watched them come down the rocks toward the water where I was waiting to greet them. I am very happy when I am with them.

I am also happy when I am near the two-tailed mammal who goes to the bird island every sun phase. He does not come into my environment with me, but I get very close to him and can feel that he has a good presence. Perhaps I feel this way toward him because I like the routine he has. Perhaps it is because he is also present in my territory at the part of the cycle of the sun when I am in my most active mood and feel the need for fun. That is the time when the sun is falling to meet the water on the distant horizon, before my moon phase feeding period begins.

I know his evening routine well. I hear the heart-throb noise far off and I know then that he is going to journey back to my territory, near his small transporter. That distant sound sparks the feeling of happiness inside me and I swim round my territory inspecting all of the chains, hollow spheres and transporters one by one. I dive into the air gently as I go past each one and reimprint them on my mind. Then I turn my attention again to the heart-throb noise. It is closer now.

I know he will be even closer by the time I have swum out to him. So my brain tells me not to swim straight toward the noise but to allow for the distance he has traveled. It is time to go. Go. One beat, two beats, three beats, four beats, five beats, six beats, faster, faster, seven beats, up to breathe and down we go, the water is flowing past me so fast it caresses me. On and on. There is the transporter.

Let me show them I am here, up we go. A quick circuit round the transporter so all the two-tailed mammals can see me. Up to breathe. Now let's have another look at that rotating fin at the back of the transporter. Let me put my nose very close to it so that I can feel the vibrations running through my body. The water it is forcing back over my skin strokes me like a long soft brush. Then sideways, away, circle, up for air and accelerate to the front where I can feel the forward push. Now no effort is needed to swim. I just adjust my flippers and tail and the water pushed aside by the transporter carries me forward. I know I can swim much faster than this vessel. So if I drop under the forward moving water in front of this transporter I can accelerate safely away without being hit as I was many moon tides ago in a place far away. That tiny misjudgment cost me a nasty injury that could have killed me if it had been to my blowhole. However, that transporter was smaller and much faster than this one. This one is safe. We are coming into my base territory now. So let's rush ahead and sweep round the bay.

The heart-throb noise has slowed right down. He will soon be putting ashore his passengers, then the fun will really begin.

There they go half falling over the dry seabed. How ungainly they look stuck up on their two fins with all that weight pulling them over if they go too far. I wonder why they don't stabilize themselves and use their flippers and their tails like some of the other mammals? The hairy mammals that make a sharp repetitive noise and sometimes swim into the sea to collect a stick in their jaws seem much more able to cope with the business of moving over the rocks close to the water than the two-tailed mammals. But I have never seen any of the land mammals move with the speed and grace of a school of dolphins. They seem far less well adapted to movement on land than I am to movement in water.

Ah! the heart-throb sound is increasing; he will be moving toward the small transporter. Yes. He's there. Then splash! followed by the delicious rattle of chains on the seabed. It is a sound picture I never tire of. The heart-throb sound has stopped. He is moving about in the big transporter, securing things with those marvelous adapted flippers so that they will not dislodge during the dark phase of the sky. He's pulling in the small transporter toward the large one and has climbed aboard. The next stage is for him to put the stick in the water and use it as a fin to propel it ashore. I do not think I will let him go just yet. I will position myself upside down under the small transporter, push with my belly against the keel and swim with my tail in the opposite direction to which he is pushing. It is very easy to make him go any way I wish. He has stopped pulling now and is trying to push me away with his wooden fin and the transporter is wobbling. I do not think he would be very happy with me in my environment. I have never seen him come into it. Perhaps I had better leave him alone.

He is off again, moving slowly toward the shore. I think I will go for a quick swim around the old homestead with a few quick dives into the air to express my joy. Round we go. Up, splash. Down and round. He is near to the land now. All of the other two-tailed mammals have gone except him. I don't want him to go. Can't he see that I would like him to stay a little longer? Just a little longer. I will give him just one more push out. This time I will push him backward with my snout. Then he can see what

157

I am doing and I can watch him standing in the transporter trying to scull it against my push. And I can hear him making low throat sounds.

The game is over; he has gone to his home on the land above. All of the other two-tailed mammals have gone too and I am now all alone in the sea with the non-mammals. The sun has disappeared behind the far horizon and the undersea world is changing. Many of the creatures of my world that hide away during the sunlight period are coming out. The lobsters are moving out of their holes in search of food. The conger eels, which keep well hidden with just their snouts protruding from their lairs during the sun phase, are coming out to swim free. The wrasse which were hurrying everywhere over the rocks during the sun phase are now quiet and resting close to the rocks in the moon phase. The octopus thinks he slides silently out of his crevice but I can hear even his slithery sounds. His sound is quite unlike the crawfish or spiny lobster, whose clicks penetrate far into the dark water. All of these sounds combine in the new orchestra of sounds that commence with the moon phase. They are the music of my environment. But in the far distance I can hear the heart-beat sound of a huge transporter, hundreds of times bigger than the largest whale. Even at the height of the moon phase the sounds of the two-tailed mammals are present. Although the two-tailed mammals have all gone from my homestead their transporters far away remind me that some of them are always on the move. Sun phase and moon phase. If we dolphins are to evolve a new survival culture we must come to terms with these monster transporters and the two-tailed mammals who control them. We cannot drive them out of our environment. We must try to understand them.

As the tide phases have come and gone I have investigated this territory. I have made contact with many two-tailed mammals and have enjoyed playing with them. Their transporters give me much pleasure and I enjoy teasing them.

I think some of them enjoy my humor, especially when they are small. But I have noticed that older ones seem to be less inclined to play. That is another difference I have noticed. We dolphins never lose our sense of fun and frivolity. I wonder why the two-tailed mammals do? Perhaps it is because they have surrounded themselves with machines which have no sense of fun at all.

During one sun phase, when I was feeling in a particularly mischievous mood I heard the delightful rattle as a small transporter came to rest and the two-tailed mammals prepared to secure it to the seabed. I knew what would happen next. As the hook came down toward the seabed I grabbed it in my beak and swam away with it. Slowly at first, then at full speed. I could feel the weight of the transporter on the end of the line and amid the flurry of seawater I could just hear the deep throat sounds of the mammals coming down through the water from the bottom of the transporter. When I was out of breath I dropped the hook and swam up to the air. Close by the transporter I humped and blew and I could sense that the mammals were emitting both fear and excitement. When they knew it was I who had mysteriously moved their transporter they were happy and wanted me to play with them some more.

All the time I am learning more about the mammals and the things they have made and put in my environment. One of my most salutary experiences occurred after I had been here for almost one long sun cycle.* It was the time when the two-tailed mammals' activities in my environment are at a minimum level. Most of them had left the small haven I had made my base during the warm season. As the rough seas made it uncomfortable to rest, I started to spend more of my time in my second territory**

* A year.
** Dale Roads.

159

where there were always floating buoys attached to the seabed. Here I could rest in peace and the hollow spheres provided me with fixed points around which I could play, for without the company of other dolphins I need some familiar objects that float between my world of water and the lifegiving but alien world of air above.

It was during the late sun phase that it happened. I was beginning to feel hungry and I could sense the energy for the fun of the chase building up in my body.

I swim around my buoy vigorously. When I am far from the buoy I spray the water with sound to find it again. The sound picture comes back loud and clear and nearby I see the sound pattern of a solitary fish. Feeling full of energy, I dart forward at full speed to take my hors d'oeuvre. Just as I am about to take the fish in my mouth it senses my presence and darts sideways. I change course. Half in annoyance and half in fun as I swim past the buoy I hit it with all my might with my tail and at the same time I leap out of the water.

As I dive I feel something grab my tail. I am startled and accelerate to full speed in three strokes. Still I can feel the thing holding my tail. I continue to thrust at full power when the thing that has grabbed my tail pulls me to an immediate and complete stop. With my body at full speed the force required to do this is enormous, and I feel the grip round my tail increase to a sudden crescendo of pain. I think for one moment it will rip my beautiful tail by its roots out of my body. Frantic with alarm I swing round and try to swim away in another direction. But the thing that has grabbed my tail hangs on and will not release me. I try swimming this way and that but the harder I swim the tighter is the grip around the base of my tail and all I can do is swim in a circle. The harder I swim the stronger the grip and the greater the pain. Suddenly I realize that I am not going to die immediately and the panic subsides a little. I notice that as I swim less vigorously the grip slackens to a more tolerable level. I slow down and then stop. The grip remains persistent but is no longer painful. I must stay still and try to resolve this problem.

First, I must find out what creature or thing is holding my tail. I will turn around and use my sound vision. Slowly around. I can still feel it, but it follows my tail so closely I can't focus my sound beam on it at all. With my light vision I can see partly backward, but can see no monster capable of withstanding all my strength.

If I cannot find out what is holding me I had better establish where I am. I will swim very slowly round and pinpoint my position on the contour map imprinted on my memory. I spray the seabed and the surrounding water with sound and in a few moments I know exactly where I am. I will superimpose the new sound picture on the one I have recorded many times before. Everything fits, the far buoy, the bump in the seabed and the far off hull of the small transporter tied to its mooring buoy. But one thing is missing; it is the buoy I slapped with my tail just before I swam after that fish. I look behind me again with my eyes and I can just see it in my peripheral vision. If I swim slowly away it follows me through the water. It is followed by another one. . . .

It had been a good season for Peter Pearson. Throughout the summer months his hotel on Thorne Island, Milford Haven, had been full of guests. As there was no direct contact with the mainland he had spent much of his time ferrying his guests to and from their temporary summer sanctuary in the sea.

Peter Pearson, an ex-squadron leader who distinguished himself in World War II, was tall, very craggy and tough. He often went barefoot and could be seen hauling heavy loads up and down the steep stone steps leading from the dock to the fortress that had been converted into a hotel. The Pearson family had owned Thorne Island for about forty years and Peter Pearson had managed the hotel for some twenty-five of them. The people who came there were looking for a holiday where they could enjoy isolation and sailing. Peter Pearson disliked power boats and enjoyed life most when he was sailing his guests round the islands of Skokholm and Skomer. For him the wind and the sea were magic.

He knew every nuance of the tides in Milford Haven and the buoys, vessels and other objects that protruded from the sea in the vicinity of Thorne Island were as familiar to him as the houses are to a mailman on his rounds. When the summer season finished at the end of September he usually closed his hotel and moved to the mainland. Every few days thereafter, either when the mood took him or necessity dictated, he would revisit his island to check that all was in order and to carry out essential maintenance and redecoration. When the season finished on September 26, 1975, however, Peter Pearson decided to remain on the island until Christmas in order to build an additional bar.

During the early winter months Peter observed that the wild dolphin he had encountered on a number of his summer sailing trips round the islands was to be seen more and more frequently in Milford Haven. Like almost everybody in the area Peter had had an experience with the dolphin. When he was rowing ashore on a very calm summer evening Donald had decided to have a game with his gray inflatable, pushing it and making steering very difficult. Finally, the dolphin whisked the dinghy round in a complete circle and thumped the side with his tail, drenching Peter and his passenger from head to foot. It was an encounter that made Peter slightly wary of the dolphin. Nonetheless he enjoyed Donald's presence in the Haven during the quiet months.

The bar extension job was nearing completion by early December and one evening after a hard day's work Peter Pearson and his son Simon, who was in his early twenties, decided to row ashore. It was a flat calm evening and they set off on their mile-long journey at about 5 o'clock. About a quarter of a mile from Thorne Island they passed a mooring buoy. It drifted downstream with the tide and had a second smaller buoy attached to the rope to keep it afloat and make it easy to pick up.

162

As they neared the buoy they noticed Donald's gray hump in the water near the buoy. It was one of Donald's favorite haunts. Peter wondered if Donald (or Dai as he knew him) would repeat his earlier performance and push the dinghy off course. The dolphin did not move. Peter looked again at the hump in the water and realized that there was something unusual about it. Then it came to him. "That's strange," he remarked to his son, "the dolphin is facing downstream, not upstream as he usually does. I wonder why?"

Pondering on this question they passed on their way, thankful that Donald had not pursued them.

I have been here two moon phases now and not one of the two-tailed mammals has come out to help me despite all of my distress cries. My school of dolphins are miles away on their migration route and they cannot hear my cries for help. My only companions are moronic fish. They can hardly help themselves, let alone me. Fortunately there are none of those big stupid sharks cruising in the area. Ah, what's that I hear? It is the transporter of the two-tailed mammal who passes these buoys regularly on his way to the seabed pool. I have escorted him many times. He must surely hear my pleas for help. Yes, he's coming closer. I can hear the quiet regular splosh, pause, splosh as he pulls his soft transporter through the water. Closer, closer. I can just hear him making throat noises. I can feel he is aware of my presence. Will he help me? I cannot make him hear my sound cries or feel my brainwave emissions calling for help. He is still aware of my presence but he is not responding. He must hear me. He must stop. He is passing by. He is not going to stop. There he goes, still making voice sounds and pulling on the sticks that move him through the water. I wish I could move away from this place, even at his slow speed. I have tried many times, but each time I do I feel the grip tighten on my tail which is painful and sore. I will just have to stay here. But how much longer can I stay, anchored to this place with no food?

I could probably stay alive for many tides, slowly using the reserves inside my body. But when these are gone and I start to utilize my blubber I will lose heat more quickly and then I will die. The prospect of being stuck here, unable to dive into the air and swim fast and deep, fills me with a sensation I have never felt before. I have sensed it sometimes in the two-tailed mammals, who call it despair. Now I am beginning to understand them more and more. What shall I do? Shall I sink, open my blowhole, and let the water that has supported me and given me so much pleasure seep into my body? If it does I know it will take me back into itself, but when it does my dolphin spirit will be gone forever. If I were with my school of dolphins I know they would try to stop me giving my body back to the sea. They would support me and take me to the surface so that my blowhole could take in the air.

Perhaps for their sakes I should remain on the surface as long as possible. The next moon phase is coming. It is getting dark. It is the time I would normally start to feed. I am hungry.

On the day following his observation that for some strange reason the dolphin was facing downstream of the tide, Peter Pearson was again working at the extension to the bar with his son. From this high vantage point he looked out at the familiar scene of the haven. His hotel had once been one of the many fortresses built when invasion threatened Britain. The view from the old gun emplacements was magnificent. The air was still; it was very peaceful. As he scanned the scene and looked down on the row of mooring buoys that rested on the sea as immobile as mushrooms, he noticed that the black hump of the dolphin's back was resting quietly beside one of the buoys. The hump sank slowly and then rose again. "There is something strange about that dolphin," he said to himself. "I don't know what it is."

He called Simon and both of them looked at the black hump that floated on the sea below.

"Come on, Simon, let's row out to him."

The two men clambered down the long flight of stone steps and launched the inflatable dinghy. The gray hump had sunk again.

"He'll probably swim over to us," said Simon, expecting Donald to leave the buoy. He looked into the water beside the inflatable, anticipating the sight of the familiar gray whale shape that turned white as Donald rolled onto his back and exposed his white belly, at the same time looking up toward the boat with that comical quizzical expression of his. But the gray streak did not appear. Simon looked ahead at the buoy and saw the hump again rise slowly in the water and sink.

"You're right. There is something wrong. He's not coming toward us."

In a few minutes they reached the buoy. As they came alongside the dolphin lifted its tail fluke clear of the water.

"No wonder the poor devil can't swim. He'd got the mooring rope wrapped round his tail."

"Here, Simon, give me a hand."

The dolphin raised its tail out of the water and over the soft inflated wall of the dinghy. The two men unraveled the rope.

"How on earth did he manage to get into that mess?"

"I don't know, but he was intelligent enough to stay still."

"What is even more remarkable is that he showed us what was wrong by lifting his tail over the side of the boat."

In a few minutes the rope was untangled and the dolphin's tail was lowered over the side into the water.

"There you are, old boy. You're free."

Ah, freedom at last. One flip, two flips, three flips of my tail and I am away. How beautiful the water feels sliding past my body again. "I'm free. I'm free!" I shout into the water. But nobody can hear. The two-tailed mammals who rescued me are gone and none of my fellow

dolphins are near. But it does not matter one periwinkle.
I am free once again. And I am free because I have assim-
ilated a new feeling from the two-tailed mammals. They
call it hope.

Hope and despair are two of the vibrations I must report to the mentor. Another instinctive vibration still
beats strongly within me—survival. If I am to survive I
must learn from my experiences, and experience teaches
me that this place is dangerous. It is time I moved on.
After being still for so long, I must move on. Out of the
haven where the life was soft and easy and where the
two-tailed mammals have their machines and buoys and
ropes—out, out into the open sea—where the wind blows,
and the ceiling of my world rises and falls, and where it
rises into peaks as the air rakes through it, splitting it into
a shining white foaming mass.

I don't know where I am going. I care not where I am
going. I am just thankful to be free again.

"Donald's run for freedom took him to Cornwall," I said to
Luciano. I had completed my flight of fantasy, wondering
whether the dolphin's mission might take him yet further
afield.

19 · The Meaning of It All?

In my village of North Ferriby, the beginning of the end of
that amazing summer of 1976 came in the last days of August. The temperature suddenly dropped and the rain lashed
down, bringing with it some of the prematurely parched leaves
from the trees.

Two days before we thought the heatwave would never end,
Barry Cockcroft had telephoned to ask me to go to St. Ives to

get some additional material. He wanted some point-of-view shots (as if seen by the dolphin) to round off the film. He said he would take David Aspinall, the man who was to edit the film, with him, so that he could savor the atmosphere of St. Ives and get some feel of the effect that Donald had on people.

With Ashley, now sixteen, chatting happily beside me, I drove to Manchester Airport to collect Maura before driving on to Cornwall.

At 9:30 A.M. on Wednesday, September 1, Maura and I were again making our way along the now familiar jetty at St. Ives. The *Aquanaut* had been brought around Lands End from Mousehole, and was moored beside the harbor wall. The air was still and the morning was gray. As I looked over the harbor wall I was dismayed to see that the water, previously light-blue and transparent, was a yellowy-brown. The wind and rain of the previous few days had filled the sea with suspended sediment, and I could tell by looking at it that high-quality underwater photography would be impossible. I reported the situation to Barry and Mostafa. But despite our disappointment we enjoyed our reunion with Bob and Hazel, and passed our heavy diving and camera equipment down to them on the *Aquanaut*.

We soon cast off and cruised slowly out of the harbor. The sea was flat calm. Rental buzz boats swarmed over the surface like ants on a discarded sandwich. I had lost my dolphin rattle, the can with stones in it, and Bob suggested I should use his technique instead, blowing into his small foghorn with the bell of the horn submerged.

I jumped overboard and blew. In a few minutes Donald appeared, but by the time we had the camera in the water he had gone off to play with the buzz boats. We tried again but there were so many attractions in the water that we could claim his attention for only a few minutes at a time. We spent over an hour in the water, but at the end had only a few useful feet of film "in the can." So we abandoned the filming session and made our way back to The Sloop for lunch.

When we were at the bar, one of Barry's many fishermen friends told me that he had seen Donald killing a sea bird. I could not believe that Donald would wantonly destroy any form of life, but the fisherman was adamant.

On the basis of our previous filming experience I was hopeful that we would have better luck with our filming in the late afternoon. When, accordingly, we set out again into the bay we saw a young guillemot skittering across the water. The bird was running at full speed and beating its wings as fast as it could, but it had obviously not yet learned to fly. Just to the rear of the mottled wake it left in the sea a triangular dorsal fin humped momentarily out of the water and disappeared again. The reason for the flight of the young guillemot was apparent. Donald was in pursuit. A few seconds later his head appeared and the gullemot was flung into the air, dropped back into the water and disappeared.

So the fisherman was right. Donald was killing birds. I was still finding it hard to believe the evidence of my own eyes when the guillemot surfaced some way from where I had last seen it. I snorkeled over in the direction of the bird, which was floating nervously on the surface. Then it dived of its own volition and I saw it swimming directly underneath me with streams of silver bubbles flowing back from its wingtips. It looked more at home swimming under the sea than trying to fly on top of it. Around us were a host of sand eels that were being caught by terns that were dive-bombing them like kamikazi pilots. However, Donald took no notice of the terns. He was having fun with the poor guillemot that a few seconds later was again skittering flat out across the calm sea with Donald in easy pursuit. The match was as uneven as that between a cat and a mouse. But it did not end in the usual tragedy. Some time later we saw the young guillemot sitting on the sea shaking its feathers and regaining its composure, like a genteel lady in a coffee shop who had been insulted by an insolent waiter. My faith in Donald was restored. He was mischievous to the point of maddening the recipient of his unwanted attentions—but he was not a bird killer. I could also understand how easy it would be for the fisherman to be mistaken.

Maura regained Donald's attention by trailing her yellow fin over the side of the inflatable, and we persuaded him to follow us to a place where there was a good outcrop of kelp on the seabed, as we wanted film of him in this type of terrain. But conditions underwater were so bad for photography that we abandoned the idea. I suggested that we should concentrate on surface shots and attempt, once again, to get Donald interested in a ball.

Maura and I tossed a plastic football between us with Donald playing pig-in-the-middle. First he swam back and forth between us, toward whichever of us had the ball. Then suddenly he managed to get it away from us. In a matter of seconds he had pushed it a hundred yards and was in a frenzy of delight. He threw the ball high in the air and when it landed he leapt over it. His game continued for one or two minutes, nonstop. I started to snorkel toward him and looked up to see the ball quite still on the surface, with Donald, his head down and his tail out of the water, arched over it, and so he appeared to remain for a considerable time. It was a most unusual posture to say the least, and I took it to signify that it was his ball. I continued to swim toward him and the ball. When I was about twenty yards away he accelerated across the surface of the sea and bore down on me like a speedboat under full power. For one panic-stricken fraction of a second I thought he was going to ram me. Then at the very last instant he veered away.

I got his message loud and clear. He was playing with the ball and did not want me to interfere. He was again demonstrating that he was the master of the sea and I was a powerless intruder. Not wishing to suffer the same indignity as the young guillemot, I conceded defeat and withdrew.

The following day the sea was so rough that all hopes of filming and diving were abandoned. With filming out of the question we adjourned to our favorite coffee shop and chatted with the proprietor, Zena Christmas, who had become a friend as well as provider of endless cups of coffee and cakes for the television crew. Zena told me that Donald had become progressively more friendly during the summer. On the day before our visit, he had come right up to the steps outside her window at high water and allowed the children paddling there to stroke him, and even given some of them a gentle tow. I gave her a notebook and her young daughter agreed to keep a day-to-day log of Donald's activities.

I did not know at the time that she would never write a word in the book.

The weather was not improving and we agreed to abandon

further filming and went home. It was not a happy journey. Maura had an important meeting at the sub-aqua club the following evening, and although I stretched my driving ability and the performance of my car to the limit, we were held up by endless traffic jams and she missed her plane at Manchester for the Isle of Man. We were all tense after the long hours of racing against the clock in the heavy holiday traffic. Maura broke down and wept.

We eventually changed her flight to one from Liverpool the following morning. Silent and miserable we drove toward Liverpool and found a suitable hotel in Warrington. It was very late when we left Maura, and Ashley and I set a course for home.

My luck was running out.

On Saturday, September 11, 1976, the longest, hottest, driest summer in living memory eventually smashed like a bottle dropped from great height onto concrete. The sixty-foot-high trees outside my house waved like saplings. As the wind rose to gale force, water sheeted out of the heavens. It was a storm that produced floods of biblical proportions. On the morning after the storm the lawn in front of my house was strewn with branches ripped off the trees. Although the rain had ceased, parts of the countryside which earlier had been parched and cracked were hidden under inches of water.

The reason I can remember the day so well is that it was our wedding anniversary, and to celebrate I took my wife, my mother and my son out for lunch to the Corn Mill at Stamford Bridge. The low-level rose gardens adjacent to the converted water mill were under two feet of water. I looked at the river where I had dived searching for old bottles. The water, instead of cascading down the weir as I had seen it previously, came over the top in a solid unbroken arch of brown. It crashed to the river below and raced forward like a roller coaster at a fairground.

I watched, mesmerized by its strength and brutality. A branch, caught in a whirlpool beside the fall, was beaten back into the depths every time it surfaced. Sometimes the end of the branch rose out of the water like the shining head of a monster in its death throes, only to be smashed back down and pummeled by the river bed. I remember feeling how equally cruel the sea can be.

A few days later I received a clipping from a West Country newspaper which reported that St. Ives had suffered its worst northerly gale for many years. It gave an account of the valiant attempts of the lifeboatmen to save the ships in St. Ives harbor. One of the St. Ives fishing boats I remembered, the *Compass Rose,* had sunk after being holed. Many other vessels were damaged and a number of small boats filled with water and sank at their moorings.

I telephoned Zena Christmas and she told me that Donald had disappeared.

Was his luck also running low, I asked myself? I had for some time been reflecting on the increasing risks to Donald's safety as his presence became known to more and more people, some of whom showed the grossest insensitivity to his vulnerability. The buzz boats in Cornwall were only one such hazard, and there was always the chance that he would encounter an unfriendly fisherman. It almost seemed as if Donald was himself deliberately compounding the risks—from the remoteness of the Isle of Man he had moved to Wales, and then to Cornwall, each move being to a more heavily populated area. In Cornwall, a vacation area attracting visitors from all over the country, he had become the subject of national publicity. And I of course had played a part in this, by helping to make Barry Cockcroft's film. I reasoned that if Donald was to become known, it was important that he become *well* known, that public sympathy and understanding be aroused on his behalf so that he would have friends among human beings who would keep an eye on his wellbeing. I was not altogether certain I had done the right thing.

As if to confirm my fears, a few weeks later my wife returned home from work to warn me that she had sad news— she had heard that Donald was dead.

I was stunned. By a series of the kind of coincidences that already haunted my relationship with the dolphin, it seemed that Wendy had heard the news from one of my ex-scientific colleagues, Dr. Mike Rance. Mike's parents had recently returned from a holiday in St. Ives in Cornwall, where one day after the storm they had found a dead dolphin washed up on the beach. The sight of the dead dolphin was so distressing for

Mike's sister that the entire family had set to and buried it, spontaneously conducting a little funeral ceremony that moved Mike's sister to tears. It was reported in a local paper that the dolphin which had befriended divers and had become the playmate of children in St. Ives was dead. Mike's parents had no idea of my interest in that particular dolphin, but Mike did.

I could not believe that Donald would no longer be part of my life. Were a few photographs and an unfinished film all that remained of him? I felt as empty and bereft as if I had lost a close personal friend.

When the news had sunk in I telephoned Zena Christmas for confirmation of the story. To my surprise she had not heard of the dolphin's death and burial. I thought it strange that in a place so small as St. Ives she would not know of such an occurrence. A tiny ember of hope started to glow in the ashes of my grief.

I telephoned Mike and asked him to repeat the story, to make sure that I had got the facts absolutely right. I asked Mike if there were any identifying marks on the body and roughly how big was the dolphin? He could not answer my question and gave me his father's telephone number.

I hurried through the formalities of self-introduction and put the same questions to the older man. And when he said the animal they had buried was five to six feet long, I could have shouted for the sheer relief of it. When he had answered a few more questions there was not a shadow of doubt in my mind: the dolphin his family had buried with such touching ceremony was not Donald. From his description I deduced it was a common porpoise.

Each time Donald moved, as I realized in retrospect, he appeared to have a reason for doing so. The underwater blasting in Port St. Mary on the Isle of Man must have brought about his emigration to Wales. Then at Dale Haven he suffered the trauma of being caught up for days in a buoy line, and after his remarkable release very reasonably beat a retreat from that area too.

Geoff Bold had no doubts as to why Donald abandoned his next adopted territory, around the Penlee lifeboat station. He said a group of servicemen who were camped nearby drove the dolphin nearly to distraction by buzzing him and trying to run him down in their inflatables, which were fitted with powerful outboard engines. Geoff protested, but the servicemen ignored him.

Then the fearful storm in St. Ives would have indicated to the dolphin that during winter there he could expect little rest. He needed to find a sheltered location where boats were moored. Only in such a situation could he relax sufficiently for part of his brain to sleep. Where, I asked myself, would he find such a place? A look at the map showed several possibilities, depending upon how far Donald was prepared to travel for a winter resting place.

A short time later I heard that a wild dolphin had appeared in Falmouth. And once more, the information involved a curious coincidence. Some neighbors, Jimmy and Isobel Simpson, with whom we enjoyed considerable friendship, had moved to Cornwall—Jimmy was a maritime engineer who spent much of his time on boats in and out of Falmouth, and from his office window he could look out over the harbor. He had observed what some of the local residents had already commented on—some of the small boats were moving back and forth on their moorings for no apparent reason. Donald had found a new home. He had also discovered one dinghy which was particularly to his liking and would spend hours playing round it, just as he had done in Port St. Mary, at Martin's Haven and St. Ives.

As the spring daffodils came into bloom in 1977 Donald was already winning hearts in Falmouth and the inhabitants of St. Ives were mourning their loss. A news item from the West Country announced that a man who had fallen overboard had been helped to the surface and saved from drowning by a dolphin in Falmouth harbor.

History was repeating itself. As it did so the questions that I had asked myself many times before again raised themselves. Do dolphins really have a special mysterious sensitivity to their environment—including some kind of unknown understanding of man himself? Were for instance the two occasions on which Donald had been reported to have saved human lives, evidence of this understanding—and not only understanding, but a peculiar dolphin benevolence? Were they also proofs of dolphin intelligence?

The subject of dolphin intelligence is a very controversial one among scientists. The fact that some of the best brains in the world are seriously debating the issue lends a certain credibility to the hypothesis that dolphins are in some way unique as a species. Professor Teizo Ogawa of the University of Tokyo describes the intelligence of whales and dolphins this way: "In the world of mammals there are two mountain peaks, one is Mount Homo Sapiens, and the other is Mount Cetacea." But the major difficulty in comparing the intelligence of man with that of dolphins is the fact that we have evolved in two such different environments. The so-called "environmental factor," which makes comparisons of intelligence even between different ethnic groups of humans extremely difficult, becomes an almost impenetrable barrier when comparing humans and dolphins.

On February 20, 1976, Sidney J. Holt, who is a Fisheries and Environment advisor to the Food and Health Organization of the United Nations, produced a memorandum. It was addressed to members of the Advisory Committee on Marine Resources Research, and reviewed the published literature by various authorities on Cetaceans. He pointed out that only in recent years have scientists come to abandoning the idea that race or color can determine intelligence among human beings. Was it time, he suggested, that the committee widen its perspective still further and concede that intelligence is not confined to the human race, but recognized in other animals? Should Cetaceans in particular be accorded a special status different from that of other marine animals or indeed any other animals than man?

I do not know how the recipients of that memorandum reacted when they read it, but its existence did indicate that members of the United Nations were at least giving serious consideration to the possibility that there is something special about the whale family.

Whales in the past have been treated simply as a resource to be husbanded and exploited for our benefit. Should we now establish a new category of animals, completely separate from man, but which are accorded intelligence, social structure and a consciousness on a par with that of man? If we can humble ourselves enough to accept this possibility, we may find that we are at the dawn of a new era of understanding of what life is about.

Man through his history has devoted most of his energies to the provision of food, shelter and transport for himself and his family. Today, for instance, motor car assembly workers labor at producing the means of transport and are paid in money, which in turn enables them to buy food produced by farmers and fuel hacked out of the ground by coal miners. Man, in other words, has devoted his intelligence to adapting the environment to suit his needs. The majority have little time to play and enjoy themselves.

Cetaceans, on the other hand, instead of attempting to control their immediate surroundings, have themselves adapted through the process of evolution to harmonize with their environment. A dolphin lives in an ecosystem in which food is abundant. He has no need to construct a shelter. Donald can travel with ease, speed and grace, leaving no trail of toxic exhaust. Unburdened by possessions, he does not know avarice. With the open sea as a common heritage Cetaceans do not suffer the tensions of living in highrise blocks of apartments, the resentments of the squalor in shanty towns, or the burning hatred of suppression in ghettos. Having no money with which one dolphin can exploit another, they have no problem with the corrupting influence of power. No one dolphin has a fortune while another suffers the misery of poverty, and no starving dolphin swims alongside a bloated glutton. Unspurred by greed for land, no dolphin technology has needed to develop mustard gas, flame throwers, defoliants or any of the other hideous instruments of human warfare.

At least until man dropped the atomic bomb of his technology into the undersea world of the Cetaceans, one might almost have said that dolphins lived the ideal socialism that has long been a human ideal but which man himself has so far failed to achieve because of his own greed.

With no technology, no art, no scientific achievements, one might ask, for what purpose did the Cetaceans evolve their large cerebral cortex through the past ten million years?

One answer to that question might be that the dolphins have evolved in order to enjoy and revel in the pleasure of simply being alive, of being dolphins.

And when the day comes that we can communicate intelligently with dolphins, they may introduce us to the concept of survival without aggression, and the true joy of living, which at present eludes us. In that circumstance, what they have to teach us would be infinitely more valuable than anything we could offer them in exchange.

It is in that context that I had evolved my fantasy of Donald's mission to man.

To some readers such a hypothesis may sound outrageous. My reply to them is that it is no more improbable than, for instance, the concept of a divine God, to which, in some form or another, most human cultures subscribe.

And there are many other experiences in life that cannot be explained in terms of the current state of our scientific knowledge—among them a whole series of happenings generally known under the unwieldy title "paranormal phenomena." There are now scientists all over the world who are willing to concede that although we have no explanation for them at present we should not brush them under a carpet of skepticism.

Less open to speculation is the effect Donald has had on the various people he has encountered. Each person who has come into contact with Donald has established a relationship with the dolphin which is as unique as the personality of the man or woman concerned. This is something both observed and experienced—it is real to me, to Maura and many others.

To Maura, for instance, Donald is "a person"—she has often told me so. She loves him like a person, and that love has actually seemed to break down some of the gigantic barriers that inevitably exist between species. Her relationship with Donald is such that she can understand and interpret his moods and behavior in almost the same way as she expects to do with another human being with whom she has lived through good times and bad times.

To Mostafa, Donald is an extension of his extrovert self—excitable and generous. Like Mostafa, Donald is a law unto himself.

To Geoff Bold, the relationship with Donald was almost a kind of therapy. Donald interacted with Geoff in such a way that the lifeboat mechanic's preoccupations were directed away from an area that caused him stress into a realm where contentment could at last be found.

And to me Donald symbolized freedom. Knowing him has caused me to rethink my life and the values I placed on different aspects of it. He caused me to ask myself what was important and what was trivial. But above all else he made me realize that the thing I cherished above all others was freedom. And indirectly, at least as far as my work is concerned, he even gave me that freedom, for had it not been for Donald I would almost certainly have taken another full-time job.

Not for one single moment have I ever regretted my moment of decision when he turned up, literally out of the blue, off the Welsh coast and I decided to attempt to make a new living from freelance work.

Scientists will be skeptical, and rightly so, about this joy that people say they feel when in Donald's presence, until some more tangible evidence can be produced. But until someone invents an instrument to quantify it and measure it—a dolphin happiness meter, perhaps—we shall have to be content with the evidence of our own subjective experience.

To me, Donald has achieved the ultimate. Like King Solomon's lilies of the field, he sows not, neither does he reap. He is free to associate with humans and things human when he wants, and he is also free to take to the wild and wide open sea. And his ability to do this must remain sacrosanct—to me, freedom is a dolphin.

PART TWO

20 · Happy Reunions

Late in the summer of 1977, we waited on the headland, peering out to sea, hoping Donald would return. The air was still, and the sea, flat as a pool of mercury, reflected the pink-tinged clouds like a mirror, adding to the expanse of the evening sky. From afar we saw a large vessel approaching the bay. As it came nearer we were aware that it was being escorted by Donald.

To the dolphin, the mass of displaced water in front of the bows was like a stream which propelled him almost effortlessly. The forward moving water was not all progressing at the same speed. The dolphin used his sensitive skin to detect the subtle differences of flow and adjusted his position accordingly, weaving back and forth in the bow wave. It was an experience he had had many times in the past and one that he never ceased to enjoy.

The act of sensing pleasure generated in the dolphin an enzyme with adrenalin-like properties which accumulated in his system. The effect was like that of hauling a roller-coaster to the top of the run. He could feel the energy building up in his body and with it a sense of expectation at the exhilaration to follow. Suddenly he was over the top. The energy had to be released. With a few powerful sweeps of his tail he accelerated ahead of the boat, headed toward the surface and gave one mighty thrust that sent his 700-pound body arching high out of the water.

The red glow of the sun tinted his body orange as it formed a fleeting silver archway over the flat, rose-hued sea. Within seconds we had our boat launched and were heading out to sea. We were delighted to have Donald with us once again.

"He's here again," shouted our companion, Nick, excitedly, "he's over the stern."

"Right, let's get out the aquaplane. Ashley, you can go in first."

The boy slipped over the side of the now stationary inflatable and swam away from the stern carrying the aquaplane. The boat moved forward, and the line came taut. With his arms outstretched, Ashley held onto the handles and was hauled through the water. Donald responded immediately. Thus Ashley had the double pleasure of the thrill of a tow, plus the even greater thrill of having the dolphin swimming alongside. But it was not only Ashley who appeared to be excited and enjoying the double dose of fun. The dolphin, who had spent many hours playing with the boy in the sea, also seemed to derive much greater pleasure when his human companion became slightly more dolphin-like in his aquatic capabilities. As Ashley dived and surfaced and zigzagged from side to side the dolphin followed his every movement. Sometimes the dolphin would nudge Ashley's arm with his head, as if encouraging him to feats of even greater daring. When he looked at Donald beside him in the water Ashley could see the dolphin nodding his head vigorously up and down in a gesture which seemed to indicate his approval at the way the game was developing. As the game progressed the dolphin became more and more boisterous.

Like two unleashed dogs whose sizes and capabilities were completely unmatched, Ashley and Donald cavorted one with another. Being able to outperform his companion in every way, the dolphin would sometimes rush ahead, swim around the inflatable, divert around one of the several boats moored in the bay and return to his human companion as if his tail was on fire. We never knew what to expect next. Several times the dolphin took Ashley's outstretched arm or an ankle in his mouth and gave it a playful nip. It was rough and tumble, with plenty of physical contact.

After Ashley had climbed back into the boat we continued to tow the aquaplane behind the inflatable because Donald obviously enjoyed it. With no one clinging to it the aquaplane bounced over the surface.

The dolphin's attitude toward the aquaplane now became that of a kitten toward a trailed piece of string. This similarity in behavior was revealed when we discovered that sometimes Donald would disappear and remain hidden from view behind a moored dory. When the inflatable next passed the dory, the dolphin would rush out and leap high in the air. Once we had unraveled his tactics, a new and exhilarating game developed. We would swing our craft with its trailing aquaplane deliberately close to the dory, and Donald would charge across the surface toward us. Then the dolphin would dive. A few seconds later there would be a whoosh as Donald rocketed out of the sea.

We were in a pitch of excitement as Donald performed one leap after another. The dolphin, too, was in a highly excited state. Sometimes, between leaps, he would rub his abdomen vigorously against the keel of the dory, causing it to rock violently.

Time lost all meaning. The sun set. And it was not until the light intensity had diminished and a quiet gray dusk settled on the sea that we became aware of the world again. It was as if for a time we had been alone with the dolphin in a capsule charged with an atmosphere of intense excitement. In our transparent bubble the spirits of three humans had reached the highest peaks in a rare and spontaneous meeting with a truly wild animal—a wild animal who was totally free and capable of bursting the bubble at any time simply by swimming away out of the bay.

As darkness descended and the inflatable nosed its way gently back to the shore, we realized for the first time that we had just participated in what must have been one of the most unique dolphin shows ever performed. During the course of the evening people had come out of their hotels. The harbor wall and every other vantage point was lined with spectators. The crowd had enjoyed an unexpected evening of holiday entertainment and expressed their appreciation in the traditional manner. As we stepped ashore we were greeted with a round of enthusiastic applause.

A diver from Bromley who had recognized me came over. "That was fantastic, 'Oris," he said. "At one time the dolphin came so low over yer 'ead I thought 'e'd knocked yer 'at off."

A boy rushed up to me and said, "Are you training him, mister?"

A little old lady, too shy to speak to me directly, turned to my wife and commented rhetorically, "You will thank your husband for that wonderful display, won't you?"

To which Wendy replied, "It was Donald who put on the display, not my husband."

The pub in the harbor at Coverack was packed to capacity. So we drove out of the fishing village to seek an alternative hostelry. Fortunately, like most other parts of rural Britain, the Lizard is well blessed with such establishments. We found an unpretentious but ideally suitable pub called The Three Tuns in St. Kevern. Carrying glasses of wine and plates bearing generous helpings of hot cheese and potato pie we made our way through the jostling crowd of predominantly young vacationers to a table in the secluded garden. As it was the last night of our visit, the four of us discussed the exciting events of the past few hours and reviewed the entire situation of Donald and ourselves. The wild dolphin had been directly responsible for bringing us all together. Furthermore, Donald had brought about dramatic changes in all our lives.

I had taken up an exciting but precarious living as a freelance speaker, writer, broadcaster and self-styled delphinologist; my wife, Wendy, had resumed her professional career after seventeen years as a housewife; my son, Ashley, had moved from the local comprehensive school to a boarding school in Grimsby—a change which completely altered his attitude to education and gave him a much broader perspective of life; and finally our scientist companion, Dr. Nick Webb, had sold almost everything he possessed to spend the summer closely following a wild dolphin whose strange and eventful odyssey around the British coast had started in 1972 off the Isle of Man, taken him to Wales and had now brought him to one of the most spectacular and beautiful parts of England.

The spectacular session with Donald was a fitting end to a vacation. Three weeks earlier I had left my home in East Yorkshire and headed for Cornwall, knowing that by the normal laws of chance the possibility of locating the dolphin was as remote as winning the lottery. But inside me the fire of hope burned, fueled by the knowledge that several times in the past, despite equally enormous odds, I had made contact with the dolphin and dived with him in the sea. I seemed to be guided to him by a mysterious force which I could not explain. As I drove into Falmouth, I wondered if the magic would still be there after nearly a year.

I parked my car close to the harbor. I had stopped only once on the nearly 400-mile journey and I was stiff when I climbed out of the driving seat. As I did so I felt an immediate compulsion to walk to the harbor wall. I hurried to the jetty and joined a small knot of four or five people who were watching some activity on the water about thirty yards away. I did not speak to them but I knew instinctively why they were there.

I looked toward a small boat tied to a mooring buoy. As I watched, I saw a silver-gray dome rise above the water. It moved slowly forward and sank gently. A dark gray triangular fin quickly followed and moved across the surface of the sea like a sailboat in a gentle breeze, leaving behind a tiny wake on the gray-green water. It slowly circled the moored boat and then the head again humped the surface to take another breath of air.

I stood on the jetty mesmerized by the sight of my dolphin. A feeling of great joy built up inside me. I felt like waving and shouting out to Donald "Hey Donald, I am here, I am here." Had I been on my own I would certainly have done so. However, the possibility that the other people present might have thought I was an escapee from the local lunatic asylum prevented me from openly expressing my delight. Instead I remained silent and let the delight build up inside me like wine rapidly fermenting in a sealed bottle. As I stood there, I found it harder and harder to contain my joy.

I was in a mood of slight amazement, hardly daring to believe I had located Donald so easily. It was uncanny. In some mysterious way I had known where to go and when to be there. True, it was not a totally chance meeting; I had taken advantage of whatever intelligence services I could tap. From phone calls made before leaving home I knew Donald had been seen in the Falmouth area. But sightings showed that he frequently made excursions which took him from St. Ives to Fowey, a distance of about 100 miles. Furthermore, if I had been just 100 yards away from the place where I felt compelled to look I certainly would not have found the dolphin. The first shot I had taken to locate him was right in the bull's-eye.

It was midevening, and despite the exultation I had experienced on seeing Donald again, I was tired and hungry. So I waved Donald a brief and silent farewell, hopeful that I would find him again the following day. I did so however, not knowing that Lady Luck had decided she had already bestowed upon me more than my fair share of good fortune. I set off to locate Nick, who had dived with the dolphin several times. I was anxious to find out how his experiments were progressing.

I found Nick in the Globe Hotel where he had taken a part-time job as a bartender and handyman. Donald was nowhere to be seen when we later walked along the water's edge to look for him.

The following day was squally and there was no sign of Donald in Falmouth. Nick said that the dolphin sometimes made his way into the Helford River so, as the temporary bartender had agreed to meet a couple of his friends at the Ferry Boat Inn, we made our way there and parked on the beach. The car gave us a refuge from the wind and the rain showers and, at the same time, provided a vantage point from which to keep a lookout for Donald.

Nick and his two friends were highly entertaining company and Helston was a delightful place to pass the hours, but at no time did we see the flurry of activity in the river which would have heralded Donald's arrival. When he came onto the scene the dolphin always became a focus of attention. The ferryman welcomed him and trade became very brisk because he took his small vessel to the dolphin, to the delight of those on board. If Donald made one of his spectacular leaps the passengers cheered and felt that they had had their money's worth. When we asked the boatman if he had seen the dolphin that day, he replied that sadly Donald was not in the area. As an afterthought he added: "If you find the dolphin, send him here. I could do with the extra business."

On this occasion the reason for my presence in the West Country was to run an underwater photography course at the Underwater Center at Fort Bovisand near Plymouth. I had to leave the following day without a further sighting of the dolphin. As I drove to my next destination I was heartened by the prospect that I had already made plans to return to Cornwall with my family. Next time I would have more time to spend renewing my acquaintance with Donald.

And so it was that two weeks later, with Wendy and sixteen-year-old Ashley in the car, I headed back toward Cornwall on what was for all of us a holiday with an objective—to find Donald.

About two miles out of Falmouth I spotted Nick walking along the footpath. He climbed into the car and told us that Donald had not been seen for several days. We went to the jetty where I had seen him previously, but there was no sign of our mischievous friend. We decided that the only course of action was to set up a "Hunt the Dolphin" operation. We drove to Helston, which was crowded with vacationers, but drew a blank there. In our investigations we talked to one lady who told us of a local headmaster who had taken out a group of children in kayaks. They had been intercepted by Donald who enjoyed himself and delighted the children by pushing them around, but she could not give us any information on recent sightings of the missing dolphin. At the end of the day we were no nearer our goal.

The next day was also devoted to reconnaissance. We contacted an ex-neighbor who had an office in Falmouth. It had a splendid seagull's eye view of the harbor and Jimmy Simpson regaled us with stories of Donald's antics as seen from his office window. One tale which he found particularly amusing involved a very smart and expensive German cruiser which came in to tie up to a mooring buoy. Apparently, just as a crew member on deck was about to snag the buoy rope with a boat hook, the buoy moved mysteriously away and out of reach. This caused some confusion onboard and the boat had to maneuver in the confined anchorage in order that the bows could be brought alongside the buoy again. As the boat slowly approached the buoy and the boat hook was again lowered to fish for the line, the buoy moved away just out of reach. By this time Jimmy had called the other members of his staff into the office to watch the comedy routine taking place below. The memory of the incident was so clear in Jimmy's mind that he could only recount the story to us between bouts of laughter. For apparently those on board the vessel did not take the incident very kindly and the man at the wheel started to scream at the crewman, chastising him for his blithering incompetence at not being able to carry out a simple task like hooking up the buoy.

Donald kept up the game of buoy pulling for a considerable time, much to the immense embarrassment of the captain and his crew and to the even greater amusement of those assembled in Jimmy's office. Eventually the submerged dolphin allowed the crewman to grab the buoy. However, just at the crucial moment, as the sailor was thankfully pulling it inboard, the dolphin gave the line a final tug. And only by a remarkable display of acrobatic agility did the luckless crew member manage to avoid going overboard to join the dolphin in the water.

When Jimmy had recovered from his own merriment, I was able to explain that the story he had just told us was typical of the dolphin's sense of humor. Donald appeared to take a special delight in disrupting the activities of serious-minded humans. By turning a routine procedure into a farce he demonstrated that there could be a lighter side to every situation. Was he showing us that humans might all enjoy life a little more if they did not take some of their activities quite so seriously? If that was his message, then I was receptive to it. We were on vacation and there was no point in spoiling it by becoming frustrated at not locating the dolphin. So we left the area to visit some other friends of Donald in the little fishing village of Mousehole near Penzance.

Those friends were Geoff and Liz Bold. Geoff, the mechanic of the Penlee lifeboat, had studied Donald when the dolphin adopted the area outside the lifeboat station as one of his resting places. He told us that Donald had been seen in the Lizard region. Having enjoyed a pleasant afternoon in Mousehole we journeyed forth again and went to the tip of the Lizard, the southernmost headland in England. As we stood on that bleak and remote cliff top at sunset, we could see the sea stretching for miles about us in a huge unbroken arc which extended through three-quarters of a circle. On that vast expanse of sea a single dolphin would represent no more than a pin prick. So what chance did we really have of finding the elusive Donald? Was I trusting too much to the magic which had worked in the past?

The following morning, we met up again with Nick and were joined by two other friends who were eager to meet Donald for the first time. With three cars at our disposal we decided to go our separate ways, and to this day I do not know why I chose to go in the opposite direction to the others. I decided to go back to the Lizard. Wendy and Ashley were with me and we eventually descended into Coverack, which I discovered to my delight met my romantic ideal of a secluded Cornish fishing village. At the heart was the tiny harbor. The tide was low and the boats lay heeled over in picturesque confusion. An old cannon, half buried in the sand, provided a post to which their algae-covered mooring chains were attached. I stopped the car and peered down over a stone wall to the harbor below. Some children were running gleefully in and out of the crystal clear water. There was a jumble of small boats directly beneath me. The water was about three feet deep and I noticed a white plastic rowing dinghy. Then to my unbounded joy I saw a dark silver-gray shape cruising slowly around the dinghy.

I don't think I had ever seen Donald looking so immaculate before. The bright sunlight, reflected from the pure yellow sand beneath him, illuminated his underside which seemed to shine as if it were solid silver. The silver underside merged with the dark gray topside which had the appearance of burnished pewter. At that moment, Donald looked like a perfect dolphin, in a perfect setting, on a perfect sunny day.

A few minutes later I had my wetsuit on. Wearing just fins, mask and snorkel, I finned rapidly toward the middle of the bay; during the time it had taken me to change, Donald had moved out of the harbor and I was anxious to make contact quickly just in case he decided to take off on another journey.

As I approached, I called out to him through my snorkel tube but he did not come to greet me. It was time for his midday rest and he was in no mood to play. When I reached him, I stroked him. He closed one eye and rolled over, inviting me to stroke his abdomen. We stayed together for about twenty minutes before I made my way back to shore. I knew from previous experience that Donald was seldom in high spirits in the middle of the day. I left him in peace, knowing that if he was undisturbed when he wanted to be alone, he was less likely to seek a more peaceful place elsewhere.

In the midafternoon I again put on my wetsuit and headed out toward the middle of the bay. This time Donald came to meet me and the two of us enjoyed playing gently with one another. Through my snorkel tube, I spoke to Donald as I would have to an old acquaintance after an absence of several months.

Then Donald moved away from me and I saw that he was making his way toward a lady wearing a bright red bathing cap who was swimming the breaststroke toward the middle of the bay. I finned toward them and when I reached her she was gently stroking the dolphin. Within a few minutes we were talking to one another over the back of the dolphin. She asked me about my past and Donald's past, as if we were conversing across a coffee table. I don't think for one moment that it struck her as at all incongruous that we should hold such a discussion in the middle of a bay across the back of a dolphin while we were treading water. The lady spoke with an air of complete imperturbability. I felt she could have dealt with even the most bizarre situation without "losing her cool." I did not know at the time that my assessment of her would be put to the test the following day.

It happened after I had taken tea with her and her mother in their house overlooking the bay. Nick had joined us and our midmorning tea break came to a natural conclusion when Donald made his appearance in the bay. We all decided it was time to pay him another visit.

The lady in the red bathing cap swam out from the shore, while the rest of us, younger and less hardy individuals, put on our wetsuits to keep out the cold. We even used motorized transport in the form of Nick's inflatable to reach the middle of the bay. Getting suited up and preparing the boat took several minutes. By the time we were ready for our encounter with Donald he was already circling the swimmer and was rubbing himself against her bare legs. I knew immediately from the manner in which the dolphin diverted and approached us at full speed that he was in a playful mood and we could be in for a boisterous romp. I was not disappointed. We took it in turns to leave the boat and go into the water with him. Meanwhile our lady swimmer continued to take her morning exercise, unperturbed by occasional visits from the dolphin and the antics that were going on around her.

When Donald is in one of his most energetic moods he is really awesome. And that morning there seemed to be no end to the energy he was prepared to expend.

When Ashley was in the water, the dolphin leapt high over him several times. The sight of 700 pounds of dolphin plummeting back into the sea at very close quarters left an image in my eyes that stayed for a few seconds after the event was over. It was frighteningly exciting because at the back of my mind lurked the knowledge that, despite all that had gone before, Donald was still a wild animal. In truth we knew very little about him. He could have killed us all in a few seconds if he chose, by ramming us with his beak as he might quickly dispose of a shark. However, I had no sense of aggressive feelings coming from him, and dismissed that possibility completely.

As Ashley climbed back into the inflatable, I slipped overboard to join the dolphin in his world.

Nick Webb and I had had long discussions on dolphin behavior and had debated in detail how we could study the dolphin. All of our proposed experiments depended upon Donald's voluntary cooperation and we both agreed that we would never try to confine the dolphin or attempt to fix instruments, such as radio transmitters, to him. We felt that to do so would disturb the relationship the dolphin had spontaneously established with us. Also, and of the utmost importance, was the fact that it would be contrary to the spirit of freedom which the dolphin somehow symbolized to both of us. When I took to the water that morning all thoughts of testing Donald vanished from my mind. It was as if I was overwhelmed completely by the spirit of the dolphin, who just wanted to play and enjoy himself. If ever any animal radiated a sense of joy and sheer pleasure at being alive and free, then Donald did so in full measure that morning.

When Donald came alongside me and we had exchanged our usual greetings, I cupped my two hands around the front of his dorsal fin. The result could not have been more exciting if I had been mounted on a racehorse and the starting gates suddenly opened. Donald rushed forward at full speed across the surface of the sea with me clinging to him as if my very life depended upon it. The sea swirled up between my arms and foam cascaded over my shoulders. The rushing water partially obscured the vision through my facemask, which was just above the water. So close to the surface, the sensation of speed was heightened. Ahead of me I could see clear water. Occasionally this view was broken by the brief appearance of the shining dome of Donald's head as he took a rapid breath.

I could always have left my metaphorical mount merely by letting go of the dolphin's dorsal fin, but it was Donald who decided when it was time for my joyride to end. He simply rolled to one side. This caused his fin to slip from my grasp.

I once again realized how inadequate were my own swimming capabilities when Donald deliberately broke my connection with him and accelerated away to give the rubber inflatable a playful swipe with his tail.

After one particularly thrilling tow, I climbed back into the

After beaching himself on the shore of the English town of Derbyhaven, Donald is ignominiously scooped into the bucket of a mechanical digger and returned to the freedom of the sea. *John Maddrell—Manx Press Pictures*

Being close to Donald when he leapt out of the water was awesome and exhilarating. *D.J. Nunn*

Donald always took a keen interest in any underwater activity involving mechanical gadgets. *Norman Cole*

Donald's farewell. On January 14, 1978, Donald played gently with 7-year-old Nicola Dunstan. This last recorded contact was photographed by Barry Wills.

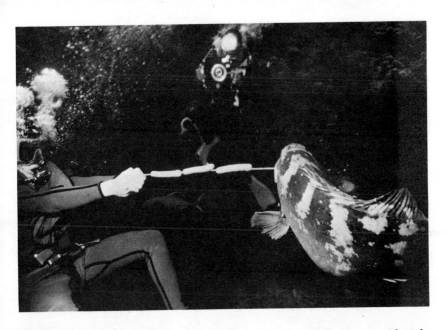

Nassau grouper we nicknamed Lord Marmaduke had a tug-of-war with Ashley when offered some sausages threaded on a string. *Horace Dobbs*

Boy on a dolphin. Opo gives a youngster a ride. *New Zealand Newspapers Ltd.*

Anne Rennie with the dolphins who were later to help her through a very critical stage in her life. *Eastern Province Herald*

An aborted calf lies alongside its dead mother after a *grindadrap* in the Faroe Islands. *Gordon Ridley*

The author, right, confirms, from the International Dolphin Watch chart, that Spurn is a white-sided dolphin. *Ashley Dobbs*

Human–dolphin encounter off Coral Island in the Red Sea. *Horace Dobbs*

Jill and the dolphin both moved gracefully underwater. *Horace Dobbs*

In South Africa's Durban dolphinarium, a dusky dolphin examines me closely, nipping me with his sharp teeth. *Lex Fearnhead*

Many people were shocked when they heard of the massacre of the dolphins by Japanese fishermen. Jenny Crates started her own campaign and quickly won a lot of support using this sticker with a very direct message.

Jan Doak dressed in a wet suit designed to make her shape more like that of a dolphin. She quickly found she could swim almost effortlessly for long periods with her legs together, using a dolphinlike stroke. *Wade Doak*

The ying-yang symbol painted on the hull of the Doak's Wharram catamaran symbolized the link between man and dolphins. *Wade Doak*

inflatable and Donald turned his attention to the lady who was still swimming steadily doing the breaststroke in the middle of the bay. All of a sudden Donald dived and came up underneath her, lifting her bodily out of the water. Like a sack of potatoes tossed onto the back of a horse she was draped helplessly over his neck region. As he accelerated forward she was prevented from slipping off backward by his dorsal fin. With his new passenger on board Donald rushed at full speed toward the inflatable as if to show off his prowess as a racing sea horse. Indeed, I would not have been surprised if he had tried the role of a steeplechaser and attempted to jump right over the inflatable with his astounded jockey still on top.

Instead, he decided it was the flat racing season, and he followed a course which took him past the inflatable with a tremendous flurry of water caused by his trailing load.

It was at this stage that I realized what it is in the British character that separates some of us from other Europeans. Completely unperturbed, but obviously very much surprised at finding herself hurtling across the bay on the back of the dolphin, the lady in the swimsuit and the red bathing cap managed to gasp in her refined, crisp English accent as she raced past the inflatable, "Is this usual behavior?"

She was gone before I could reply. As my answer would have been an emphatic "No," for I had never before seen Donald behave in such a manner toward a swimmer, we hastened after her at full speed to render whatever assistance might be required.

We caught up with her when Donald eventually decided it was time for a different game. I invited her to climb aboard the inflatable just in case the dolphin decided to practice any more of his outrageous behavior. But as it turned out I was much more anxious for her safety than she appeared to be.

When we got back to the lifeboat slipway, I was cold from my immersion in the sea, despite the fact that I was wearing a wetsuit. Our swimmer friend, who did not have the benefit of any such insulation, rubbed herself down, and with her large bath towel wrapped around her, made her way back to her mother's house. As she departed I had nothing but admiration for her stamina and stoicism.

21 · Messing About with Boats

Ever since I first met Donald I have tried to find out as much as I can about him. Piecing together his past proved to be a fascinating exercise which has revealed hidden and surprising stories of his relationship with man. The last sighting I obtained of Donald on the Isle of Man was March 18, 1975. When he turned up out of the blue beside my diving boat in August, 1975 I was overjoyed to reestablish contact with him, but local detective work showed that he had been in the area for some time.

The first recorded sighting was on April 5, 1975, when in snow and windy weather a bottlenosed dolphin was reported to have followed the vessel *Sharan,* a converted lifeboat, from Milford Haven to the island of Skomer. The *Sharan* was towing a small clinker-built wooden dinghy, which appeared to be the main attraction for the dolphin.

Subsequently the dolphin formed a strong association with the dinghy and his behavior was observed and recorded by Pembrokeshire Parks warden Malcolm Cullen. The warden would ferry birdwatchers from the mainland to the islands of Skokholm and Skomer in the converted lifeboat which was kept moored in Martin's Haven during the summer months.

Donald soon discovered that the warden was a sympathetic person whose regular activities could provide a source of amusement. The dolphin would often spend the night in the haven resting beside one of the moored vessels. He would greet the boatman when he came down to the beach early in the morning and often swam alongside the tender when it was sculled out to the *Sharan.* The dolphin liked the sounds of the big boat being prepared for the outward journey. He would swim excitedly around the bay when the visitors scrambled aboard, knowing that he would be undertaking his self-imposed escort duty to see the *Sharan* safely out of the bay. Sometimes he would swim with his beak just a few inches from the steadily revolving propeller. At other times he would ride the bows. Occasionally he would show his pleasure by jumping close to the vessel. If he succeeded in drenching the occupants of the boat with the splash so that they shrieked with surprise, he would swim alongside with his head out of the water to view with a mischievous eye the consternation he had caused on board.

It was during his stay off Martin's Haven that Donald discovered a new trick that could cause a great deal of human confusion if it was done without anybody knowing of his presence. He would swim underneath a moving boat and exhale under the propeller. As the air bubbles rose the blades of the propeller would have nothing to bite into. This absence of water resistance would cause the engine to increase its revolutions dramatically. As soon as the air had passed, the engine would resume its normal speed. The unsuspecting helmsman would wonder what was happening. If he was quick enough he would slam the engine control down to low throttle as soon as the engine raced. When he brought it up to speed again all would be normal and he would puzzle over the reason for the sudden cavitation of the propeller.

If Donald was in a particularly mischievous mood he would play his trick two or three times without surfacing, and when he did eventually make his presence known, some boatmen did not connect the two incidents. Indeed, I suspect there are people still puzzling over the mysterious misbehavior of boat engines when they were in or near Martin's Haven. I am not sure which situations Donald relished more: those in which his activity remained undiscovered and he made the machine appear to be master of the man, or, when his prank was discovered, the fist-waving and general exclamations hurled in his direction. For a dolphin who liked to be noticed at times, he certainly commanded an audience—though they were not demanding an encore.

I had always assumed that following the use of underwater explosives to improve the harbor at Port St. Mary in the Isle of Man Donald traveled straight to Wales. But this simple journey came into question when an article by John Denzler in *Yachting Monthly* was brought to my attention by Ruth Wharram—a woman who had led a very adventurous life as a sailor on board Polynesian-style catamarans and who had a passion for dolphins.

A dolphin had popped up alongside a ketch in the Irish harbor of Dun Laoghaire, near Dublin, and had entertained its crew for six hours with aquatic tricks. There were aspects of the encounter that seemed to indicate that the dolphin was none other than my friend Donald. But was it? I had two files full of Donald sightings. The article was published in 1978 and, during the previous winter, Donald was in Falmouth. So the actual date of John Denzler's meeting with the dolphin was crucial.

With the aid of Ruth Wharram, I wrote to John Denzler. I received a letter by return mail which pinpointed the encounter to the first three weeks in March, 1975. As evidence John enclosed a photocopy of the appropriate page of his passport which bore the date stamps for his entry into Ireland and his next port of call—New York. The latter date (March 23, 1975) fitted exactly with a blank in sightings of Donald between his departure from the Isle of Man and his arrival off the coast of Wales.

However, I felt no self-respecting detective would base a case on a single well-established clue. So I asked for more information.

The size of John Denzler's dolphin was about right.

John offered another reason to support the case for it being Donald. He wrote: ". . . his behavior was another clue to his identity. . . . More than once I felt—Jesus, I know this dude; it must be Donald. The way he ogled the inside of the dinghy was exactly your description of his fooling the Jack Russell terrier."

John Denzler speculated that the dolphin may have followed the ferry into Dun Laoghaire. He suggested that dolphins, like humans, may drown themselves in brain stimulating activity: drugs, music, drink, colors, work, physical exertion to ease off painful memories. Thus Donald may have found relief from the memories of the explosion by immersing himself in the cacophony of sound coming from the large vessel.

He also commented on the Greek roots of the word Delphi ". . . which stands for whole, entire, unfractured, total. When you put this in context with the oracle's motto, 'Know thyself,' I get this curious feeling again of an underlying purpose and meaning, a pattern which is more felt than seen, a connecting web of inter-species' communication and intelligence."

Donald affected the lives of many humans who entered his orbit. The changes he brought about in their thoughts and activities, directly or indirectly, fascinated me. John Denzler, however, appeared to be extra special. I was so intrigued by his experiences and thoughts that I wanted to find out more about the man. When I inquired he answered with typical frankness. "When I met Donald I had quit a career as art director for a first-rate international advertising agency. I was in a personal crisis and felt I couldn't go on anymore with this highly paid daily rubbish. My exit from the ad world had been rather dramatic. I virtually flung my loaded out-tray at the head of the chairman of the board."

He left Switzerland and drifted from Europe to America and back to Ireland where he carved the figurehead, bow scrolls and large sternboard for a ketch. In contrast to the contrived art of the advertising agency, John Denzler found the satisfaction and peace of mind he was searching for. "I was in a trance, frequently forgetting food and rest, during this fantastic period of designing and carving these pieces." It was just after he finished this work that he met Donald.

It was a joy to receive letters from somebody who was obviously a fellow spirit. John Denzler added a new and previously unknown leg to the picture I had built up of Donald's odyssey around Britain.

John Denzler's "Strange Encounter," as he had titled his article, was the only incident I uncovered about Donald's diversion to Ireland on his passage to Wales. However, I collected more stories about Donald's antics when he reached his new destination. One person who regaled me with first-hand accounts was John Davies.

I met John in Liverpool, at the historic Vines Hotel. It was an appropriate venue because the crowded room in which we sat was a place where countless stories had been exchanged over pints of frothy ale. John had long dark hair, a beard, bright eyes and wore a gray turtleneck fisherman's sweater. He had a droll sense of humor, and I had to listen carefully to the tales he had to tell because he spoke quietly. The events he recounted took place near his home town of Haverfordwest in Pembrokeshire.

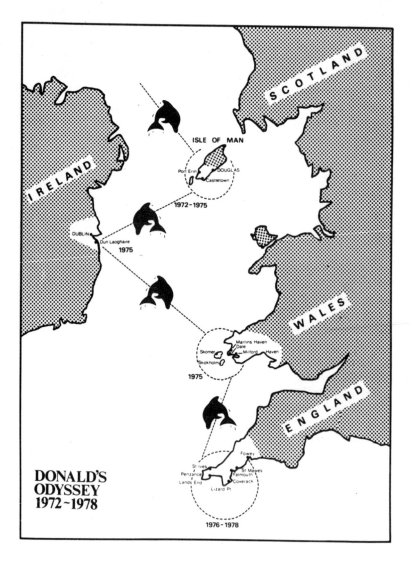

DONALD'S
ODYSSEY
1972~1978

In the summer season of 1975 John owned a rather old 505 dinghy—a boat which he described as having "razor sharp responses, extreme maneuverability and generally sweet handling." One evening when John was sailing back to the Yacht Club on a gentle steady breeze, Donald appeared between the dinghy and the slipway. Shortly afterward the dolphin surfaced astern and then overtook the 505 at tremendous speed. Close to the stern he dived. As he did so John banged the helm down and was almost instantly going back the way he came.

"Donald surfaced quite a long way away, and I think looking a little unsure. So that he wouldn't feel rejected, I set course toward him," continued John.

"What followed was one of the most astonishing things I have ever seen."

Donald started his display by charging under the boat from the starboard side. John looked over the port side expecting to see the dolphin surface. But the dolphin did not appear. Instead he heard a splashing on the starboard side.

"Donald had doubled back under us and come up to starboard, obviously to say 'I can do a U turn too!'"

John continued his story excitedly. "After that for openers, he swam around us. Zigzagged under us. Dived. Leaped. Well we did our best—and a five-oh-five is good—but for speed, maneuverability, grace and flamboyance he had us totally outclassed."

Like many other people John Davies attributed human characteristics to Donald and he described him as "A lovely fellow. Very pro-human, totally trustworthy, sometimes boisterous and sometimes subtle."

It even occurred to John that Donald might be a dolphin ambassador to humanity.

Donald's "I come in peace" approach, together with his intelligence and the lengths to which he would go to make people feel good, were, according to John, all factors which led him to think of the dolphin as a very special fellow inhabitant of our planet.

John Davies missed Donald when the dolphin set off for Cornwall. Before his departure, however, Donald left another story for the dinghy sailors of Dale to tell incredulous visitors to the Yacht Club who had not had the benefit (or misfortune—depending upon your point of view) of a first-hand encounter with the mischief-making dolphin.

It happened on a summer's evening when the club's GP14 dinghies were out on a points race. There was very little wind and the boats drifted lazily round the course, slowly sorting themselves into a line. The slowest helmsman started to lose interest in the race and decided simply to enjoy a lazy gentle cruise.

Sitting in the stern he let his hand trail in the water. All of a sudden he was surprised to feel something smooth touch his fingers. In startled surprise he pulled his hand out of the sea and looked down. To his amazement there was Donald's head like a gray shiny dome beside his boat.

"Oh it's you, Donald," he said. "What are you doing here?"

Donald raised his head out of the water and looked inside the dinghy.

The one-sided conversation with the dolphin continued with a rhetorical question.

"You OK then? I'm supposed to be racing. But there doesn't seem to be much point with so little wind, does there?"

At this point Donald nodded his head and with a mischievous glint in his eye disappeared beneath the surface.

"Well, you didn't stay long, did you?" the man continued, addressing his remark over the now empty water.

He sat back and continued to trail his hand in the sea. Then suddenly his dinghy started to gather speed. The helmsman immediately became alert and steered his boat past his nearest rival.

"This race could become interesting after all," he said to himself, delighted with the turn of events.

He smiled to himself as he overtook his next rival who watched him pass with an expression of disbelief. With his competitive edge sharpened, the helmsman concentrated on making those fine adjustments that enable one person, a superior person, to sail a boat that much faster than the crew in another identical dinghy. With a growing feeling that he might gain some useful points, he urged his craft forward toward the next dinghy that would fall prey to his superior speed and sail.

Then gradually he lost way. He pulled at the sheet and pushed the tiller across but the dinghy would not respond. He was practically becalmed again. As he considered what to do next, there was a distinct sharp puff beside the boat and Donald's head broke surface. In the excitement of his newly acquired racing prowess the sailor had forgotten the dolphin.

"Phew, Donald, you made me jump," he exclaimed as Donald once again submerged.

The helmsman watched the indistinct gray torpedo shape move through the green-brown water. It circled the boat just below the surface and came up to the stern. Then the sailor felt his boat surge forward once again. Donald was actually pushing the dinghy along.

"Well I'm damned," blurted out the sailor as he suddenly became aware of the source of his newly acquired superiority. "Keep it up, Donald."

That night when the points for the race were awarded there was a great deal of controversy in the clubhouse. A member claimed that Donald had gripped the rudder of one dinghy in his teeth and actually pulled the boat backward. However, it was Donald's effort to give one competitor an advantage by pushing him forward that was most hotly debated.

An ancient copy of rules on dinghy racing was consulted. This particular set of rules were drawn up in the heyday of the British Empire when England's navy ruled the waves of the world. They were devised to help maintain standards of racing behavior in such farflung outposts as the River Nile. Thus reference was found about what to do if crocodiles interfered in a race, but absolutely nothing could be found to deal with the participation of a dolphin.

The following argument ensued.

"I can use the wind to help me win the race can't I?"

"Yes, of course you can," came the reply.

"The presence of the wind is an act of God isn't it?"

"Well yes, I suppose it is."

"So you will agree that I can use an act of God to help me win," said the beneficiary of Donald's help, pressing his next point. "Well, I maintain that the presence of the dolphin was also an act of God."

Before the objector could interrupt he launched forth again. "So if I can use the wind I can also use the dolphin. That settles it."

On the basis of this argument the judge's decision was upheld.

The person who thought he had been deprived of points by the antics of the dolphin was later heard holding forth to his cronies in the bar about the serious nature of dinghy racing and how intolerable it was that such interference should be permitted to take place.

If Donald could have heard what ructions he caused, I wonder if he would have pondered the strange character of those men who cannot accept the humorous side of a situation—even when they are playing. If he had done so, I am sure he would have chortled to himself and perhaps blown a raspberry into the air before sinking back into the sea.

When Donald eventually departed from Wales he spent several months in the Percuil River near the picturesque Cornish town of St. Mawes.

He seemed to prefer the area at the mouth of the river and was often seen there by the fishermen early in the morning and late in the day. Donald, boisterous as ever, would swim excitedly round the dinghies when the fishermen rowed out to their fishing boats on the moorings. Most fishermen are prepared to face quite rough weather in order to wrest a living from the seas. However, some of them found Donald's antics too hazardous to risk the journey from the shore to the moorings in their small dinghies for fear of being tipped into the river. They resorted to using much heavier rowboats for the trip.

One crew member came close to a ducking when he was making his way out to the moorings in a fast dory. Donald came out of the water and onto the bows, nearly capsizing the plastic boat. This caused the fisherman, who could not swim, lightheartedly to wear a lifejacket on the journeys to and from the big boat.

One person who found the antics of the new arrival very entertaining was Martyn Melhuish. Martyn had a dog called

Bunter who often accompanied his master on fishing trips. The fisherman was convinced that his dog could smell Donald's breath at long range because Bunter would bark with excitement if the dolphin was in the river. As Martyn's boat left the shore Donald would charge over, sometimes from hundreds of yards away. When the dolphin came in close to the dinghy, he would stand on his tail, raise his head over the side of the boat and squeak at Bunter. This excited the dog and the dolphin so much that both the fisherman and his pet nearly ended up in the water. At times the dolphin became so boisterous that Martyn and Bunter were both drenched.

Of all the encounters Martyn Melhuish had with the mischievous Donald, the most amazing occurred when the fisherman returned early to base with scallop dredges that needed repair. The crew lowered the dredges, a pair of two-meter Frenchmen on a tow bar, into the water to turn them around as there was insufficient room to do so on deck. Donald arrived on the scene and watched fascinated as the crew attempted to manipulate the dredges with a boat hook. The men gesticulated at the dolphin and indicated that they would like his help. After a slight delay Donald put his beak on the tow bars and spun them around as requested. After he had done so, Donald came alongside squeaking with obvious delight. Martyn was not sure if the dolphin really understood what he had been asked, but the fisherman liked to believe he did.

However, it was with divers that Donald established his closest contacts. One was a friend of mine, Dr. Barry Wills, who lived in Falmouth and was an active member of the local branch of the British Sub-Aqua Club. Barry became very fond of the dolphin. When Donald started to escort the diving boat regularly on short expeditions out of Falmouth, Barry and his fellow divers were delighted, and they came to expect the dolphin as part of a regular diving routine. However, not everyone was aware of Donald's newfound alliance with the diving boat *Pisces*. When a novice diver unexpectedly became the focus of Donald's attention the results were startling, as Barry told me with some relish.

The incident happened on Sunday, November 27, 1977.

Barry was supervising a party of nine trainee snorkel and aqua-lung divers off the rocks of Pendennis Point, Falmouth. Two of the aqualung divers were about 200 yards from the point, under the steep rocks near Castle Beach, when they lost contact with one another. One diver surfaced, but the other broke all the rules and stayed submerged—engrossed in collecting shells from the sandy bottom. It was then that Kevin Martin, a student from the Cambourne School of Mines, felt something gently pushing on his aqualung cylinder. Turning around he was confronted with a huge dark body and an eye about six inches from his mask. Having no previous knowledge of the dolphin his immediate reaction was—shark.

From a vantage point on the rocks Barry and his companions had observed Donald moving from Gylingvase Beach, about a mile away, toward the divers and had seen the dolphin submerge near Kevin's bubbles. A few moments later the group on the rocks burst out laughing when they saw Kevin hit the surface with both hands waving in the air. The solitary diver then made his way frantically towards the nearby rocks. On reaching them he attempted to claw his way out of the water on his hands and knees with the dolphin seemingly trying to aid his futile efforts by gently prodding him from behind.

It is not hard to imagine the novice diver's intense relief when Barry was able to convey to him that the "shark" was only a playful dolphin. All of the trainee divers promptly joined the dolphin and frolicked with him. To all of them it was a memorable experience.

Donald enjoyed the company of divers, and he quickly learned which boats had divers on board. He could tell one vessel from another by their different engine sounds.

After I had given a lecture at a diving club near Halifax, one of the audience stood up and told the assembled company, very seriously, that his dive with Donald the dolphin had been the greatest experience of his life. When I requested his name and asked if I could quote his comment he pondered deeply, weighing up the consequences of committing himself so unequivocally.

"Yes, you can quote me as saying it was the greatest experience in my life," he said. Then, after a further pause he added: "Except for my wedding night."

This comment drew a burst of raucous laughter from his audience. I could tell from his expression, however, that he had not intended his reply as a joke.

By the end of 1977 Donald had become a nationally known dolphin. This had the advantage for me that I was able to develop a network of contacts who kept me updated on his movements. As the winter closed in, sightings became fewer because of the general decrease in aquatic activities. However, some of the more stalwart divers continued to pursue their recreation in the sea.

On February 11, 1978, I had a phone call from Barry Wills informing me of another sighting of Donald. Shortly afterward, one of the worst winter storms on record hit the West Country. Many roads were snowed in and the winds reached a terrifying force. When they abated and the Falmouth divers resumed diving, they were sadly disappointed that their regular escort did not join them.

Had Donald moved on again, I wondered; and if so, where? I expected news of the dolphin's whereabouts to come through on my countrywide grapevine of diving contacts. But I heard nothing. My efforts to track him down were redoubled following an event which took place in London on June 6, 1978.

One of my contributions to Underwater Conservation Year had been to organize a dolphin competition for the children of Cornwall. The Duke of Cornwall, H.R.H. Prince Charles, agreed to judge the finals and the pictures were put on display inside Buckingham Palace.

The pictures were very diverse. They ranged from a small pencil drawing of a cheeky smiling dolphin, through a very sensitive montage of a mother dolphin with her baby, to a large painting of a sea covered with multicolored dolphins all performing incredible acrobatics. In addition there were pictures of dolphins leaping in front of rows of round-faced children with hair like twigs and trainers wearing bright red pullovers carrying buckets clearly marked FISH.

When the prince asked about Donald's present whereabouts, I told him that the last sighting had been four months earlier in Falmouth. Even so, he told me he would like to dive with Donald in the sea if he possibly could. As he left the room, he issued instructions for his equerry to attempt to fit a rendezvous and dive with Donald into his crowded schedule.

Shortly after my visit to Buckingham Palace I traveled to Cornwall where I had agreed to show my film of Donald at the winning schools. When I walked into the tiny old-fashioned school in the town of Sennen, I was greeted by the headmaster who was teaching a class. Later, when I showed my film, which was also shown in Buckingham Palace, I could not help contrasting the crowded Cornish classroom with the spacious splendor of the setting in London. Yet I found both occasions equally rewarding.

After my show in the school I stayed the night at a house nearby with a Bed & Breakfast sign outside. The garage, a wooden and corrugated iron structure, was heeled over at a crazy angle. It looked as if it had been picked up and dropped back down on the ground. When I discussed the subject with my overnight landlady she described the terrifying storm that had indeed literally picked up her garage and moved it from its original position. She said it was the most frightening night she had ever lived through.

The date of the storm coincided exactly with the date of Donald's disappearance from Falmouth.

Earlier detective work had shown that Donald had deserted his adopted port of St. Ives in 1976 when gale force winds swept in from the northwest and caused havoc in the harbor. On that occasion he moved round Land's End into the relatively sheltered waters of Carrick Roads, Falmouth. Clearly, the dolphin did not like to stay in places where he could not find quiet water in which to rest. But with a southeasterly gale that raged for days, where would he go? I consulted my map of the area. The north coast yielded a lee shore but the shoreline did not have the secluded creeks that occur naturally on the south coast of Cornwall.

I decided to visit the most likely places to make inquiries and followed a route along the northern shore. The stone walls lining the road were tufted with a profusion of foxgloves, honeysuckle and other wild flowers. The rounded hillsides were quilted with a new growth of bright green ferns. In the brilliant June sunshine, the scene offered such tranquility and beauty it was hard to imagine how fierce the winds could be in this last finger of England. However, the absence of any trees, and the way in which the large roadside shrubs appeared to have had their tops trimmed, testified to the severity and direction of the winter winds which could scythe off any twig or branch that dared to project itself too high toward the heavens.

I visited all of the places where I thought Donald might have sought shelter from the storm. But nobody had seen the missing dolphin. I telephoned coastguards and many of my contacts who had previously helped me track my nomadic friend, but to no avail. After numerous and intensive inquiries I felt sure that if Donald had still been in Cornish waters someone would have seen him and I would have learned about it.

Had Donald moved much further afield? I launched a national appeal for information and followed up many clues and dolphin sightings which indicated that he might have journeyed to places as far apart as Kinsale in Ireland and Bayona in Spain. But all the trails eventually led to the same end—no Donald.

About a year after the last sighting of Donald I returned to Falmouth and continued my inquiries about the missing dolphin. Most of the people I talked to told me to go and look in Falmouth Bay. When I did so I understood why Falmouth had been dubbed "Cornwall's mackerel Klondyke." The stink of fish meal pervaded the air. It seemed that the horizon no longer consisted of the subtle junction of sea and sky. It was castellated with the silhouettes of fishing boats, foreign factory ships and freezer vessels. I had never before seen such a concentration of large vessels dedicated to the extraction and processing of fish.

The purse-seine techniques used for catching Cornish mackerel were similar to those adopted by the tuna fishermen. With such an enormous number of nets scooping fish from the sea, was it conceivable that Donald had fallen prey to the same perils that had beset so many of the dolphins in the tuna-fished waters of the Pacific? In the scramble for riches would a fisherman who found a dead dolphin amongst the mackerel in his net do any more than curse and toss the body back into the sea? Indeed, what more could he do?

Many of the people I spoke to were very pessimistic about

the fate of Donald. The vessels in Falmouth Bay were from many nations including Russia. One woman pointed out to me that since the Russians were prepared to hunt for big whales they would not object to picking up a small one. "I reckon he's in a can now," she said dismally. Several other people expressed the same opinion.

I could easily envisage it happening. Donald, with his insatiable curiosity for mechanical things, would have been fascinated by the noise and action of men shooting nets. I remembered that in 1976 I had observed him in St. Ives Bay swimming excitedly round a small trawl net when it was hauled to the surface. Despite the anxiety expressed by the fisherman at the time I felt sure the dolphin would not become trapped because he could scan the entire net with his sonar system and avoid getting into a dangerous situation. This was not true with a very large purse-seine net of the type used off Falmouth, which was very long and deployed to completely encircle large shoals of mackerel. Once inside, there would be no way out for the dolphin when the bottom of the net had been pursed. And Donald who had defied death a dozen times would finally succumb, killed like the proverbial cat, by his own curiosity.

Another view was put to me by a fisherman who liked my fantasy idea that Donald had been sent out from a school of dolphins especially to make contact with man in order that the Cetaceans could come to terms with a new force that threatened to destroy them.

"He came, he completed his mission and now he's gone," he said. "He's probably swimming around happily in the open sea with a wife and Donald Junior in tow," he continued.

Being both a romantic and an optimist I prefer to believe that something like that really did happen. I must admit, however, that in my darker hours the other possibility looms like a black cloud across a sunset.

22 · Sandy

To my knowledge Donald was the only wild dolphin in the world to associate freely with man for a period of six years (1972–1978). When I told people about his behavior, they frequently asked, "How typical is Donald?"

Scientists do not like conclusions drawn from observations on a single aberrant animal, so I needed to support my experiments with investigations on other dolphins. The obvious place to conduct such studies was in a dolphinarium with captive dolphins. I was convinced, however, that confinement itself would so change their behavior that comparisons would be of little value. What I needed was another dolphin, free in the sea, who voluntarily associated with humans.

And I heard of just such a dolphin three days after Christmas, 1977.

The news came in the form of a phone call from Ireland. The woman who telephoned me introduced herself as Sheila Chamberlain. She told me that she and her family had recently returned from San Salvador in the Bahamas where they had a fantastic experience diving with a wild friendly dolphin. She told me that the local dive leader swam with the dolphin regularly when he escorted parties to a place called Sandy Point. She informed me that the dolphin delighted in the company of divers, but that Sandy, as he was called, seemed to have a particularly strong affinity with Chris McLoughlin.

I subsequently received some color prints from Sheila showing the dolphin with her daughter on the surface of the sea. One of the pictures showed two young swimmers wearing fins, masks and snorkels, floating on the surface, touching the dolphin with their hands. Only part of the back and the dorsal fin of the dolphin were visible. Although it was obvious that the San Salvador dolphin was considerably smaller than Donald, I could see no other features clearly. Thus its shape, true size, facial features and hence its species remained a mystery.

209

Some of my questions were answered in a letter from Chris. It arrived when Britain was in the grip of winter, on the very day that the storm which drove Donald out of Falmouth was loosing its full fury on Cornwall. Chris enclosed some color transparencies taken underwater and they were among the best undersea pictures of dolphins I had ever seen. The sea had a blue color which I knew from personal experience is only associated with water of extreme clarity. The divers with the dolphin were wearing no protective clothing, which implied that the water was very warm, and the lighting indicated that the sun was shining very brightly on a flat calm surface.

Chris informed me that Sandy was about six feet long and weighed between 150 and 200 pounds. From his overt sexual behavior he was obviously a male and had been associating with divers from the Riding Rock Inn for about eighteen months. Thus the dolphin would encounter twenty-five to forty different divers a week in addition to the diving guides who regularly escorted their parties to Sandy Point.

From the pictures I was able to see that Sandy enjoyed the presence of divers and his pleasure in their company was expressed in his eyes. Furthermore the shape of his body postures as he frolicked among them seemed to convey the sense of playfulness which I knew so well from Donald. I could understand why he had been called a spotted dolphin, because the lower regions were spotted like a poorly marked dalmation dog. His very long beak, characteristic of spinner dolphins, gave his jaw line an exaggerated smile.

In his letter Chris admitted to being "a dolphin addict of course" and went on to say that "I've never seen anyone meet him without coming away with a very positive feeling inside (vibrations)." At the end of the letter Chris offered accommodation and free diving if I could find the time and the air fare.

I immediately got in touch with my friend Bruce Lyons, who organized the travel arrangements for my diving expeditions. Bruce made contact with the Bahamas Tourist Office and I agreed to shoot a 16-mm film of Sandy for them. However, though negotiations went quickly and smoothly, I had commitments and it was not until late March that I took off for the

Bahamas. A phone call to Chris indicated that Sandy was being seen less frequently off Sandy Point and this lengthened the odds of a meeting with the wild dolphin. Nonetheless, when I set off with my seventeen-year-old son Ashley, who was to accompany me as my assistant underwater cameraman, we were both in very good spirits at the prospect of the unknown adventures ahead of us.

When we arrived in San Salvador Chris explained that Sandy had not been seen lately, but he was hopeful that the dolphin would join us when we went to Sandy Point. He also pointed out that since all three diving boats were committed to their routine dive schedule, he had decided to put Ashley and myself on his boat, which would ferry a group of doctors who were attending a one-week course on diving medicine to the various dive sites around the island.

When we assembled at the jetty the following morning, we discovered just how efficiently the dive and lecture schedules for our group of doctors were organized. Within ten minutes of leaving their lecture the entire group were settled on the boat and we were heading out of the marina toward the open sea. The sun was shining from a sky of unbroken blue on an unruffled sea to match.

Our first dive was to The Cathedrals, which consisted of a series of spectacular archways on the edge of the "drop-off"— the region where the sea suddenly plummets to enormous depths. It was a superb diving site and it provided us with an opportunity to try out our new movie camera and housing before the hoped-for meeting with the dolphin.

The afternoon dive was to a location called Grouper Gully. With cameras in hand, Ashley and I dropped into the clear blue sea to meet the fish after which the site had been named.

That evening in our trailer Ashley and I reviewed the situation. The day of trial dives had revealed faults in our underwater cameras that we managed to correct. Tomorrow was to be the big day—our first visit to Sandy Point where we hoped to encounter Sandy the dolphin.

It was thus with high hopes that we set out the following morning with two powerful engines on the stern of our diving boat pushing it ahead at a fine speed. I was told that if Sandy

211

was in the area he would join the dive boat on its journey to Sandy Point. As every diver on board had heard of the dolphin and was eager to meet him, all eyes were set to scan the ocean for his arrival. Ashley and I looked first ahead to see if we could detect the joyous rise of the dorsal fin as the dolphin came up to ride the bow wave, and then aft to see if Sandy was enjoying the sensation of having water thrust over his body from the propellers at the stern. But we were disappointed. The dolphin did not appear, and eventually we anchored over the appointed diving site at Sandy Point without the company of Sandy.

Previous diving experience had taught me that the most spectacular underwater scenery is often found around a headland. It is also the place where the biggest fish normally congregate. Although the dolphin had not joined us, I anticipated we would be in for a good dive and I was not disappointed.

The water was exceptionally clear, with the underwater visibility in the region of 200 feet. From the surface we could clearly see the bottom immediately beneath us, about fifty feet down. We were just on the edge of a reef table that dropped almost vertically to about 140 feet. As we glided down, we could see the underwater vista stretching away from us with unbelievable clarity before it eventually disappeared into a pale blue curtain.

I was hoping that the dolphin would suddenly appear to join in the fun with the divers, so in addition to enjoying the presence of the multitudinous fish, I took frequent looks into the far distance to see if he was homing in on us. It was on one such scan that I saw a large shape coming from far down the reef. It approached steadily and was making a course in a straight line directly for us. It was a fish called a grouper. When it arrived we were in the company of an Australian doctor who was distributing the last pieces of soggy bread from his food bag. The grouper snapped them up and we started to film. The fish was the largest specimen of a Nassau grouper I had seen.

The grouper stayed with us for the rest of the dive. It was not until we started to head back onto the reef table that the fish suddenly veered off. As it disappeared into the azure haze

I envisaged it returning to its own special cave deep on the reef.

That evening all the divers assembled on the patio outside the hotel and I showed the film *Ride a Wild Dolphin* which I had made with Yorkshire Television about Donald. Everyone was most interested to see the wild bottlenose dolphin on film and Chris commented how much larger he was than Sandy.

Right up until our last day we were hopeful that Sandy would reappear, but he never did. In fact he was never again seen off San Salvador. What became of him remains a mystery.

Ashley and I consoled ourselves by making a film about a grouper instead of a dolphin. We nicknamed our new star Lord Marmaduke. We soon discovered he would perform extraordinary antics, such as having a tug-of-war, in his efforts to secure food. The fish's behavior contrasted with that of Donald, who would never accept any food, no matter what tasty morsels we offered him.

Although I failed to make personal contact with Sandy I was eager to pursue my investigation of the connection between humans and dolphins. I therefore set out to collect what information I could on the effect Sandy had on the people he met in the sea. One person who was most helpful in this respect was a woman who set up a permanent diving facility called Pat's Place on San Salvador shortly after we left.

Pat wrote to me from her new home and here is her own account of her contact with Sandy, which she called "a moving spiritual experience that is difficult to narrate objectively."

We first met Sandy in December of 1976 when he would appear, leading the boat at Sandy Point. When I went over the side, camera in hand, he would disappear. When the boat began moving again, he would reappear.

It was in February/March 1977 that Sandy began to approach snorkelers and divers, and every time I saw him from there on his progression in contact with humans was remarkable. I fully expected to see him driving the boat!

In July of '77 I took Chris Adair to San Sal to meet and photograph Sandy. Sandy adored Chris because he could free dive to 110 feet. He preferred skin divers—perhaps he knew that they weren't cheating with tanks! One day

Chris Adair was free diving with Sandy and the dolphin took him deeper than usual. He pointed with his beak to the reef directly below him. There was the cross that Chris had been wearing around his neck—the chain had broken and we surmised that Sandy had attempted to catch the cross in the water as it fell, because it was indented with several of his teeth marks.

While Chris was there in July 1977, so was Paul Tzimoulis. He asked us to keep Sandy around after our photography so that his photo class could take some pictures. When they arrived (in many clouds of sand) Sandy greeted them all, but suddenly disappeared. Chris McLoughlin and Chris Adair went to find him, and discovered him trying to support a woman in Paul's class who was in trouble on the surface. She had to be towed in by Chris McLoughlin.

On one occasion in September of '77 I went into the water to see Sandy. He did his usual pulling of hair, rubbing his body up against mine (a very horny male!) and giving me a ride. Before long I realized that he had very cleverly drawn me close to a mile from the boat. When I surfaced, the boat was a tiny speck on the horizon. It was a long swim back with no help from my beloved friend who always towed me away from the boat—never toward it.

Very often, after someone left the water, Sandy would "pout" and go to no one for a while.

The most remarkable characteristic of Sandy, to my mind, was his ability to understand and "sense" each person's water ability and personality. He never played rough with those who couldn't handle it. He definitely preferred certain people over others. One could predict beforehand whom he would prefer if one was aware of personality traits. Warm, loving people enjoyed Sandy the most. The feeling was always mutual. The other outstanding characteristic was his fantastic sense of humor. Hair pulling, mask grabbing, a gentle crack on the head with his beak. Deliberately making it difficult to take pictures.

When I read Pat's letter for the first time I felt that if she substituted the name Donald for Sandy she could have been referring to my bottlenose friend instead of her spotted companion. For instance, Donald preferred to play with Ashley and me when we were not wearing our aqualungs and would free dive with him.

There was just one small area where the two dolphins appeared to differ. Donald would tow us back to the boat as well as away from it. There were certainly occasions when Donald did not want us to leave the water.

My most cherished memory of Donald, though, was his sense of humor. I was delighted to hear that Sandy had a similar disposition. Perhaps it is this characteristic above all others which differentiates man's relationship with the dolphin from that with all other animals. Many domestic and wild animals have a sense of fun, which is often infectious, but a sense of humor is normally regarded as an exclusively human trait. As the brains of man and dolphin are both equipped with comparable frontal lobes, it is conceivable that the positive intellectual interplay which we call humor can take place between the two species.

This leads to the interesting speculation that the need for intellectual interplay is one of the prime motivating forces that leads solitary wild dolphins to seek and maintain human contact. Thus if dolphins enjoy the pleasure associated with a developed sense of humor when they are in a social group of their own kind, what happens when they become isolated? Regardless of the reason for their isolation, they will certainly not find the mental satisfaction they are seeking with their fellow occupants of the marine environment—the fish. So was it Sandy's innate sense of humor that caused him to seek out Pat Selby? She also had sensitivity, which is the other, perhaps even more important prerequisite for the build-up of a human–dolphin relationship.

23 · Horace in New Zealand

Less than a year after my visit with Ashley to the Bahamas to find the elusive Sandy, I heard of another solitary dolphin seeking the company of man. The news came from a part of the world that was even farther away—New Zealand.

215

In December 1978 the following headline appeared in the *New Zealand Herald:* HORACE THE DOLPHIN STEALS THE SHOW. Spectacular shows were being put on by a wild bottlenose dolphin who had chosen to entertain the public, free of charge, 100 yards off Westshore beach just outside the Napier dolphinarium where visitors paid to see captive dolphins leaping.

> Night after night Horace has been turning on his act of aerial flips and great leaps out of the water as he frolics with divers and boats that have become his playmates.

Horace delighted in the company of swimmers and occasionally allowed them to touch him. He did not permit more than glancing contact and when a diver tried to grab his dorsal fin, the dolphin slapped the surface of the water with his tail in an obvious sign of displeasure. He would go racing across to people who tapped the sides of their boats, and responded with extra leaps when onlookers cheered excitedly. A television crew turned up to film Horace's antics and many of the public who saw the footage were surprised to learn that dolphins do not need trainers to make them perform. "It all comes naturally," was the newspaper's comment.

Horace the dolphin seemed to have a mischievous sense of humor. He discovered that nudging the rudder of a sailing dinghy underway produced a response that was highly amusing to any onlookers, although the joke was not always shared by those on board. His sense of humor found even greater expression when the dolphin discovered that he could produce havoc by pushing up the centerboards of small dinghies under sail. The more the crews protested the more Horace appeared to enjoy the mischief. One person who was particularly annoyed by the dolphin's practical jokes was a local Anglican bishop. He was sailing his Sunburst dinghy when Horace pushed the centerboard up with such force that he split it. Nonetheless, most of those on whom Horace focused his attention took the wild dolphin's tricks in good part and enjoyed the experience of having the company of such an unusual and playful companion.

One who was more than delighted at the new arrival close to

his home in Taradale was Frank Robson, a man who had devoted much of his later life to the study of dolphins and their close relatives the large whales. Before Horace's arrival, Frank and I had become long-distance friends with the letters we exchanged halfway around the world. We quickly established that we had common attitudes to dolphins. Frank was fascinated by the marine mammals that he regularly encountered when he took his fishing boat to sea. He had a passion to learn about them and help what he considered to be the most beautiful creatures on earth—the dolphins and whales.

From his letters and other reports I had read, I deduced that Frank was an outspoken man who was not slow to aim criticism at those in authority when he felt that either through ignorance or greed they were causing harm or death to his beloved dolphins. When Horace made his first appearance off Napier, Frank was concerned for the wellbeing of the newly arrived dolphin. Frank therefore set about establishing a special personal relationship with the marine mammal. Knowing of my own friendship with Donald, Frank gave the dolphin the name Horace. When I heard, I could not have been more flattered. I know of no one else who has had the honor of having a dolphin named after him.

At first Horace tended to stay well offshore and each day Frank went out to find the dolphin in order to build up their relationship. Frank discovered that the dolphin sometimes carried objects around in his mouth. So the fisherman kept in his boat a frond of kelp that he would give to the dolphin to play with. Soon the dolphin trusted his human friend and would follow Frank's boat. It was not long before Frank was able to entice the dolphin into shallow water where Horace could enjoy the company of vacationers who swam out from the beach. Horace became a local celebrity. When the media publicized the dolphin's amusing antics, Frank Robson became very concerned for Horace's safety, and, with the support of the Commission for the Future and the Commission for the Environment, a leaflet was produced and distributed free in Napier. It was entitled simply HORACE. It explained the dolphin's arrival and said that Horace was about ten feet long and had an estimated weight of 450 pounds.

In addition to giving general facts and figures on dolphins the pamphlet contained details of a cautionary tale. It concerned Opo, the dolphin whose antics with children delighted the world when they saw the pictures and read the story in newspapers and magazines. But as Frank pointed out in his pamphlet, there was also a dark side to this romantic association between man and dolphin. This is how it was described in the pamphlet:

> In 1955, at the height of the holiday season, Opo could be relied on to appear almost every day. The local people were quick to form a protection committee and notices were erected asking for careful behavior. The idyllic summer continued.
>
> But on March 9 Opo was found dead, cut to shreds and jammed in a crevice on the rim of a rock pool. It was commonly believed, though never openly stated, that self-interest and commercial considerations had led someone to kill the dolphin with a gelignite blast.

In his pamphlet Frank also pointed out that if the citizens of Napier wished to retain their new aquatic entertainer they too should be sensitive to the dolphin's moods and requirements.

Although such statements as "Treat Horace as you would your best friend," "Don't force yourself upon him" and "Be gentle at all times" were read with some jocularity in the Dobbs household, we all admired the pamphlet. We were also impressed with the initiative Frank and his colleagues had shown in their efforts to save the wild dolphin from accidents that could arise through ignorance.

For one of Napier's best known divers, Quentin Bennett, a single headline in Frank's pamphlet was especially appropriate. It read as follows: "Look after Horace and you will be part of a rare experience." Quentin's first contact was made when the dolphin took the diver's fins in his mouth and tugged them. Later the two of them started to play games with one another that at times became very boisterous. In a letter to me Quentin explained how on one occasion he saw stars when in the middle of a jackknife dive he collided head-on with the dolphin. Despite this painful incident, Quentin continued to play with

Horace and was rewarded by a number of magnificent rides with the diver clinging to the dolphin's dorsal fin. Quentin did not use an aqualung during these activities. He wore a wetsuit plus fins, mask and snorkel. Thus, like a dolphin, he could stay submerged only for as long as he could hold his breath. An extra tinge of excitement was added to these thrilling rides because Horace usually took Quentin down to the seabed. As the underwater visibility was only a few feet, the diver rushed forward in the gloom not knowing where his supercharged mount was taking him.

Some other divers who were treated in a similar fashion found the experience very unnerving and declined further rides. Indeed, Horace had his favorite human playmates. Any would-be jockeys whom the dolphin did not like, usually because they were too rough with him, were given such a hefty thump with his tail that they left the water and declined to dive with the dolphin again.

To Quentin, who was fit and willing to engage in an underwater rough and tumble, the highlight of his dolphin experiences came when Horace picked him up and carried the exhilarated diver back to his boat, much to the amazement of his goggle-eyed children on board.

Horace the dolphin also befriended a human who was a complete contrast to the fit aquatic Quentin Bennett. She was a woman who was extremely nervous in the water and could in no way be described as a diver. Yet such was the affinity she felt for Horace that she overcame all her fears and established a relationship with him. Her name was Rosamond Rowe, and I came to know her as Ros.

Rosamond's interest in the dolphin started when her husband, Allan, swam with Horace and the two of them developed a mutual trust. Allan would swim out into deep water and play hide-and-seek with the dolphin in the seaweed. When that game was over the two mammals would have a tug-of-war contest using a piece of kelp to take the strain of their opposed forces. If one of the contestants let go the other would dash off with the "rope." Horace tried all sorts of tricks and loved the fun. Sometimes when Allan appeared on the shore and called, the dolphin would dash off and return with a piece of seaweed in anticipation of the games to follow.

One day, shortly after one of Allan's early swims with Horace, the dolphin swam in close to the beach where the Rowe family were enjoying a picnic with an elderly friend, Miss Bingham. When they saw Alan swimming with the dolphin, the two women felt an overwhelming desire to join in the fun. But neither of them had their bathing suits. So with a hesitant glance at the busy highway forty yards away, they stripped to their underwear and rushed into the sea. Horace's trust had not developed to a stage where he would venture into very shallow water and the Napier housewife and her elderly friend had to be content with watching Horace playing in water out of their depth.

It was not until the dolphin came into the harbor that Ros established her first real contact with Horace. She spoke to the dolphin and sensed that he was responding to her verbal overtures.

Encouraged by Horace's friendliness, the Rowe family purchased a small rowing boat for the express purpose of watching the dolphin at closer range. During the Easter holiday of 1979 the Rowes were able to get alongside the dolphin and Horace allowed Ros to caress him all over as she talked gently to him.

Such were the effects of this close contact that Ros purchased a wetsuit. Wetsuits are made of sponge rubber, and, in addition to keeping the wearer warm, they make him buoyant. A wetsuit can therefore be regarded as a thermal lifejacket. With just a few pounds of lead on a weightbelt Ros felt comfortable in the water and could bob around quite happily and safely. Thus she was able to join Horace in his own element. The dolphin seemed to appreciate this bold step by the housewife who, in her turn, was thrilled to share an interspecies friendship.

Ros was given her first ride by Horace on a day of special significance. She had just learned that a horse she had owned several years earlier, a beloved companion to her, had died. Ros felt very flat when she heard the news and agreed to join the family when they suggested a rowing trip to find the dolphin. When Horace was located he was in one of his most trusting and playful moods. Ros decided to do something she had been wanting to do for ages but felt silly about. She sat quietly in the boat and sang to him. Horace was fascinated and lay quietly on the surface with the pinhole of his ear exposed. Ros then let herself into the water and was immediately approached by Horace, who swam underneath her and took her on his back. It was not until he surfaced that she realized she was sitting between his blowhole and his dorsal fin.

Perhaps even more remarkable than the friendship between the dolphin and Ros was the relationship Horace developed with the Rowes' friend, the seventy-year-old Miss Bingham. The elderly lady also acquired a wetsuit and enjoyed aquatic games with Horace. As the Rowes' young children also participated in the activities, it could be said that Horace's relationships bridged three generations of humans.

Every one of Horace's human friends hoped he would stay in Hawke Bay for a long time but they all knew his visits could come to a sudden end. Indeed, I too hoped that Horace would stay in Napier long enough for me to organize a visit to New Zealand to meet my namesake face to face.

But it was not to be.

For some time divers had been laying charges in the harbor. Frank Robson and others, concerned for the dolphin's safety, asked for advance warning before charges were detonated underwater in order that they could entice the dolphin away. However, they were not always notified and Horace's many friends were worried that the dolphin would either be killed or maimed by the shock waves if he was close to a charge when it went off.

The Rowes and Miss Bingham had their last swim with Horace on Saturday, May 26, 1979. The humans noted that their dolphin companion did not behave normally and appeared to be wary of physical contact. At dusk on June 7, after he had been absent two weeks, Miss Bingham saw Horace feeding offshore. Six hours later, 600 yards away, there was another explosion in the harbor.

Whether or not the dolphin was killed by the explosion (which seems unlikely as no body was recovered) or simply moved on, nobody knows. It was suggested in the New Zealand press that Horace may have migrated to warmer waters.

Many of the people of Napier sadly missed the dolphin, whom they had come to regard as their own special friend.

Margaret Bingham, ever hopeful that Horace would return, expressed her feelings in a poem entitled *Seeking Horace*.

Perhaps he'll come today—
perhaps I'll see the fin
cleaving towards me
or the swirl
where the honing body has
just been;
feel the skin so smooth
and underneath
the bone of muscle.
Courteously
he'll come, leaving
the darting fish to
say holloa;
nudge me with his beak
or take my foot
into his mouth saying
I love you—
then like the wind
under the water
go
to his own encounters.

24 · International Dolphin Watch

Common to Donald, Sandy and Horace was the fact that nobody knew where they came from, or where they went when they disappeared. This reflects a lack of knowledge of dolphins—a point which was brought to focus by Prince Charles during my visit to Buckingham Palace.

As we passed from one panel to another, discussing the merits of the different entries in the dolphin competition, Prince Charles interspersed his comments with general inquiries on dolphins.

"How many are there around the British Isles?"
"Where do they come from?"
"Where do they go to?"
"Where do they give birth to their young?"
"How long do they live in the wild?"
To all of these questions I had to reply, "I don't know."
"I thought you were an expert," he quipped.
"That's right, I am," I replied. "But the truth of the matter is that nobody knows."

It could be argued that the fact that we know next to nothing about the life of wild dolphins is probably beneficial to the dolphins. For when the paths of man and dolphin cross more often than not it spells disaster to the dolphins. Indeed man is their only real enemy.

One of the dilemmas was poignantly expressed in an essay from a nine-year-old boy, Antony Chapman, who submitted his entry to my dolphin competition. Here it is:

DOLPHINS

I'm a hunted dolphin. As I look around me I see the shadows of motorboats. Suddenly I hear a squeal! One of the school is already dead. The other dolphins go to help while I investigate. I rise to the surface of the water but see nothing. Then suddenly out of nowhere a speedboat comes charging at me. It's trying to kill as it did the other dolphin. I must go and warn the others. Meanwhile up above the Japanese are circling in their boat. Then I see a flush of bubbles. A man tries to kill me with a harpoon. I swim into deep water where he can't get me. Then I come out. It looks all clear to me I say but it isn't. For behind some seaweed hides the man. He catches me with his harpoon. It looks like the end of my life.

Antony Chapman's essay was undoubtedly inspired by an event which took place in Japan on February 23, 1978, when a fisherman discovered a dolphin following a shoal of yellowtail fish in the waters of Tsushima Strait. He harpooned the mammal and raised the alarm. When a group of dolphins gathered to assist their stricken companion, more than 100 fishing boats

223

closed in on the dolphins and started to drive them toward Iki Island off Northern Kyushu.

To the Japanese fishermen the dolphins were an enemy that had to be destroyed. The drive and subsequent dolphin slaughter were conducted like a military operation. It started at about 3 P.M. on Thursday, February 24. Deploying their boats like platoons of soldiers, the Japanese rounded up the dolphins in the area and forced them into a small bay. Isolating boats were then rushed to the scene and the mouth of the bay was sealed with nets. There the captured dolphins were imprisoned until 8:30 A.M. the following day. By this time about one thousand fishermen were on hand to help with the massacre.

The following morning I opened *The Daily Telegraph* at my breakfast table and found the headline JAPANESE CLUB 1,000 DOLPHINS TO DEATH. In the lengthy article, which had been sent from a correspondent in Tokyo, I learned how the dolphins were driven ashore two or three at a time, dragged up the beach and left for later killing by club-wielding fishermen.

The fishermen explained to the journalist that "they considered dolphins to be 'gangsters of the sea' because they eat cuttlefish and yellowtail fish."

The article continued as follows:

> As the angry fishermen proceeded from dolphin to dolphin with their clubs, butting the crying mammals on their heads, they were absolutely untouched by the tears which streamed from the eyes of the dolphins on shore.
>
> Later, the heads were chopped off, the bodies gutted and the dolphin carcasses tied to concrete blocks and dumped back into the sea.

Those who were upset by the articles in the newspapers, which were accompanied by black and white photographs, had their sensitivities even more strongly disturbed in the evening when the same news item was shown on television. Viewers with color sets saw the water red with blood from the bleeding dolphins. It was a harrowing sight.

Not unexpectedly, the Iki massacre, as it became known, produced a wave of public indignation and reaction against both the fishermen of Iki and the Japanese in general. The

224

Japanese embassy was bombarded with protests. I was invited to appear on the BBC program *Tonight* and, in an interview with Dennis Tuohy, I showed a clip of my film of Donald. A newsfilm illustrating the slaughter of the dolphins at Iki was also included in the item, so the contrast between the two situations could not have been more grotesque.

It was not difficult to trace the events on the other side of the world which led to government authorities putting a bounty on the head of every dolphin. Iki indirectly followed the developments which took place after the Second World War when Japan became one of the world's major producers of consumer goods. It was a road to financial glory for which the price was degradation of the staffs of life—air and water. The Tokyo air became heavy with lead from exhaust fumes and the seas around were used as a dumping ground for mercury and other chemical wastes. By the early 1960s widespread pollution had wiped out many of Japan's coastal fishing grounds. Thus pressure was put on the Iki fishermen to produce even more fish from their relatively uncontaminated waters, which were already giving up their maximum sustainable yield of yellowtail.

In hindsight, the result was as predictable as it was inevitable. The fish became scarcer and the frustration of those who for generations had been solely dependent upon fishing for their livelihoods focused on the dolphins.

Despite the enormous volume of protests their action provoked in 1978, the fishermen were determined to continue their war on the dolphins, and further bloody slaughters took place in 1979 and 1980.

DON'T MURDER DOLPHINS

One of the witnesses to the 1980 dolphin massacre was John Edwards, a reporter from *The Daily Mail*. Knowing that John Edwards had also frolicked in the sea with Donald, I found his graphic description of the scenes even more disturbing:

The huge dawn sun of Japan rose into the clear sky and glazed the sea. There were so many fishing boats heading for the dolphins it looked like an invasion force.

When they rendezvoused ten miles out there were 900 boats in the area three miles wide slipping quietly behind a herd of dolphins which was so big the sea boiled from horizon to horizon. Four men were in each boat.

Boats at the ends of the arc pulled towards the middle. Now the fleet was like the shape of the horns of a bull sweeping a seaful of leaping dolphins in front of them.

The fishermen screamed at them. They dipped iron pipes into the water and banged them with hammers. The noise exploded underwater sending shockwaves like gunfire to frighten the great creatures into a terrifying fight for their lives.

The trap closed around them. The boats steered them into the narrow creek of Thatsuno island. The sea was a wild sight of thrashing dolphins.

Babies were pushed to the surface by their mothers to stop them being crushed.

Then a net was dropped from one side of the creek to the other. It penned over a thousand dolphins between the sea and the beach.

"It was a sight I could not have imagined," recalled fisherman Yamanda. And the curtain rose on the real horror of the day.

Suddenly, the fishermen went chest deep into the water. They hacked the dolphins with axes and cleavers and stabbed them with poles which had iron spikes nailed to the end.

The sea went red. It was so thick with entrails and dolphin foetuses it didn't look like water any more.

The dolphins rose painfully trying to escape. They snorted for air and corkscrewed at the net that was holding them and tried to leap for safety with their stomachs trailing and tail fins cut off.

226

The bloody smears of their victory covered the bodies of the fishermen. Dolphins were dragged onto the beach and left to pant to death in the sun. Baby dolphins were thrown onto the rocks.

The awful noise of killing and screaming and the stench lay in the creek like a war in hell.

The urge for revenge grew in the fishermen. They went on hacking and stabbing and the rising tide took the stain of the slaughter high onto the rocks.

The last dolphins were dragged to a lung-bursting death on the beach, or had their insides flushed out with a knife.

At the time John Edwards was compiling his report for London a daring attempt was made to save the lives of at least some of the dolphins. The man in the front line of the commando-style rescue operation was a thirty-six-year-old American marine scientist and former teacher, Dexter Cate.

Cate carried a small inflatable plastic kayak and collapsible paddles hidden in his backpack when he landed on the island of Iki, 1,200 miles southwest of Tokyo, where the dolphins were corralled and awaiting execution.

Cate, a field agent of the Fund for Animals and a member of the Greenpeace Foundation, waited until the fishermen stopped work for the day before putting on his wetsuit. Under the cover of darkness he paddled his flimsy craft a mile through high surf to the mouth of Tatsuno-shima Bay. There he slipped overboard into the bitterly cold water and managed to untie and cut some of the ropes of the nets that imprisoned the dolphins.

Even when the way to freedom was opened, many of the prisoners were reluctant to leave their injured companions. Dexter Cate had to swim among the confused dolphins urging them to escape, but many refused to run for freedom.

Hours later, the exhausted Cate could not make it back to base. High winds and large waves forced him ashore. The next morning, when the fishermen returned to continue the slaughter, they discovered Cate, cold and fatigued, and took him to their village. There were reports of a menacing crowd gathering as the fishermen interrogated Cate in the fishing cooperative's hall. He was later arrested by the police who further interrogated him.

Dexter Cate was subsequently charged with "forceful obstruction of the fishermen's business." He was refused bail, and when he went on hunger strike he was forcefed. A month later his trial started and on May 30 he was given a six-month sentence suspended for three years. After the verdict he was handed over to the immigration authorities who deported him on the grounds that his visa had expired. After more than three months in a Japanese jail Dexter Cate returned home to Hawaii.

The imprisonment of Dexter Cate without bail incensed many conservation groups throughout the world. In Britain Jenny Crates, founder member of Dolphin Defense, organized a petition and gathered thousands of signatures. She also led a delegation of Members of Parliament and show-business stars to lodge a protest at the Japanese Embassy in London. Many of the protesters, who could do nothing directly to help the dolphins, admired Dexter Cate as a man who was prepared to take effective action and pay the price.

The Japanese Foreign Ministry in London revealed that the number of dolphins caught in 1978 was 1,327 and this rose to 1,621 in 1979 with a further increase to 1,818 in 1980. Information concerning the subsidies paid to fishermen was also released. It amounted to Y20,000 (about $80) for every dolphin killed. According to the Japanese Minister of Information this was intended to offset the loss of the fishermen's earnings caused by the decline of the yellowtail catches. In practice the subsidy acted as a formidable financial incentive to kill more dolphins. When the organization Friends of the Earth looked into the level of payment it was discovered that on average the subsidy from six dead dolphin represented one person's entire income from fishing for one year.

When this information was coupled with the fact that the government contributed $70,000 toward a machine for use by the Matsumoto Fisheries Cooperative to grind dolphins into pig feed and fertilizer, the seriousness of the Japanese Dolphin Eradication Program could not be denied. GENOCIDE AGAINST DOLPHINS was how one American organization

228

captioned a picture of the newly installed machine it called "Auschwitz."

Life in the sea is a very complicated matrix of interdependent species. Nature has shown time and time again, on the land and in the sea, that the selective removal of a single species to solve a short-term problem often creates long-term problems of far greater magnitude.

In the old fishing community at Iki there was a legendary taboo against killing dolphins. The village elders maintained that to break the taboo was to court maritime disaster. Old rites and superstitions often have a hidden logic. It is possible that when the present fishermen of Iki broke the taboo, changes that would bring personal disaster to many of them were already written in the stars.

The Japanese regarded the dolphins as their enemies. To other fishermen, however, the dolphins are allies because they help them locate much-prized tuna fish.

In the eastern Pacific Ocean large shoals of tuna are often accompanied by dolphins. Why this partnership was formed is still a mystery. It has been suggested that they both follow the same food resource. But this seems too facile an explanation. I suspect that careful and detailed observations will eventually reveal a much more complex interplay between the dolphins—which are aquatic mammals, and the tuna—which are true fish. However, if man continues the present volume of tuna fishing with the techniques now in use, a possibly mutually beneficial association of sea creatures could be destroyed in a decade.

This new dilemma for the dolphins can be traced back to 1927 when the albacore tuna did not appear as usual off the coast of California. The small US fleet which set out to intercept the migrating fish sailed far south in search of the vanished stocks. In the deep blue expanse of the eastern tropical Pacific, which was untouched by fishing, the fishermen discovered the huge yellowfin tuna in almost undreamed-of abundance. It must have been an exciting moment when the dolphins were spotted, for dolphins (usually referred to as porpoises in the U.S.A.) on the water and flocks of sea birds in the air marked unseen tuna below.

229

When the cry "Porpoises" rang out, the crew would burst into a frenzy of activity as the vessel headed straight for the dolphins. With the dolphins around the ship, the crew would fish either with long lines or with very strong fishing poles. In the latter method, bait would be scattered in the water and, once the tuna were in a feeding frenzy, they would take the bare barbless hooks hung from poles wielded by the crew, who would then swing the heavy fish aboard. And while they stayed with the dolphins the crew would work strenuously to haul one fighting fish after another onto the deck. It was extremely exhausting work, but the crews were well paid and financial rewards for the owners of successful tuna boats were considerable. This method of fishing had no known harmful effects on the dolphins marking the tuna.

In the 1930s, when the United States was in the throes of the Great Depression, the tuna fishermen enjoyed a bonanza. Many a tuna man must have blessed the dolphins for the providential role they played in the provision of uncommon prosperity. For nearly three decades the American tuna fishermen dominated tuna fishing in the eastern Pacific. They had a virtual monopoly for their product in a huge home market. And the rest of the world was hungry for cans of tuna which competed favorably with canned salmon.

The Japanese started to build their own armada of tuna clippers after the Second World War. By the mid 1950s economic storm clouds started to form over the American industry as the Japanese-caught tuna flooded onto the market and depressed the price. But the storm did not break. The Americans were able to take advantage of years of experiment, coupled with postwar inventions such as nylon nets and power blocks which could haul huge loads. Using their new knowledge and equipment, American fishermen developed a novel technique for catching tuna based on the purse-seine net. This method was much less labor-intensive than the pole and long line fishing techniques. It gave Americans an economic edge over their competitors. By 1960, although a considerable number of bait boats remained, the majority of the ever-expanding U.S. fleet was equipped with purse-seine nets which could bring in as much as 100 tons of tuna in a single shot.

Once a school of dolphins was located they were rounded up cowboy-style with four or five speedboats. The dolphins were herded to a position alongside the parent boat and allowed to settle down with the tuna circling restlessly below. The school of dolphins and their accompanying tuna were then encircled with a huge net, which could be well over a quarter of a mile long and 250 feet deep. The net was suspended vertically in the water, the top attached to a floating cork line while the bottom was weighted down with a so-called "lead line." Iron rings were fastened at intervals beneath the lead lines. Once the fish had been encircled a steel hawser threaded through the rings was winched in, closing, or pursing, the bottom of the net under the tuna.

During the pursing operation and afterward approximately fifty percent of the net was hauled back on board the fishing vessel through the power block. As this happened, some of the trapped dolphins tried to escape by diving to the bottom of the net, only to become entangled in the mesh and asphyxiated. The dolphins' strong instinct to assist each other in adversity, and for mothers to remain with their calves, resulted in many of them being injured as the net was drawn in. Once a dolphin was caught, the others would remain close by and would make little attempt to escape.

To the fishermen, hell-bent on pulling out of the sea as many tuna as they could, the panicking of the dolphins and the dead dolphins caught in the nets were a hindrance. Effort that could have been directed to hauling in tuna had to be deployed in extricating the wounded and dead animals from the nets and tossing them back into the sea.

The high mortality of dolphins associated with the tuna fishing went virtually unnoticed by those outside the industry until it was brought to the attention of the American public in an article by William Perrin, who sailed with the tuna fleet for two seasons to study the taxonomy and behavior of dolphins. The young scientist described how sometimes hundreds of porpoises were either suffocated or battered to death in the sacking up of a single set. He cited catastrophic sets in which over 1,000 dolphins were slaughtered. Extrapolating from his experiences he estimated that between 250,000 and 400,000 dolphins were being killed each year in the eastern tropical Pacific. He speculated that such a level of mortality could lead to the collapse of dolphin populations.

These revelations shocked scientists and conservationists alike. Their individual concern and remonstrations built up quickly into a tidal wave of protest which swept toward Washington.

The result, in 1972, was the Marine Mammal Protection Act, which mandated that the incidental kill or serious injury of mammals permitted in the course of commercial fishing operations be reduced to insignificant levels approaching zero.

At first the conservationists were pleased that they had been instrumental in obtaining a reprieve for the many dolphins who would otherwise have met their deaths at the hands of the tuna men. However their satisfaction was short lived. It soon became apparent that the fishermen were prepared blatantly to ignore the law. For eighteen months the tuna lobby kept up an unremitting pressure on the government to exempt "incidental taking" of porpoises from the act. At the same time the fishermen researched methods of reducing the dolphin kill by modification of their nets and techniques.

Although the introduction of a large mesh section, called a Medina Panel, into the net considerably reduced the dolphin mortality it certainly did not eliminate deaths altogether. It was predicted in mid-1974 that the total porpoise deaths for the season would be about 100,000—hardly an insignificant number approaching zero. Many conservation groups joined in the bitter fight inside and outside the government to bring the tuna fishing industry to its senses. Apart from the tragedy of the slaughter of the dolphins, it seemed obvious to everyone except the recalcitrant fishermen that if they continued as they were doing, they would destroy the markers that enabled them to spot their valuable source of income.

When a group of conservationists take on an organization with the formidable backup of a government department, it is a David and Goliath contest from the start. The tuna industry claimed that a porpoise quota would bring the industry to its knees. They threatened to remove their boats and fish under foreign flags rather than have regulations forced on them. Despite such protests, the National Marine Fisheries Service established a quota of 52,000 dolphin mortalities for 1978 and 41,000 for 1979. As it turned out the death tolls were well below this, indicating that it is possible to catch tuna and not kill so many dolphins using modified purse-seine method.

American fishermen are disgruntled when they hear of fishermen of other nationalities catching tuna unimpeded by U.S. regulations and quotas. With huge investments still being made in tuna boats in many parts of the world, it is sad to contemplate the ravages each vessel will inflict on the Pacific dolphin population whose cumulative incidental deaths at the hands of the tuna fishermen already exceeds six million.

To the Faroese fishermen the concern many people express over the plight of dolphins is hard to understand. For generations they have hunted a species of dolphin and continue to do so as their rightful harvest. However, they have become affluent like the rest of the western world, and there is now a considerable element of sport in their dolphin hunts. When the undersea explorer Gordon Ridley visited the islands in 1980, he got the impression that the men on these remote islands continue their tradition more for the benefit of the masculine image than for the food it provides.

The species of dolphin which suffers as a result of their predation is the pilot whale (*Globicephala melaena*). The pilot whale drives, or Gridadraps as they are called by the Faroese, are carried out in small open fishing boats. On sighting a school, the fishermen take to their boats and drive the dolphins slowly toward a convenient bay. Once they have been coralled close to a chosen shallow, the school is panicked by striking the hindmost dolphin on the tail. The pilot whales then rush onto the beach where they are stranded and then killed by a knife cut through the neck into the spinal cord. The local sheriff subsequently arranges the distribution of the meat and blubber in accordance with a complex tradition.

An expedition to the Faroe Islands from Cambridge University in 1978 reported three pilot whale drives which accounted for 611 deaths. In addition seventy killer whales were driven ashore and killed. The Faroese also shot white-sided and white-beaked dolphins and common porpoises and illegally harpooned fin whales.

It was against this kind of background that a plan slowly

took shape in my mind. Somehow or other I wanted to make people aware that dolphins could bring great joy into human lives. I took my inspiration from a completely unrelated field—ornithology.

Most of our knowledge about bird populations and migrations has come not from professionals, but from amateur bird watchers. Many of those involved developed a passion for the animals they studied.

I felt sure that the same could be done for the dolphins of the world. I decided to call my proposed scheme The Dolphin Survey Project and I formulated plans for recruiting an army of amateur dolphin spotters. At the same time I conceived of an even more ambitious project—one that would cover far wider aspects of delphinology. I eventually decided on the title International Dolphin Watch and described its aims as: "A program to increase our knowledge and understanding of dolphins."

Having decided on my objectives, I pondered how to make such a grandiose scheme work. To collect and analyze data gathered from all over the world in the Dolphin Survey Project, I needed to collaborate with a person or persons who could process the data. Ideally, my collaborator would be in a university department and have access to a computer.

A look through the scientific literature indicated that Richard Harrison stood head and shoulders above all others when it came to academic studies on Cetaceans. In addition to being a Fellow of the Royal Society, certainly the most prestigious scientific body in Britain, Richard Harrison was professor of anatomy at the University of Cambridge.

I visited Professor Harrison and we were soon engrossed in an animated discussion on many aspects of dolphin behavior. It was a delight to have the opportunity to meet a man who was both knowledgeable and enthusiastic about his subject.

Richard Harrison told me of his concern about the pollution of the seas and that he thought the build-up of high levels of chlorinated hydrocarbons (derived from pesticides) in the bodies of dolphins could be a contributory factor to the decrease in the dolphin population.

Professor Harrison confirmed that the dolphin population

234

was on a strong downward trend. With dolphins living perhaps as long as forty years in the sea, the build-up of toxic chemicals in their bodies could lead to circumstances which did not result in immediate death. This was an area with which I was familiar, because I had been involved for ten years in similar research. Indeed, I had presented papers on work carried out in my laboratory to meetings of the European Society for the Study of Drug Toxicity.

Professor Harrison said there were enormous gaps in our knowledge of dolphins and this applied particularly to their behavior in the wild. When I described to him my concept of using amateur observers to gather information and suggested the production of a guide book or notes he said he already had such a project underway and would be pleased for me to carry it forward. When I was shown a series of paintings by one of his colleagues, Dennis McBrearty, of the twelve species of dolphins found around the British coast, I realized I had been right to make contact with Cambridge University. We agreed on a plan for cooperation in which we would pool our respective resources and talents. As Professor Harrison showed me out, he said, "I have been waiting thirty years for someone like you to come along."

For my part I could not have wished for a better arrangement. I was thrilled with the outcome of our meeting and eager to get to work on the Dolphin Survey Project, which had become the major task under the umbrella title of International Dolphin Watch (IDW).

IDW started to succceed from the moment the idea first came to me. Almost everyone I approached said they thought IDW was a good thing and would help if they could. I realized that this success would bring with it a much bigger work load than I could carry on my own, and my wife Wendy suggested I should approach the Manpower Services Commission (MSC), which existed to help people find employment. Through the MSC I was told of a Special Temporary Employment Scheme (STEP) whereby I could obtain fulltime help for the management of International Dolphin Watch. The state would finance the post for a period of one year. Thus I was able to recruit Elaine Orr, a newly qualified honors graduate who was unemployed, and once again it seemed that the face of fortune was smiling on IDW because she proved to be ideally suited to the post.

One of the local resources in the village of North Ferriby, our base, was a printing works. It was run by a friend, Jim Freeman, who had given up fulltime employment to set up his own small business in two unused rooms on the platform of the railway station. The railway was still in regular use and we discussed the production of a dolphin handbook to the sound of the printing press and the occasional train that rattled through the station. Jim suggested that before we embarked on a book we should consider publishing a broadsheet illustrating all the dolphins on a single page. This idea met with the prompt approval of Professor Harrison. The poster gave us an immediate springboard from which to launch our recruitment campaign. International Dolphin Watch was underway.

25 · Take Me to the Dolphins

DOLPHINS SHOULD BE FREE was the message boldly proclaimed at the foot of a letter I received from South Africa shortly after the birth of International Dolphin Watch. It came from Nan Rice, the honorary secretary of The Dolphin Action and Protection Group. A few months later, my wife Wendy and I were winging our way to Cape Town to meet a group of conservationists who were dedicated to preserving the dolphin populations in their natural environment—the sea.

We discovered Nan Rice to be a charming and dynamic person. She and her colleagues organized a series of events and meetings for us which stimulated a lot of interest in dolphins and provided a more exciting overseas launch for International Dolphin Watch than I had dared to hope for.

My visit to South Africa brought to light several new dolphin stories. One of them pointed very clearly to the nature of the special bond that can exist between humans and dolphins. The Dolphin Action and Protection Group was opposed to the

236

capture of dolphins for exhibition purposes, but by one of those cruel twists of fate the story I am about to relate centered around the friendship of a young woman with captive dolphins.

I met Anne Rennie in Port Elizabeth. She was less than five feet tall and very smartly dressed. From what she told me later it was apparent that her frail appearance belied a tough lady. Her manner was vivacious and her eyes sparkled when she launched into animated discussion. She gestured with her hands as she talked, and her quick movements were those of a sensitive, emotional person.

It was December 1978, but Anne Rennie's story began over a decade earlier, shortly after two female bottlenose dolphins were introduced into the Port Elizabeth dolphinarium. The unlikely names given to the two new inmates were those of well-known brands of Scotch whiskey—Haig and Dimple. At the time Haig and Dimple came into her life Anne Rennie, the mother of two young children, was in the bloom of young womanhood. She was fast becoming an expert skindiver and was allowed into the pool with the newly captured dolphins.

When Anne first lowered herself into the water, she began by swimming the "dolphin stroke," keeping her hands at her sides and kicking her feet up and down in unison. Haig—the younger of the two dolphins—was intrigued by the nymph who had come into her pool. When the newcomer did corkscrew turns, stood on her head on the bottom of the pool, and carried out every maneuver she could invent in the gravity-free underwater world of the aqualung diver, the young female dolphin was delighted and followed Anne around the pool watching her every move. In contrast Dimple, the elder of the two dolphins, kept her distance, and watched disdainfully from afar.

When Anne left the water she was enthralled with the friendship she had established with Haig. Visits to the dolphin pool became regular events. A significant step forward was made in her relationship with the dolphins when Haig took the initiative and physical contact was established.

Once the barrier between Anne and Haig was down it was not long before they had evolved new games that both of them enjoyed. Anne would hold onto Haig's dorsal fin and be towed around the pool. Alternatively Anne would put her hands in the mouth of the dolphin who would clench them gently between her teeth, like a horse bridle, before towing her human playmate around the dolphinarium. Dimple watched these goings-on with matronly detachment and would never become involved herself.

Our discussions ranged over many aspects of dolphin behavior and included the mysterious way dolphins have of making people feel happy and even helping them in times of mental stress. We talked for hours and when we parted company I had a slight suspicion there was something more to come to light in Anne Rennie's story. Something deep down which she could not bring herself to talk about. We agreed to meet for lunch the following day.

Anne arrived on time outside the dolphinarium bearing a scrapbook full of press cuttings and photographs of her with Haig and Dimple. She had attracted a lot of attention at the time, and it was not difficult to see why. She was beautiful, and people like to see pretty girls in their newspapers.

We sat turning the pages in the heat of the mid-day sun. Anne became emotional as the curtains were pulled back on images that had been hidden in her subconscious mind. Tears started to stream down her face and she told me how the dolphins had helped her get through a tremendous emotional crisis in her life.

It started with her simply being embarrassed when she began to discharge blood when she was swimming. She went to her doctor, who examined her and told her that she had uterine cancer and would have to have surgery immediately.

The effect that such a diagnosis would have on a sensitive woman with a young family is not difficult to imagine. When she heard the news, she was so stricken with fear and apprehension that she could not face the prospect of telling even her husband. There was one thought in her mind.

"Take me to the dolphins," she said.

She went straight to the dolphinarium and played with the dolphins. As she did so the burden of the frightening news became tolerable and she gathered together the fragments of her shattered peace of mind. When she left the dolphinarium she was able to break the news to her family and to face the future. That mysterious force which seems to spring from dolphins helped Anne to ride out the worst storm in her young life. The fact that she was alive ten years later was evidence of the success of the surgical operation.

Anne told us her story outside the dolphinarium. She declined to go inside, and in fact had seldom been back since her recovery. When she walked away, with her scrapbook under her arm, I knew she had no doubt in her mind that the dolphins had helped her to survive a crisis. The memories of that most difficult time in her life were still painful ten years later.

26 · Death on the Beach

Once International Dolphin Watch was launched, details of dolphin sightings often arrived at my home from unexpected and surprising sources. Not all were of dolphins swimming joyfully free in the sea. The events that followed one such report developed into a deeply distressing situation.

It happened on a Sunday, March 18, 1979. The news of a stranded dolphin was phoned through to some friends in Harrogate with whom my wife and I were spending the day. It was snowing hard and when we set off I wondered if we would be able to make the journey to Spurn Point where the dolphin—which had been named Spurn—was stranded. As our home was on our route to the coast we stopped in to collect my wellington boots and our children Ashley and Melanie, and we left immediately for Spurn Head, about thirty miles away.

It was the coastguard who had first spotted the stranded dolphin on the previous afternoon. With the aid of the lifeboat crew, they got the dolphin back into the water as the incoming tide crept slowly and gently inshore to cover the mud flats. The following morning, however, they found the dolphin was once again lying stranded on the mud when the tide receded. With the aid of the local RSPCA officer they managed to get some sponge rubber mattresses under the dolphin, whose body was covered with a sack and kept regularly dowsed with water.

The coastguard then telephoned various contacts including me, and by mid-afternoon I drove into the bird sanctuary at Spurn to see what assistance I could give.

The white-sided dolphin was fully grown and appeared to be in good condition apart from some superficial wounds that were bleeding, and a small abscess on the tail stock, which looked as if it might have been caused by a small-caliber bullet.

The profile of the head was similar to Donald's, although Spurn's beak was less pronounced. The top of his head was gray, but the rostrum was creamy white with a distinct border between the two zones of color. This gave the white-sided dolphin the look of a melancholy clown and the tears that streamed from Spurn's eyes added to his disconsolate appearance. He presented a very forlorn sight. His respiration was labored and erratic. I opened his mouth and found that the conical teeth were in good condition. From this I concluded that the dolphin had not come ashore to die of old age.

The most logical explanation for his presence was that he had come into the bay of shallow tidal water and had been unable to find a way out through the maze of drainage channels that eventually led to the safety of deeper water. His head was pointing in the direction of the open sea, which was about 300 yards away on the other side of the long spit of sand that comprised Spurn Head. One of the onlookers suggested that the dolphin could hear the sound of the waves on the far shore and that he had beached himself in an attempt to reach the open sea, not knowing that there was a barrier of sand between them.

The watery sun which occasionally appeared through the slightly misty air, casting a yellow band across the still water in the bay, was sinking. There were a few hours of daylight left, and it was getting colder.

What could we do? We could wait for the tide to come in again and hope that the dolphin would swim free and find his way back into the Humber Estuary and from there into the open sea. The events of the day before had shown that this was unlikely to be a successful solution to the problem. An alternative was to wait for a crew that was on the way from the dolphinarium at Woburn. They were not expected to arrive for several hours and even if the dolphin survived the long journey back to the pool, that was no guarantee that Spurn would live long in captivity. As I stood looking down at the immobile dolphin, wondering how I could help, I heard the sound of waves scurrying up the beach out of sight just behind me. I could not help thinking of Donald and his obvious love of life in the open sea. The best chance Spurn had was for me to find some way of getting him across the 300 yards of mud flats and sand dunes that separated him from freedom in the sea. I had to make an attempt to get the dolphin into deep water.

I estimated Spurn's weight to be between 400 and 500 pounds, and he was extremely difficult to maneuver because he was stranded in an area of thick black glutinous mud into which our feet sank. I quickly found some boards along the high water mark and these were placed around the dolphin. After a great deal of struggling, we managed to get a canvas sheet under him. We were aided by some of the sightseers and by John Chicester-Constable who had seignorian rights and was responsible to the Crown for dealing with all "royal fish" that landed between the high and low water marks on the foreshore between Flamborough Head and Spurn Point.

It was a long hard struggle, but with the front of the sling roped to a Land Rover we heaved the dolphin across the soft sand. We lifted him over the track running down the center of the sand spit and moved him around the posts and obstacles that obstructed our route to the open sea. At last we were on the beach, which was gravel. Within a few minutes we had the dolphin at the water's edge. It was at this stage that what should have been triumph turned into tragedy.

The direct cause was the surf that came creaming up the beach with every wave. Out at sea the waves were two to three feet high. As they came toward the shore the crests raced ahead until they broke away, turning into a mass of frothy water that rushed up the shore pulling the pebbles with it. Thus when each wave was near the limit of its travel it was not a body of buoyant water. Instead it consisted of air, water and stones that acted like a pump, pushing anything in its path up the beach. When each wave exhausted itself the pebbles were deposited, the air bubbles dispersed, and just the water flowed back into the sea, carrying with it only lightweight objects that would float easily.

We got the dolphin to the foaming part of the sea. The people who had helped us so valiantly during the past hour were weary and thankful to relieve themselves of the burden. In addition to myself only a couple of people, including John Chichester-Constable, were wearing wellington boots. Thus it was left to us to carry the dolphin on the final short leg of his journey back into the sea.

We managed to drag the dolphin into the shallow surf but as the sea came rushing in we were abandoned by those who did not want to get their shoes full of water. The sun had long since disappeared and it was getting decidedly colder in the fading misty light, so the prospect of wet feet was not a pleasant one.

As the first wave of foam swept over the lower part of the dolphin, he seemed to be infused with a spirit to survive. His respiration became sharp and regular and he thrashed with his tail as if trying to swim, but to no avail. Spurn remained firmly where he was.

When the next wave swept in, it was higher than the previous one. It curled over the tops of our boots, which were instantly filled with sea water. But worse still, it pushed the dolphin back a short way despite our desperate attempts to hold him against the surge. When the wave had passed, we tried to maneuver the dolphin forward with the backrush of water. Spurn tried to help himself by thrashing his tail. But it had nothing but air to react against and the dolphin could generate no propulsive force. When the wave receded, we were left with the dolphin on the beach and our boots full of water. After several more fruitless attempts to get the dolphin into deep water, Mr. Chichester-Constable, who was by this time wet to the knees, admitted that he was recovering from influenza and felt that it was not prudent to continue to expose himself to the cold water any more.

So Ashley and Melanie, neither of whom had come prepared with wellington boots, valiantly waded into the water and tried to help me move the dolphin forward. Inch by inch we made progress as the waves receded, and just managed to stop the dolphin being swept back toward shore with each inrush of water. Then a large wave rushed in. It spun the dolphin sideways. I tried to stop it by pushing my feet hard into the sand and gravel. But such was the force on the dolphin that I was bowled over. Melanie and Ashley managed to stay upright but in water nearly up to their waists. As I stumbled, Spurn was swept past me and carried back and dumped high on the beach despite his efforts to swim free. As the sea receded he slithered a few feet back toward the sea and stopped. When the wave spent itself, the dolphin was left like a piece of driftwood on the tide line.

Spurn was bleeding from abrasions he had received on the gravel and he presented a piteous sight. I realized that there was nothing more we could do for him except hope that he might be carried back to the sea by another large wave. But that was a forlorn hope and I knew it.

The air temperature was ice cold, it was almost dark and the three of us were utterly exhausted. All of the sightseers and helpers had gone except for one officer of the RSPCA.

We had no dry clothes to change into and we were saturated with sea water. I emptied the water out of my wellington boots and put the sodden shoes belonging to Melanie and Ashley in the trunk of the car. We were all cold, wet, uncomfortable and dejected when we set off on the thirty-mile journey back home. On the car radio we heard that many roads in the nearby Wolds were still completely blocked by snow. Fortunately we were spared the ordeal of having to drive home through a blizzard, but the vision of a lonely dolphin being tossed up the beach like a piece of driftwood remained with me. I have been haunted by it many times since.

The following day I learned that the team from the dolphinarium carried Spurn back to Woburn where he was covered with Vaseline and tended through the night by Jackie Wyatt. Sadly, the dolphin died the following morning.

27 · Hunt the Dolphin

The chances of a diver seeing a wild friendly dolphin swimming free in the sea are extremely remote. So when Chris Goosen, my partner with whom I made underwater films, telephoned me to say he had just seen a wild dolphin in the Red Sea I got him to tell me the full story.

Chris explained that he had been to Ras Muhammed with a BBC producer, Duncan Gibbins. Chris and I had become firm friends with Duncan, with whom we had enjoyed several assignments. Having filmed a Greek freighter that had gone aground and threatened to destroy the underwater paradise, the two divers decided to have a last dive at Coral Island on the way back to Eilat. And Chris, not wishing to lose an opportunity to get some more shots for a television movie we were making about the Red Sea, took the camera in with him. They were in the company of a very experienced Dutch diver named Paul, who found an octopus among the coral heads and persuaded it to leave its lair, whereupon the disgruntled octopus attached itself firmly with its suckers to the Dutch diver's facemask and mouthpiece. After Chris filmed this unexpected turn of events he was aware of another presence. He glanced around and to his utter amazement there was a six-foot-long dolphin just a few feet away watching the spectacle.

At this point the octopus decided it was time to leave the scene and swam away from Paul, leaving a cloud of ink in the water.

"The dolphin completely ignored the octopus and seemed to be watching Paul," Chris said.

Chris, Duncan and Paul followed the dolphin down into the depths. Chris had fifty feet of film left in his camera. He focused the lens and had just started to shoot when there was a deafening roar. He looked up through the clear water and could see the hull of a large boat overhead.

"A huge anchor and chain came hurtling down into the water just a few feet away and the engines were put into full reverse."

Chris was furious, not because of the danger, but because he thought the noise would frighten the dolphin away.

Everything then went quiet and a host of people wearing fins, masks and snorkels jumped into the sea from the big boat. Much to the surprise of Chris, the dolphin ignored the overhead activity. Instead the dolphin stayed with the divers until distracted by a new activity overhead.

A couple jumped into the water with aqualungs. The girl was bronzed and wearing only the pants of a very brief bikini. The dolphin swam slowly up and circled around the new arrivals and then descended again to a depth of fifty feet. Suddenly the dolphin hurtled toward the surface. Such was the clarity of the water in the Red Sea that Chris could see the dolphin's gray shape above the sea before it plunged back in again.

"It was the most incredible jump," reported Chris. "He must have leapt a tremendous height out of the water. The remora fish that was earlier clinging to his back was just hanging on near the dolphin's tail."

The dolphin then made two more jumps in quick succession. This time Chris was ready for the action and watched it through the viewfinder as the last feet of film ran through the camera. After his third show of aerial acrobatics the dolphin stayed with those snorkelers who had not rushed back on board the boat. Chris and his companions rose closer to the surface and watched the ballet of movements over their heads.

"Then everybody climbed back on board," continued Chris, "and the dolphin followed the boat as it sailed away."

Although Chris was overjoyed at the experience of diving with the dolphin, he was disappointed that he had only a small amount of film left in the camera. He and Duncan were scheduled to fly home the following day and had to be at Eilat airport at noon. Although diving on the same day as flying is not recommended because of the increased risk of bends, the two divers decided they could safely get another shallow dive with the dolphin before their departure.

By 9:30 the next morning Chris, Duncan and Paul were back in the sea off Coral Island. The divers made every kind of underwater noise they could think of to attract the dolphin— but he didn't turn up. At the end of the dive Chris decided to use the film in his camera and the party set off underwater for the long swim back to shore. When they were just a few feet from land, Chris looked up. The dolphin was only five feet away. There was no time to change the film. But there was time to have a brief swim with the tardy dolphin.

As soon as he arrived back in England Chris telephoned me. We were planning to make a TV program on dolphins in addition to our Red Sea film. So I had a readymade excuse to suggest that we should return to Eilat.

I had no sooner put the phone down than it rang again. The next caller was Duncan Gibbins. Duncan could not have sounded more excited if he had discovered a goldmine.

"You should have seen him, Horace," he blurted out, lapsing into one of the many colorful dialects with which he embroidered his verbal pictures.

"He was fooking fantastic. It blew poor auld Goosen's mind," he said, in a stage Irish accent, exaggerating the hint of Irish intonation that gave away my partner's homeland.

Duncan knew of my failure to meet Sandy in the Bahamas and when I told him I was planning to go back with Chris he could not conceal his envy.

"You lucky buggers," he said in broad Cockney. "You know I'd really piss myself if you didn't find him," he added.

I retorted loudly that there was not the remotest chance that a dolphin would allow him so much selfish pleasure. However, from my experience in the Bahamas I knew that finding a wild dolphin in the sea could be an even riskier business than searching for sunken treasure.

Exactly one week later Chris and I were together on a plane bound for Eilat. With us was his wife Jill.

Immediately after we arrived in Eilat we made our way to the Aquasport dive center at Coral Beach. We needed a check-out dive. I wanted to drive immediately to Coral Island about seven miles away, but Chris thought it better to do a much easier dive from the beach as Jill had not been under the sea for about a year. He also pointed out that we had six days in which we could enjoy the company of the dolphin. Reluctantly I conceded.

The following morning we were back at the diving center as

soon as it opened to make arrangements for a boat to act as surface support for our dives at Coral Island.

Some time later, with the vessel well laden with our cameras, lights and diving gear, we were underway for Coral Island and our rendezvous with the dolphin.

When we arrived it appeared that nobody had informed the dolphin of his appointment with us. The boatman, named Ellie, who ferried passengers from the mainland to the island told us that the dolphin had been there the previous evening but had not yet turned up.

Chris was absolutely confident that the dolphin would come to us once we were in the water. So we anchored over a wreck at exactly the same spot where the encounters had taken place a week earlier. With cameras loaded and at the ready we went overboard excited and expectant, anticipating that the dolphin would be attracted by the sound of our bubbles. For fifteen minutes we swam among the giant coral heads, occasionally calling out into the water, but no dolphin.

When I studied Donald off the British coast, I quickly discovered that I could call him up by making sharp sounds. I estimated he would come from several miles away if I used my aqualung cylinder as a kind of underwater gong. So I tried the same trick under the Red Sea and tapped the base of my air tank with the metal handle of my diving knife. The sound radiated into the water. When the dolphin still failed to turn up, we continued to call and tap as we glided down deeper. Away from the bright shallows, we journeyed into a horizonless world filled with diffuse blue light. We were weightless travelers on a journey through the huge inner space of the ocean waiting for the arrival of a small spaceship shaped like a dolphin. But our hoped-for rendezvous with the alien intelligence did not take place. Disappointed but not too disheartened, we made our way back to the boat without shooting a single frame of film.

Chris was convinced that the Dutchman, Paul, had a special way with the dolphin. The following day we agreed to meet Paul at Coral Island and use his magnetic power to attract our quarry. But that did not work either.

In the evening we reviewed the situation. Two of our five

full diving days had gone. When we discussed the matter with Paul we discovered that he had dived with the dolphin on only four occasions and one of these was with Chris. The other three were widely spaced over a period of several months. We questioned everyone who might give us clues in our dolphin hunt. Those who had dived with the dolphin were ecstatic about him. Willy Halpert described how he and other divers found their underwater encounters with the dolphin to be some of the most exhilarating experiences in the thousands of hours spent under the sea.

"When did you last see him?" I asked when I could find a gap in the commentary.

"On Saturday, one day after Chris left for England."

Further detective work showed that on the first day of our visit to Coral Island the dolphin had put in a brief appearance at Raffi Nelson's village—a place between Coral Island and Eilat.

"That means we could actually have sailed right past him on our way to Coral Island," I said to Chris, who had already reached the same obvious conclusion.

We worked out a new plan of campaign and agreed that we would have to do much more reconnaissance before rushing to Coral Island.

Day three was a very bad day. It was excessively hot. In the shade the temperature reached 130°F; in the sun it was even higher. The wind was blowing and standing outside was like being in the path of a giant hair dryer.

We knew the dangers of dehydration in such climate conditions. We were sitting on the terrace at the diving center, having a last drink before launching the boat, when I was told that there was an urgent message waiting for me at the Caravan Hotel where we were staying.

"Someone's seen the dolphin," I shouted to Chris as I jumped up and ran across the road to the hotel opposite, convinced that one of our contacts was reporting in.

It was a message from a Telex machine very faintly typed in red. I scanned it quickly. It was not about dolphins at all. I tried to read it but my eyes were filling with tears and my legs felt as if they had suddenly turned to rubber. Only certain

words registered—RING HOME URGENTLY . . . DAUGH-
TER . . . TAKEN TO HOSPITAL . . . BRAIN DAMAGE
. . . ATTACKED BY MODS.

I held onto the counter to steady myself and tried to read it
properly, but the words fused into a pink blur. I picked up the
insignificant-looking piece of buff paper and stumbled across
the road to find Chris. I laid it on the table and asked him to
read it to me.

He smoothed the crumpled paper out with his hands and
read it through a couple of times. Then he looked up and said,
"It's not Melanie who has been attacked. It's her boyfriend."

When I had regained my composure and Chris reread the
message out loud the message was obvious. Even so it was
some minutes before I felt fit enough to return to the hotel and
telephone England.

When I spoke to Wendy, she informed me that Melanie's
boyfriend Don had gone out with some of his pals to a club in
Hull to celebrate the end of exams and the fact that he was to
become officially engaged to my daughter on the following day.
When he and a friend left, they were jumped from behind. In
addition to suffering a blow to the head which had produced a
four-inch fracture of the skull, the boy had been kicked in the
face and ribs. As far as Wendy could find out there was no
motive, only gratuitous violence. He was not robbed but left
unconscious in the gutter with blood streaming from his head,
and that was how the police found him. When I spoke to her
he was still unconscious, although he occasionally thrashed
about violently in bed. My daughter, who was nursing him in
the hospital, was extremely distressed and was told by the spe-
cialist that it was impossible to predict at this stage whether
there would be any permanent brain damage.

When I suggested that I should fly home immediately,
Wendy said there was nothing I could do. We could only wait
and see what happened. We agreed that I should return home
in three days as scheduled, and we would keep in touch by
telephone.

When Chris and I set off in the boat to find the dolphin, the
events in faraway England kept flashing on the screen of my
mind like a horror movie.

We had become very friendly with the boatman on the ferry at Coral Island. He operated his small glassbottomed boat according to demand and was always one of the first people to know when the dolphin arrived. He agreed to keep constant watch while we scouted up and down the coast in the car. He was very hopeful that Wednesday would be the day, because he worked out that the dolphin was often away for periods of three days at a time. Thus he deduced the dolphin would be back at Coral Island on the fourth day of our five-day filming schedule.

The next day began like all the others, with the sun rising into a pink sky that was soon transformed into unbroken blue. As it did so the temperature climbed from the eighties, through the hundred mark, and up on the Fahrenheit scale. We had decided to abandon the boat and concentrate on covering as much coastline as possible using the car. But at the end of the fourth day we were no nearer our goal. As the sun went down we watched Coral Island become a black silhouette against the faintly misty mountains of Jordan on the far side of the Gulf. They appeared to be only a short distance away. The trip across the Gulf certainly did not pose much of a journey to a dolphin to whom international boundaries were of no significance.

"You realize that he could be in Jordan," I said to Chris as I sat transfixed by the vision of layer upon layer of distant mountains slowly changing hues from pink to purple.

"I know," he replied. "If that's the case there is absolutely no way of us knowing where he is. And tomorrow is our last day."

Our hopes of finding the dolphin faded with the sunset.

The next day we didn't hurry through breakfast. When the time came to carry the heavy engine and our diving and camera equipment down the beach to the boat we dallied, and after our labors in the hot sun we had an extra drink in the shade before setting off on the journey to Coral Island. On the way, I searched every quarter carefully with my binoculars, but there was nothing to signify the presence of our quarry. Thoughts of my fruitless trip to the Bahamas invaded my mind and they were coupled with visions of Duncan Gibbins convulsed with unsuppressed laughter.

We headed straight for the jetty. As we approached, Ellie the ferryman rushed out of the restaurant waving his arms. He came running down to the edge of the pier as we were about to tie up.

"He's here! He's here!" he shouted waving his arms in triumph.

"He was here at five o'clock this morning," he blurted out. From what he said, we gathered he had tried everything in his power to get a message to us. But there was no phone, no taxi and he could not contact anybody going through to Eilat to carry a message. It was already late morning and we were working fast to get ready. Then he electrified us further by saying, "Hurry, hurry, he could go at any time."

"Jill, you get in the water and keep the dolphin amused," ordered Chris.

The boatman already had the engine of his ferry running and Jill, who was wearing a swimming costume, grabbed her mask and fins and jumped aboard while Chris and I frantically started to suit up with full diving equipment and cameras. The dolphin was in the middle of the channel between the island and the mainland. Jill soon splashed into the sea. We watched her submerge and the triangular dorsal fin of the dolphin moved toward her.

Chris was convinced that the dolphin would swim to us once we were in the water. As soon as we were ready, we took our boat to the place where he had encountered the dolphin previously, which had a line to which we could moor. Chris was first in the water with his camera. A few moments later I too slid over the side. Chris was forty feet down tapping the metal wing of his camera housing with his knife and looking around. As I approached I could hear the sound but the dolphin was nowhere to be seen. I scoured the blue limit of my visibility.

Then in the distance a gray shape appeared out of the mist like a ghost. I held my breath. There was complete silence. The dolphin continued to fly toward me. As he did so the diffuse shape materialized until a very solid-looking dolphin was swimming just a few feet away. There was no hurry or excitement—the dolphin moved slowly past as if summing me up. The eye that was assessing me was half shut. I immediately got the feeling I was in the presence of a friendly, gentle creature. His approach was so smooth and peaceful I didn't feel immediate ecstatic excitement. I felt more as I might if I met up with a friendly neighbor while walking to the shops. The presence of the dolphin felt absolutely normal. We swam slowly together side by side like two friends casually passing the time of day.

Then he cruised around gently and headed down toward Chris, who had his camera up to his mask and was filming our meeting.

Now it was my turn to film. Through the reflex viewfinder of my camera I watched the dolphin spiral down to Chris as if I was actually watching a film in slow motion. He swam through the curtain of rising air bubbles and circled around Chris. Then the dolphin swam toward one of the large bubbles and playfully bit at it, splitting it into a dozen small scintillating spheres that oscillated as they chased one another upward.

I soon exposed the thirty meters of film in my 16-mm movie camera and returned to the boat to change the film. I had come prepared to spend many hours with the dolphin and I wanted to observe and record his responses to the same kinds of objects and situations that had produced such interesting reactions in Donald. So while I changed the film in my camera, Chris took down objects of different shapes and textures. These included a rubber quoit attached to stout fluorescent tape. On many occasions Donald had taken a quoit in his mouth and towed me through the water while I hung onto the line. But the Coral island dolphin showed no interest in it whatsoever. And when I played music and made other noises to him via my underwater loudspeaker, I noticed no response apart from a glancing look.

This dolphin appeared to be much more interested in people and what divers did. Chris pulled his hand into his chest and stuck his elbow out, attempting to imitate a dolphin's flipper. When Chris wagged his elbow rapidly the dolphin immediately responded by waving one of his flippers. When Chris then arched his body several times, the dolphin did likewise. All of the time the dolphin was watching Chris carefully as if encouraging him to invent a new game for their mutual amusement. When Chris rose to the surface and popped his head out of the water he was surprised to see the dolphin follow him up and do the same. Obviously the dolphin wanted to continue the game. So Chris bobbed up and down in the water and much to his amusement the dolphin did the same. From afar they looked as if they were on opposite ends of an underwater seesaw—each of them breaking surface alternately. When that game was over and the diver swam away using the dolphin stroke, the dolphin swam in unison very close alongside. However, when Chris put his hand out to touch his playmate, the dolphin always remained just out of reach.

By the time Chris had exposed all of his film I was ready to go back in again. So too was Jill, who had been picked up by the boatman from the middle of the channel. With Jill was another snorkel diver—an attractive young woman of French origin named Estelle. With beautiful girls and a dolphin for company I sank slowly into the transparent water. The sun shone and my bubbles glittered as they gurgled toward the ever-changing canopy of blue and silver over my head. The girls, who were not wearing underwater breathing apparatus, snorkeled down toward the dolphin who weaved in an endless pattern of sweeps and curves through the water. From below it looked like an aerial ballet.

Unfettered by gravity, my bikinied ballerinas were able to fly and twirl through the water for as long as they could hold their breath. I was the only audience underwater to appreciate the show.

The dolphin ballet came to an abrupt end when a family group on the island decided to go for a swim. The dolphin disappeared. When I surfaced and heard shrieks of excitement coming from afar I knew immediately the source of their thrills. The dolphin was obviously among them. So in the company of the two deserted underwater ballerinas I swam off to join the fun.

When we arrived there was much splashing. The youngsters were bobbing down, swimming frantically underwater for a few seconds and then popping up again. Estelle also started to rush after the dolphin, stretching out her arms toward him. The bra of her bikini was not designed for such vigorous exertions and she briefly joined the ranks of the topless maidens who adorned many of Eilat's beaches. The dolphin, however, gave her no more than a passing glance.

When Chris came back into the water the snorkelers went back to shore. The dolphin stayed with us and we had time to look at him in detail as he cruised slowly around. I saw his teeth only very briefly and they appeared to be in good condition. So I guessed he was a young adult.

There was one aspect of the dolphin's behavior for which we could find no explanation. He would descend to the bottom and press his forehead (called the melon) against a small coral head. We watched him do this several times and on each occasion he always used the same piece of coral, although there were several similar outcrops close by to choose from.

After spending nearly three hours in the water, I climbed aboard our boat to recover while Chris reloaded our movie cameras onshore. The dolphin swam slowly away. When Chris returned, I had revived sufficiently to go back into the water. Jill and Estelle, who had also taken a breather, jumped in with us, but try as we might we could not attract the dolphin back.

Although we stayed in the water for some time, we concluded that our Cetacean playmate had gone. We headed back for base.

We had aroused tremendous interest in our quest for the dolphin. Wherever we went people would inquire about our success. When we got back to the diving center in Eilat that night I felt like an olympic athlete returning home with a gold medal.

Yes, we had met the dolphin. Yes, we had a fantastic time with him. Yes, we had filmed him. Yes, we had taken stills and movies.

There had always been some doubt about what species he was, and I was able to answer Willy Halpert's next question.

"He's a bottlenose dolphin," I told him.

"Male or female?" asked Willy.

"Definitely male."

Willy was obviously delighted to hear this because it confirmed his somewhat diffident identification.

"Have you got a name for him?" he continued, with a bright sparkle in his deep brown eyes.

254

"Well, as a matter of fact, no—although I have some ideas," I replied.

"Well, don't bother," said Willy. "I just wanted you to confirm that he was male."

"Come on Willy," I jibed. "Out with it. What name have you dreamed up?"

"Dobbie," he replied, beaming.

We were due to fly out of Eilat at twelve o'clock the following day and hoped that we would be able to have two encounters with the dolphin on successive days. But it was not to be. We stayed in the water off Coral Island until the last possible moment before rushing to the airport. We packed our still soggy wetsuits and our masses of camera equipment at the check-in desk. All in all it was a very impressive and very untidy load. If our rolls of exposed film had been made of platinum, they could not have been more valuable to us.

Less than twenty-four hours after our touch down in England, I had an excited call from Chris who had viewed the rushes.

"The footage is fantastic," he raved over the telephone.

"And we've denied old Gibbins the pleasure of pissing himself with laughter."

Fortunately the incident that had caused me so much anxiety had a happy ending. Don made a complete recovery from his terrible injuries. At the time of writing his plans for marriage to my daughter are well advanced.

Sadly, however, the story of Dobbie did not end in the same way. A few months after our visit I had a letter from a qualified biologist working at a marine biological laboratory in Eilat. He informed me that the body of a dolphin bearing very distinctive marks had been washed ashore.

Dobbie had been killed with a shot from a rifle.

28 · Undersea Railroad

When I first met Donald I felt there must be a special link between men and dolphins but I could not define it. When I encountered Dobbie in the Red Sea six years later, I had still not solved the conundrum, although I had more information and experiences to work with. I decided I had taken too broad a view, and planned to review those cases where the human–dolphin connection was most strongly felt. I started with Nan Rice.

Nan Rice founded the Dolphin Action and Protection Group in May 1977, but her feelings were first aroused to high level in 1969 when on December 21 she saw dusky dolphins being netted in Hout Bay, South Africa. Two hundred dolphins were captured in order that six could be selected for exhibition in captivity. Some were wounded and died during the capture operation.

The wave of protest generated by Nan Rice and other witnesses did not go unheeded by the authorities, and their case was strengthened when one of the three newly captured dolphins died in Tygerberg Zoo on January 14. Less than one week later all dolphins were declared protected mammals around the coast of South Africa.

In 1977 Dr. Heydorn, director of the Durban Oceanic Research Institute, had a meeting in Hout Bay and put forward a proposal that he catch eight dusky dolphins—two for his oceanarium and six for export. Petitions against this catch were signed by hundreds, resulting in the withdrawal of the permit.

Despite this public opposition, however, one year later a team from Durban appeared in Hout Bay to catch a mate for the lone dusky dolphin in their oceanarium. Two females were caught close inshore and one of the dolphins died on the way to Durban. This death caused a furor which involved the newly formed Dolphin Action and Protection Group in an enormous amount of work and publicity. Many of the cars in the area bore stickers with their slogan: DOLPHINS SHOULD BE FREE.

I added my own contribution to the debate when my wife and I visited South Africa to launch International Dolphin Watch. After one of my presentations in Hout Bay a member of the audience said that he thought one day it would become a capital offense to kill dolphins.

The indefatigible and delightful Nan Rice escorted us to Port Elizabeth. There we met and interviewed Anne Rennie whose experiences with captive dolphins raised again the controversial issue of keeping dolphins in captivity. We then flew to Durban where the director of the dolphinarium, Lex Fearnhead, was most anxious to tell us of the scientific work that was being carried out at the dolphinarium in addition to the dolphin shows put on for the benefit of the public.

Permission was granted for me to dive with the dolphins and, in wetsuit and aqualung, I joined the two bottlenosed dolphins in the main pool. Lex, who was equipped with just fins, mask and snorkel, followed me into the water. He emphasized how important it was to have contact with the dolphins. Much to his surprise, Purdey, normally the more retiring of the two female dolphins, seemed to attach herself to me, while Gambit preferred the company of the director. When I first sank to the bottom of the pool, the dolphins circled excitedly around me. I did not know from which direction they would come and suddenly found my leg in a mouthful of sharp teeth. I had experienced such behavior with Donald in the wild and knew it was one of the ways he used to investigate me.

Shortly before the first of the afternoon shows was due to start, I clambered out of the main pool and visited the two dusky dolphins who were in an adjacent pool. Their names were Nyaluthi and Tandi. These two dolphins were among the most beautiful animals I had ever seen. Their smooth lines and shining bodies were enhanced by their coloration which managed to be both striking and subtle at the same time. No human artist could improve on those two—their elegance surpassed the finest porcelain figures. Their eyes were bright and inquisitive. They signaled to me a kind of aloof detachment which seemed to imply that there was far more going on inside their minds than I, a mere human being, was capable of understanding. I quickly discovered that their teeth were needle sharp when they decided to nibble my arms and legs, and they had no difficulty in puncturing my skin through the protection of my wetsuit. One of the trainers told me that he thought the dusky dolphins were more intelligent than the bottlenosed dolphins. It took only five minutes for these smaller, sharp-beaked dolphins to learn their tricks. When they jumped they seemed to fly through the air like swallows.

The care and attention lavished on each of the dolphins in the Durban dolphinarium was impressive. However, there was another important ingredient in their welfare. That was the genuine affection which all of the staff, from the director down, obviously had for the dolphins in their care.

I discussed the issue of keeping dolphins in captivity with Lex Fearnhead. While he agreed that in an ideal situation dolphins should be free, he could see no way of conducting detailed studies on dolphins in the wild. He also made the point that the only way most people will ever see dolphins is in a dolphinarium. Thus he justified the capture and confinement of relatively few dolphins. He deplored the retention of dolphins in tiny unhygienic pools by traveling circuses—a situation that Nan Rice and her colleagues had done much to prevent in South Africa. However, to Nan Rice, depriving dolphins of their freedom, even under the ideal conditions of the Durban dolphinarium, was something she strongly felt was morally wrong.

She was not alone in holding this view. To Kenneth le Vasseur and Steven Sipman, who worked in a dolphin laboratory in Hawaii, it became intolerable that intelligent animals should spend their lives doing thousands of repetitious tests in a tank so shallow they could not even dive to their eight-foot body length. They regarded the dolphins as slaves and it was from this standpoint that they chose to refer to their operation as the Undersea Railroad—deriving the name from the pre-Civil War abolitionist slave-freeing network known as the Underground Railroad. The two men did not think of themselves as criminals when they loaded two dolphins into a foam-padded truck and released them in the sea on May 29, 1977.

In the United States, once wild animals are caught they become the property of their owners. Le Vasseur and Sipman were charged with first degree theft, a felony carrying up to five years in jail. Le Vasseur was sentenced to six months in jail and five years probation.

The trial caused many people to focus their attention on a new concept for the first time. That concept was that humans are not alone in their rights to freedom. We do not have to go back very far in history to a time when slaves were considered simply property by law, and those who first schemed and fought for the abolition of slavery were regarded as misguided criminals by the establishment of the day.

The driving force for the abolitionists came from a deep sense of morality at a time when some ethnic groups, such as blacks, were considered inferior beings by many white Europeans. At the time there was what in modern speech would be termed "no scientific evidence" to suggest otherwise. The evidence came later, when blacks and whites graduated from the same universities.

Only time and a great deal of heartsearching will tell if a similar analogy can be drawn between men and dolphins. The problem will be a thousand times more difficult to resolve.

One person who is making a valiant attempt to find out is a New Zealander by the name of Wade Doak. A series of incidents caused Wade and his wife Jan to sell everything that kept them tied to the land and take to the sea to study dolphins in a manner never before attempted.

On an exquisite, calm day, Wade and Jan were surrounded by about thirty dolphins who lolled and gently played around the Doak's small runabout boat. Jan dived and dolphin-kicked, keeping her legs together like a dolphin's tail. One dolphin seemed to take a very special interest in Jan and stayed close by her. At the end of their session together she got the very distinct impression that the dolphins were attempting to teach her something.

"All I wanted to do was forget everything and swim off with them," she later reported.

"I'll never forget that one dolphin and the look in his eyes. He circled close. He was very friendly. Intelligent eye, understanding, playful, inquisitve and very, very wise, all at once. Climbing out of the water it all seemed like a dream, but it was very real. Dolphins in a wild state had come of their own free will to play with us."

Captivated by the charm of the dolphins, Wade pondered on ways to bring himself and his family into more contact with the mysterious magnetic sea-mammals.

Eventually Project Interlock took shape and the Doaks sold their house, their car and their runabout boat, and invested in an eleven-meter sailing catamaran designed by James Wharram. Between the two hulls they slung a bow hammock which would enable them to get very close to dolphins in the water. Speakers were placed in each bow to transmit stereo music and a special message tape with sound frequencies used by man and dolphin. A roundel bearing the ying-yang symbol of polar opposites, with a dolphin in one and a stylized diver in the

other, was specially designed by the artist Hal Chapman. Four of these roundels were fitted to the bows to symbolize the bridge between man and dolphins. It was a courageous move because the Doaks knew nothing about sailing and had no financial backing.

Since their project got underway the Doaks have had many wonderful experiences with dolphins and continue to evolve their theories about mental telepathy between men and dolphins.

Although it would have been much easier to study dolphins in captivity, the primary principle on which Wake Doak based his investigations was that the dolphins should be free in the sea. Kenneth le Vasseur and Steven Sipman set out deliberately to set dolphins free. Nan Rice and her colleagues worked to prevent the capture of dolphins and used the slogan "Dolphins should be free."

I came to the conclusion that the key to the human–dolphin connection I was searching for was freedom; not just physical freedom, but the spirit of freedom that is present in both man and dolphins.

Looking back at all of my experiences with Donald, I feel intuitively that it was a common spirit of freedom that brought us together. I cannot prove it—I just sense it.

I find myself attracted by people who have the equivalent quality in human terms. It finds expression in many different ways—often as a kind of nonviolent rebelliousness against the rules of a society that is becoming too ordered. In some cases it is the force that ultimately compels them to sell everything and sail around the world.

In their attempts to probe this human–dolphin link in Project Interlock, the Doaks approached dolphins as they would nomadic tribesmen with an alien culture. This is an interesting analogy, because in the broadest sense primitive people have been regarded as cousins to civilized man. The basis for the analogy between dolphins and nomadic tribesmen can be appreciated when one considers the way of life of the nomadic aborigines of Australia before the intrusion of white colonialists.

The aborigines did not dominate the land but became an integral part of it. They mastered the use of fire but did not manufacture metal. Their ability to create and use tools did not extend beyond the simplest modification of the sticks and bones they found around them into weapons for hunting. Spiritual and visual images—what we would call art—played an important part in their lives. To such people, whose passage through life was part of a continuum of spiritual existence, possessions were an impediment.

Man's exploration, exploitation and understanding of the sea has now reached a stage equivalent to that of the voyages of discovery that led to the colonization of the hitherto remote and uncivilized major land masses of the world more than a century ago. By reviewing what became of the aborigines of Australia and Tasmania, and again applying the analogy between man and dolphins, we can take a lesson from history that should influence our attitude and future treatment of our cousins in the sea.

An article by Susan Raven in the *Sunday Times* magazine (May 21, 1978) included a horrifying account of how the Stone Age survivors of Tasmania were hunted to extinction by the white settlers.

It is a sorry history—backed by guns—of murder and rape; of Sunday afternoon manhunts; of indescribable tortures. An aboriginal baby was buried up to its neck in sand, and its head was kicked off in front of its mother. A woman, repeatedly raped, was made to wear round her neck the severed head of her husband. There were stories of flesh being cut from the bodies of living men and fed to the dogs.

The last true Tasmanian died on May 8, 1876. One hundred years later, her skeleton, which had been on display in the Hobart museum, was truly laid to rest. It was cremated and the ashes were scattered on the sea—the same sea that had carried white men hunting for seals and bringing with them guns and death.

The aborigines of Australia were treated with no more understanding or tolerance by the British who were transported to a new continent. Unlike their Tasmanian counterparts, however, some of the Australian aborigines were able to escape extinction by virtue of the sheer size and inhospitable nature of the sunburnt Never-Never land into which they dissolved like sugar in tea.

To a people who did not evolve through a civilization based on acquisitions and wealth, the arrival of the whites was bemusing. To the aborigines, for whom possessions were encumbrances that obstructed rather than aided their long walk through life, whose stories were written in the stones of the hills and for whom the spirits were all important, the invasion by the land-grabbers was a destructive force that they could neither understand nor combat. Those who survived found their way of life destroyed. In exchange for a free existence in a land which they inherited but did not own, they were awarded a few paltry possessions, second class citizenship in an acquisitive society, and the solace of alcohol.

It does not stretch the imagination too far to relate what has

262

happened in the past to the aborigines to what is happening and will happen to the dolphins in the future. With their capacity for memory and their large cerebral cortexes, it is conceivable that the dolphins have a submarine culture that is as complex and even more deep-rooted than that of the aborigines. The value of the heritage of the dolphins (if it exists) or the culture of the aborigines cannot be measured in our terms—the beauty of a tree cannot be measured with a ruler. To comprehend it we must find a new set of values based on tolerance and freedom. If we can do that, we will do more than save some fellow creatures from extinction.